FAMILY HISTORY FROM PEN & SWORD

TRACING YOUR FAMILY HISTORY ON THE INTERNET

A Guide for Family Historians

Second Edition

Chris Paton

Pen & Sword
FAMILY HISTORY

First published in Great Britain in 2011
Second edition 2013 by
PEN & SWORD FAMILY HISTORY
an imprint of
Pen & Sword Books Ltd
47 Church Street
Barnsley
South Yorkshire
S70 2AS

Copyright © Chris Paton 2013

ISBN 978 1 78303 056 9

Typeset in Palatino and Optima by
CHIC GRAPHICS

Printed and bound in England by
CPI Group (UK), Croydon, CR0 4YY

Pen & Sword Books Ltd incorporates the imprints of
Pen & Sword Books Ltd incorporates the imprints of Pen & Sword Archaeology,
Atlas, Aviation, Battleground, Discovery, Family History, History, Maritime,
Military, Naval, Politics, Railways, Select, Social History, Transport, True Crime,
and Claymore Press, Frontline Books, Leo Cooper, Praetorian Press,
Remember When, Seaforth Publishing and Wharncliffe.

For a complete list of Pen & Sword titles please contact
PEN & SWORD BOOKS LTD
47 Church Street, Barnsley, South Yorkshire, S70 2AS, England
E-mail: enquiries@pen-and-sword.co.uk
Website: www.pen-and-sword.co.uk

CONTENTS

GLOSSARY

Blog	short for 'web log' – an online diary
BMD	Births, marriages and deaths
Cloud	an online data storage area
FHS	Family History Society
GEDCOM (.ged)	a file format, short for GEnealogical Data COMmunication – used to store and transfer information between different family tree software programmes
GRO	General Register Office
IGI	International Genealogical Index
MI	Monumental Inscription
NAI	National Archives of Ireland
NRS	National Records of Scotland
NHS	National Health Service
OPC	Online Parish Clerk
OPR	Old Parochial Records – commonly used term to describe Scottish parish records
OS	Ordnance Survey
PCC wills	Prerogative Court of Canterbury wills
PDF (.pdf)	Portable Document Format – a data file format requiring an Adobe based reader programme to access
Podcast	a digitally based audio or video file which can be downloaded to your computer to view or listen to
PRONI	Public Record Office of Northern Ireland
TNA	The National Archives
URL	A website address – stands for 'Uniform Resource Locator'

INTRODUCTION

When the first edition of this book was published in early 2011, it attempted to pull together some of the main online genealogical resources that could help those wishing to research their family history within the United Kingdom of Great Britain and Northern Ireland. By the very nature of the remit, not everything could be covered – the worldwide web is, in a classic definition of understatement, just a wee bit big. The book did, however, identify the key online resources – the genealogical gateway sites, the mainstream vendors, and many of the simply brilliant amateur sites that have come from a collective volunteer community across our four nations.

A lot can change in the world in two and a half years, and the online genealogical scene is no exception. The rise in online Irish resources, for example, has been dramatic enough to warrant a sister title to this work, *Tracing Your Irish Family History on the Internet*, published in early 2013. Many of the sites recorded in the first edition of this book have changed – some by simply moving to a new web host, others beyond recognition – whilst a few have simply disappeared. Cyberspace has moved on, and this new edition once again takes the pulse of online genealogy in a new environment.

Many new types of genealogical tools are also emerging. A good example is websites linking maps to genealogical datasets, allowing extraordinary new ways of carrying out research. In London, for example, Locating London's Past (p.93) allows me to search a Google map to locate all instances of crime on a particular street, as recorded in the online court records of the Old Bailey; in Edinburgh, a search on the brilliant Addressing History platform (p.150) can similarly allow me to locate all occurrences of a particular surname and plot them on a contemporary map. Several sites have also appeared online that allow global searches across many platforms, ranging from the Connected Histories portal site (p.4) to the relatively new Mocavo search engine (p.4). Social networking remains a powerful force, with new platforms now in existence such as Google Plus (p.188). As with society, the internet will not stand still.

Whilst such records and methods can help us to access our past in new ways, the warnings must still remain. Not everything is online – and all the documentation that is online came from another source, whether that was an archive collection or exhibit, an out-of-copyright publication, or simply a person's recollections. The ease with which we can access material remains seductive and dangerous if we do not remain in control of the research process and understand the nature of the records that we are consulting.

This new edition is once again not about the etiquette of online research or the various technical considerations of using the internet. Some websites have very long URL addresses, and for this reason I have again on occasions resorted to using the Tiny website (**http://tinyurl.com**) to shorten them. The biggest offenders tend to be local government institutions, not only in the length of such addresses, but in the frequency with which they keep changing. If such a site suddenly ceases to work, try returning to the home page of the relevant authority (usually the first part which ends in '.gov.uk/') and try to find the desired library or archive site from there. The websites noted in this book were all functional at the time of writing (August 2013). If they cease to function, look for the collection of interest on a search engine such as Google (it may simply have moved to a new host platform), or try a site that may have cached an earlier version (see p.2).

Many thanks once more to the Pen and Sword team responsible for commissioning, editing and publishing this new edition, and to my wife Claire, and sons Calum and Jamie, who remain a great support.

Good hunting!

Chapter 1

GATEWAYS AND INSTITUTIONS

Genealogical information comes in the form of both primary and secondary sources, and the wealth of information found online is no different. Primary sources are original documents, recordings or testimonies, whilst secondary sources are those which provide a story 'second hand' or which create a 'finding aid' to the original. It is always preferable to find a primary source, to see for yourself the most immediate record of any event.

It is worth bearing in mind that all documentary records can only be as good as the information given to the writer who presented his or her account of the proceedings. Records can in fact mislead – a wrong age given by the vain, an incorrect marital status by the serial bigamist, a false claim to the aristocracy in the name of social advancement. It is therefore important to check and double check any records found, wherever possible, against other sources.

Also bear in mind that you may find an entry for someone in an index with the right name in the right location at the right time – but that this does not necessarily mean you have found the right person! In times past, the pool of personal names was more limited, and you may not be looking at a complete record set.

Sometimes when we experience problems, the fault is not with the record or the website, but in our expectations. Surnames have not always been spelt the same way, for example, and geographical boundaries have changed constantly across time. We may need to be more lateral in our approach, by using name variants, wildcards and other search techniques, or by being better educated about the environments within which our ancestors lived.

Understanding the nature of the records found on a website, and the scope of the material included, is extremely important. Above all, despite its great strengths and advantages, never forget that not everything *is* online, and what is not yet available on the internet can be equally as important as what is. The internet is simply a library of resources, but there are many others, and you may neglect them at your peril!

Recording information

No matter which websites you consult, keep a note of their addresses and whatever information you have gleaned from them. You can save website addresses ('URLs') on your browser's *Favourites* tool, meaning that you don't have to retype the addresses on future visits. Be aware that some may change from time to time, particularly those from local authorities, and that information remains online in most cases only so long as the host platform is still around, or whilst the person who created the resource is still maintaining it.

It is always advisable to make a copy of any information discovered as soon as you find it. You can type out relevant portions, cut and paste text, save the web page as a file to be consulted offline, print off the page, or take 'screen grabs' (using your 'Print Screen' button). If a site does go down for any reason, all may still not be lost – some sites, such as the Internet Archive's Wayback Machine (**http://archive.org**) or the British Library's Web Archive (**www.webarchive.org.uk**) actually save many sites for posterity at regular intervals, allowing you to see earlier versions of the required page before its eventual demise.

You can choose to save your family tree and your research notes online through various genealogical social networking sites or online tree providers (see p. 189). Be wary of what you place online, however, most notably when it comes to the issue of privacy. Some people may not be happy about having their family details made available for all to see; some vendors will in fact not allow it and prevent such information from being made public. Others will offer a facility to share your family history project only with those that you have invited to participate. As a rough rule of thumb, do not place details of people online if they are still alive and/or were born less than a century ago and you should be covered.

Gateway sites

There are many free 'gateway sites' that can help you to locate useful resources for your research. For the lay of the land with regard to the location of the archives, libraries and records in the British and Irish genealogical world, the multilayered GENUKI website (**www.genuki. co.uk**) is the grandfather of them all. This allows you to search at several regional levels for resources, and includes details for the Channel Islands and the Isle of Man, as well as the UK and the Republic of Ireland. It also includes the GENEVA genealogical event listings page (**www.geneva. weald.org.uk**), mailing lists, and many other projects. Its strength depends on the input of the local co-ordinators, with some regions providing fairly basic information, and others providing the most extraordinary details. Similar to GENUKI are the Ireland and United Kingdom GenWeb Project (**www.iukgenweb.org**) and the UK and Ireland Genealogy Records Online site (**www.ukisearch.com**).

The 'UK' family of sites from Ian and Sharon Hartas are a series of free-to-access directories providing links to resources from both a county or subject-based search. They include UK Births, Marriages, Deaths and Censuses on the Internet (**www.ukbmd.org.uk**), UK Genealogical Directories and Lists on the Internet (**www.ukgdl.org.uk**), and UK Military Family History on the Internet (**www.ukmfh.org.uk**). There is a degree of overlap to the links reported between the sites, but all should be consulted. Another site worth consulting is Cyndi's List (**www.cyndislist.com**), a vast directory of resources which provides links to all the latest genealogical websites, blogs and forums, which is searchable both geographically and thematically.

UKBMD is a constantly updated directory site for British resources.

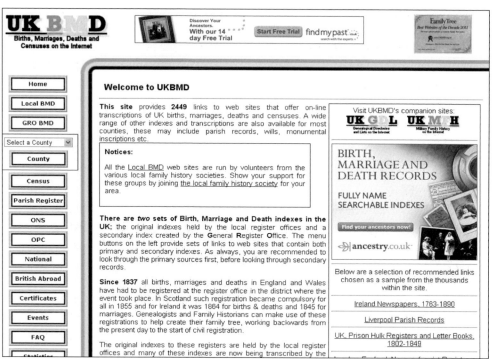

Specifically for England, a useful list of over 500 useful sites is hosted at the Price and Associates website (**www.pricegen.com/english_genealogy. html**), whilst the Scotland's Family site (**www.scotlands family.com**) is also worth visiting for resources north of the border, such as parish maps and records indexes.

Ireland is well served by the Fianna web project (**www.rootsweb. ancestry.com/~fianna/county/index1.html**), the Irish Ancestors site (**www.irishtimes.com/ancestor/browse/counties**), the From Ireland pages (**www.from-ireland.net**) and the Irish Genealogical Project (**www. igp-web.com**). On a pay-per-view basis Irish Family History (**www. irishfamily research.co.uk**) has many impressive databases.

The Mormon Church has gone to extraordinary lengths to secure and photograph copies of records from around the world, including parish records, probate papers, maps and more. Its FamilySearch website (**https:// familysearch.org**) importantly hosts the International Genealogical Index (see p.19), as well as many other useful collections in its United Kingdom and Ireland section. Some of the digitised collections can be viewed for free, though due to licensing agreements between FamilySearch and some of the archives which supplied them several can only be viewed at a FamilySearch family history library (see site for details of your nearest). In some cases FamilySearch has also created separate indexes to collections digitised by partners such as FindmyPast (see p.9). These are free to access, and in some cases are more detailed than equivalent indexes offered by the original host, but you will then be redirected to the partner site to view the original image (usually at a cost). There is also a powerful catalogue of its resources, listing items which can be ordered and consulted in microform or other formats at a FamilySearch Centre, and a useful 'wiki' based section with in-depth articles on various subjects to help you navigate your way through the genealogical landscape.

An interesting portal site is Connected Histories (**www.connected histories.org**), which provides a single federated search system for many online digitised projects, such as The Proceedings of the Old Bailey 1674–1913, British Newspapers 1600–1900, House of Commons Parliamentary Papers, and more, all of which will be discussed later in this book. Whilst the federated search is free, some of the content will require subscriptions to access.

Finally, whilst many search engines can be employed to look for material online (and it always pays to go beyond just using Google!), a dedicated genealogical search engine site called Mocavo exists at (**www.mocavo.**

co.uk). This examines a vast range of materials, including genealogical blogs, and although stronger for US-based research, it is becoming increasingly more useful for British and Irish-based searches.

Key Institutions
There are many important national repositories across the United Kingdom which hold a great deal of genealogical material, and which are increasingly finding ways to make their holdings accessible online.

National archives
The National Archives (TNA) is the main archive for the United Kingdom, predominantly for England and Wales, though holding material for all four nations. Its website at (**www.nationalarchives.gov.uk**) contains various research and resource guides, digitised records, downloadable lecture

The National Archives website.

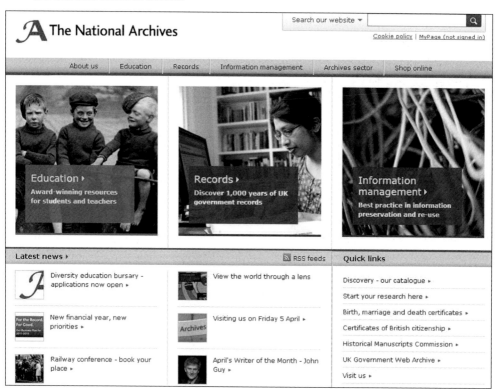

podcasts and its main holdings catalogue, called Discovery. Several other important catalogues are also hosted on the site, such as the Manorial Documents Register (**http://nationalarchives.gov.uk/mdr**) and the Hospital Records Database (**http://nationalarchives.gov.uk/hospital records**). For several years the institution has been forming strategic partnerships with many online commercial vendors in order to digitise its most commonly used materials – a full list is available at **www.national archives.gov.uk/records/catalogues-and-online-records.htm**. The site also offers a useful palaeography tutorial site for early forms of English handwriting, at **www.nationalarchives.gov.uk/palaeography**.

The National Records of Scotland (NRS) is the equivalent repository north of the border. Formed in April 2011 by a merger of the National Archives of Scotland and the General Register Office for Scotland, at the time of writing it still maintains its online presence via the websites of the two former institutions, though there is a new combined site at **www. nrscotland.gov.uk**. The archive site at **www.nas.gov.uk** does not carry digitised records, but has an impressive catalogue and detailed research guides. The facility is digitising some resources in partnership with other bodies and making them available through sites such as ScotlandsPeople (see below) and ScotlandsPlaces (p.X), most notably church records, wills, maps and tax records.

The Public Record Office of Northern Ireland (PRONI) freely provides a wealth of digitised and indexed materials on its site at **www.proni.gov.uk**, including the 1912 Ulster Covenant, nineteenth-century street directories, a post-1858 wills database, its Name Search facility, Valuation Revision Books, freeholders' records, and an online catalogue, as well as several resources guides. It is planned at the time of writing that the site will in due course be migrated to the Northern Ireland Direct government platform at **www.nidirect.gov.uk**, though the implications for current links to the site's various collections are as yet unclear.

The National Archives of Ireland (**www.nationalarchives.ie**) revamped its website in early 2012, integrating various freestanding databases into its new catalogue facility and continuing to offer several research guides. In partnership with Library and Archives Canada (p.179) the institution has also digitised the surviving census returns for 1901 and 1911 and placed them online at a new digital records platform at **www.genealogy.national archives.ie**, along with other resources such as First World War Soldiers' Wills and Tithe Applotment Books (1823–37), with many more to come in the near future, all free of charge.

Local archives
The ultimate locator for UK-based local archives is the ARCHON Directory (**www.nationalarchives.gov.uk/archon**), with links to websites, contact details, and some information on holdings. Equally useful for England and Wales is the Ancestor Search site (**www.ancestor-search.info/LOC-INDEX.htm**) which provides directory information for all county-based libraries, record offices, family history societies and research centres. My Time Machine may also help at **www.mytimemachine.co.uk/archives .htm**.

Many locally based archives, museums and libraries in England and Wales have made their catalogues accessible via a central facility entitled Access to Archives or 'A2A' (**www.nationalarchives.gov.uk/a2a**), with the Scottish Archives Network (**www.scan.org.uk**) the northern equivalent. The National Register of Archives (**www.nationalarchives.gov.uk/nra**) is a database listing some 44,000 unpublished lists and catalogues detailing the locations of additional material held across the UK, much of it in private hands, and again there is a Scottish equivalent, the National Register of Archives of Scotland (**www.nas.gov.uk/onlineregister**). In Ireland you can use the Research and Special Collections Available Locally database, or 'RASCAL' (**www.rascal.ac.uk**), or the Irish Archives Resource (**www.iar.ie**). The Learn About Archives site at **www.learnaboutarchives.ie** also provides a handy map to locate over eighty-five different repositories across the island.

Further centralised searches can be performed at the Archives Hub (**www.archiveshub.ac.uk**), representing collections from 220 academic institutions across the UK, and the Gateway to Archives of Scottish Higher Education site (**www.gashe.ac.uk**). The Archives Wales (Archifau Cymru) site (**www.archivesnetworkwales.info**) allows a keyword search through records held in twenty-one archives across the country. For materials held within the Greater London area, the Archives in London and the M25 Area (AIM25) facility at **www.aim25.ac.uk** provides an equally useful gateway, with much to offer.

Libraries
The British Library in London holds millions of books, journals, patents, sound recordings and more. Its website (**www.bl.uk**) hosts several online exhibitions, catalogues and digitised examples from its holdings, and several dedicated sites for particular collections such as its newspaper holdings or its Indian records holdings, some of which require a subscription. A useful page to bookmark is the Help for Researchers section

at **www.bl.uk/reshelp/findhelprestype/catblhold/all/allcat.html**, which lists all of the facility's online catalogues.

The National Library of Scotland (**www.nls.uk**) hosts many equally important digitised record sets, including maps, gazetteers, post office directories and more. The site also has a Digital Gallery area at **http://digital.nls.uk/print** with additional fascinating projects such as Scottish History in Print, which hosts various transcribed historic publications, and two volumes of MacFarlane's *Genealogical Collections Concerning Families in Scotland 1750–1751*. The library also has a dedicated platform on the Internet Archive at **www.archive.org/details/nationallibraryofscotland**, which hosts many additional digitised resources not found on its own website.

The National Library of Wales (**www.llgc.org.uk**) has an equally well-developed online presence, presented in both English and Welsh, with many useful catalogues and digitised collections, including wills, the National Screen and Sound Archives of Wales (at **www.archif.com**), and more. The site is very user-friendly, and probably the easiest to navigate around of all the British-based national libraries – it also has a dedicated blog.

Amongst the offerings of The National Library of Ireland (**www.nli.ie**) there is the Sources database (**http://sources.nli.ie**), which lists names found in manuscripts held by the institution up to the 1980s, Irish manuscripts catalogued between the 1940s and 1970s in other institutions across the world, and in over 150 Irish periodical titles up to 1969. There's also a Digital Photographs section at **www.nli.ie/digital-photographs.aspx** with some 30,000 freely accessible images sourced from several major Irish collections at the institute. For Northern Ireland there is no national library, but Belfast's Linen Hall Library has much to offer at **www.linenhall.com**.

The essential platform for locating items of interest within various overseas libraries is WorldCat, located at **www.worldcat.org**.

Societies
The umbrella bodies for family history societies in the UK are the Federation of Family History Societies (**www.ffhs.org.uk**), the Scottish Association of Family History Societies (**www.safhs.org.uk**), the Association of Family History Societies of Wales (**www.fhswales.org.uk**) and the North of Ireland Family History Society (**www.nifhs.org**). Not every society in the country will be affiliated to these, however. In the Western Isles of Scotland, for example, societies known in Gaelic as 'comainn eachdraidh' exist independently – a general list of these can be found at **www.smo.uhi.**

ac.uk/gaidhlig/buidhnean/eachdraidh. Most society sites have some online resources, though they vary considerably in what they provide.

The London-based Society of Genealogists (**www.sog.org.uk**) hosts a catalogue of its library holdings, and various databases for members only. The Edinburgh-based Scottish Genealogy Society (**www.scotsgenealogy .com**) has an online Family History Index outlining some of the private papers which have been deposited with them, as well as a downloadable index to its journal *The Scottish Genealogist*, from 1953–2005. The Ulster Historical Foundation (**www.ancestryireland.com**) has many subscription-based databases online exclusively for members.

Local History Online (www.local-history.co.uk) also provides details of history societies across the British Isles, many of which have useful web resources. The British Association for Local History site (**www.balh.co.uk**) has a particularly good links section for equivalent historical societies across Britain.

Commercial vendors

Family history is a fairly competitive business for vendors, offering a vast range of genealogically useful online materials either by subscription or on a pay-per-view basis. In addition, many offer free-to-use tree-building software capabilities. The following are the largest and will be constantly referred to throughout the book.

Ancestry www.ancestry.co.uk

Ancestry.co.uk is the UK arm of the American-based Ancestry.com corporation, and it is probably fair to say that you would be almost guaranteed to find something on the site of use to your family history, no matter where in the British Isles you might be from. Amongst its most useful and impressive holdings are birth, marriage and death indexes for England and Wales, probate records, British censuses, army records and more. The site also hosts online discussion forums and users' family trees. Additional records from around the world are available via a worldwide subscription.

FindmyPast www.findmypast.co.uk

FindmyPast.co.uk is owned by Brightsolid Online Innovation, and focuses primarily on English and Welsh records, though some collections are useful for the entire United Kingdom. Its major holdings include births, marriages and deaths indexes, parish records, British censuses, migration records and newspapers, and it will soon be adding the useful PERiodical Source Index

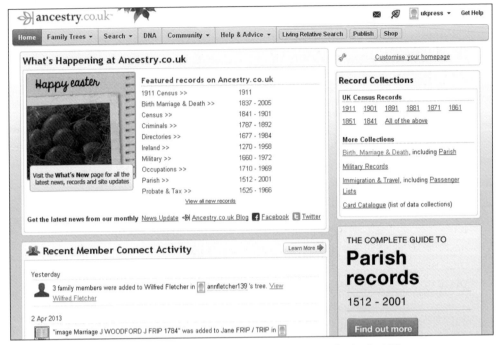

Ancestry.co.uk is the largest online commercial genealogy vendor in the UK.

(PERSI) for genealogical literature, in partnership with Allen County Public Library Genealogy Centre in the US. There are additional FindmyPast platforms in Australia (**www.findmypast.com.au**), the USA (**www.findmypast.com**) and Ireland (**www.findmypast.ie**), whose holdings can also be accessed through the British site via a worldwide subscription.

The Genealogist www.thegenealogist.co.uk

The Genealogist is another site primarily useful for English and Welsh research, with a handful of Scottish and Irish resources. As with Ancestry and FindmyPast the site also works with partner agencies and archives to provide digitised content. Its major collections include English and Welsh civil registration indexes, parish records (including Nonconformist parishes), naturalisation and denization records, and much more. A subsidiary site, **www.bmdregisters. co.uk,** also carries its unique Nonconformist records collections.

The National Archives www.nationalarchives.gov.uk

About 5 per cent of the records held at the National Archives in Kew have been digitised, with many available for purchase online through the site's

Our Online Records portal (or from search results in the Discovery Catalogue). They are supplied in downloadable PDF files, most notably for naval records, army war diaries and PCC wills. Some collections are also available for free, digitised from microfilms held at the archive – you will find these at the Digital Microfilm page at **www.nationalarchives.gov.uk/ records/digital-microfilm.htm** – with offerings including many Home Office, Inland Revenue, War Office and Admiralty collections, with gems such as the 1851 Ecclesiastical Census Returns for England and Wales.

Origins Network www.origins.net
The Origins Network provides various resources for British and Irish research, available in separate subscription packages – Total Access for all of its holdings; Irish Origins for records in Ireland; British Origins for English and Welsh resources; and the free-to-access Scots Origins. Some of the site's biggest projects include the National Wills Index, and a major initiative to place online almost 500 Irish street directories, particularly for Dublin.

MyHeritage www.myheritage.com
MyHeritage originated in Israel and has slowly grown to become a major player in the worldwide genealogical scene. Originally established as a platform offering a tree-building facility and network for genealogists, it has in recent years acquired many data providers, most notably World Vital Records in late 2011. At the time of writing it also provides access to English and Welsh census records from 1841–1901, as well as English and Welsh BMD indexes from 1837–2006.

FamilyRelatives www.familyrelatives.com
FamilyRelatives.com offers records for the UK, Ireland, and elsewhere in the world by subscription, as well as social networking tools and an online family tree hosting capability. Amongst its collections are military research materials, parish records, and free access to the GRO's overseas birth, marriage and death indexes (p.14).

Genes Reunited www.genesreunited.co.uk
Genes Reunited hosts user-submitted family trees and offers a powerful networking tool for those seeking to find connections with relatives. It works by allowing you to upload your family tree, or create a tree from scratch, and then alerts you to potential 'hot' matches between the data in your family tree and that found on others, though the definition of 'hot' can sometimes

be open to question! The site is also increasingly offering digitised records resources, primarily for English and Welsh research, such as censuses and BMD indexes.

The Original Record www.theoriginalrecord.com

The Original Record has millions of useful records on its site, though it has a somewhat unusual access set-up. The site allows you to perform searches by surname and year – you can buy an annual subscription to view search results returned for that surname for £100, or for two surnames for £180, and so on, though you can also purchase individual records. It can be pricey, and would seem to be geared more towards those researching for a one-name study (see p.19), but a great deal of rare material is hosted on the site that is not available elsewhere.

Forces War Records www.forces-war-records.co.uk

Forces War Records is a subscription-based military records site that has various rolls of honour, medal rolls and other useful military materials (including officer's lists from the Home Guard). Free offerings include a medieval database and a Prisoner of War collection. The site also carries an online digital library of historic documents, books, newspapers and magazines, some of them more than a hundred years old.

ScotlandsPeople www.scotlandspeople.gov.uk

The ScotlandsPeople website is a joint venture between the National Records of Scotland, the Court of the Lord Lyon and Brightsolid (the Dundee-based parent company behind FindmyPast and GenesReunited). Uniquely in the UK, it offers digitised images of the civil registration records for births, marriages and deaths, and is the only site to offer digitised images for the Scottish censuses. Other holdings include Church of Scotland and Roman Catholic parish records, wills, Scottish land valuation rolls and records on Scottish heraldry.

Deceased Online www.deceasedonline.com

Deceased Online commenced operations in 2008 and offers access to many digitised burial and cremation records from across Britain, as well as cemetery maps in many cases. Searches are free, but credits need to be purchased to view the full result (a forthcoming annual subscription option is being promised at the time of writing). Information on funeral applicants within the last seventy-five years is restricted for data protection reasons. The site also offers access to many Scottish gravestone records, as supplied from Scottish Monumental Inscriptions (p.22).

Genhound www.genhound.co.uk

This site is not so well known, but contains a range of useful resources from Britain, particularly for Scotland, where it provides access for early sasines indexes and Registers of Deeds. There is also an extensive amount of material from England and some overseas resources. The site requires you to purchase credits, and you will need a PDF reader such as Adobe, as records are supplied in that file format.

Magazines

The print-based *Your Family Tree* (**www.yourfamilytreemag.co.uk**), *Family Tree* (**http://family-tree.co.uk**) and *Who Do You Think You Are?* (**www.who doyouthinkyouaremagazine.com**) magazines provide free online resources on a monthly basis, as well as regular news and discussion forums. Digital editions for iPad are also available for *Your Family Tree* and *Who Do You Think You Are?*, whilst *Your Family Tree* has both Apple and Android tablet-based versions. Discover Your Ancestors (**www.discoveryourancestors.co.uk**) is a recently established online only monthly magazine, though there is an accompanying 'bookazine' produced annually in print. At the time of writing, *Discover Your History* (previously *Your Family History*) had announced a new website at **www.discoveryourhistory.net**, though content had yet to be added.

Irish Lives Remembered (**www.irishlivesremembered.com**) is a free monthly magazine which can be read online or in PDF format. *Irish Roots* (**www.irishroots media.com**) is also available in digital bi-monthly format, and carries a free online preview for each edition.

Various societies produce their own newsletters, one of the best being the Federation of Family History Societies' free bi-monthly e-zine at **www. ffhs.org.uk/ezine/intro.php**.

Chapter 2

GENEALOGICAL ESSENTIALS

Before adding the flesh to your family tree, it helps to establish the bones, and in this chapter I will look at the key basic records and sites that will help you to get your research underway.

Births, marriages and deaths
England and Wales
Civil registration of English and Welsh births, marriages and deaths commenced on 1 July 1837, and copies of certificates can be obtained from two main sources – the General Register Office of England and Wales, and local superintendent registrars' offices. Copies that were recorded locally have been indexed by the relevant authority for the area (see **www.ukbmd. org.uk/genuki/reg/index.html**), but copies were also transmitted to the national GRO every three months up to 1983, and annually from 1984, from which the GRO then compiled its own indexes. The two sets of indexes are not compatible, and so a local index entry cannot be used to order from the national GRO, and vice versa. Barbara Dixon's detailed overview on the different types of certificate and the information you will find in them can be read at **http://home.clara.net/dixons/Certificates/indexbd.htm**. A useful list of additional GRO-held records, including various overseas collections and oddities such as births and deaths registered on hovercraft, is available at **http://tinyurl.com/d2w9oqd**.

The easiest way to search for civil registration events is to use the national GRO indexes. The volunteer-based FreeBMD website (**www.freebmd.org. uk**) is working to provide free transcriptions and images of the indexes from 1837 to 1983. At the time of writing the database is making good progress into the 1960s. Users are also increasingly adding 'postem' messages to the indexes, with transcribed details of content from many records (see **www. freebmd.org.uk/postems-help.html**).

Commercial vendors such as Ancestry, FindmyPast and The Genealogist have developed their own index databases, allowing searches by name, year,

The impressive FreeBMD platform.

quarter, mother's maiden name, and registration district. As with any transcriptions, though, the indexes are not immune to errors. Once you find the right entry, take a note of the reference number and then order the record from the GRO at **www.gro.gov.uk/gro/content/certificates/default.asp**, for a standard rate of £9.25 per record. Always order certificates directly from the GRO, as some online vendors can charge up to three times the cost per certificate if obtained through them.

As noted, the national indexes were compiled from copies of the original local registers. Errors sometimes occurred in the copying process, and so you may find that the local registrar has the record even if you cannot find it nationally. Not every local registration office has placed its indexes online, but many are increasingly doing so. To find out if this is the case, consult UKBMD (**www.ukbmd.org.uk**).

Several certificate exchange sites exist where people are willing to swap details of certificates already purchased. For England and Wales these include www.certificate-exchange.co.uk, and http://aztecrose.tripod.com/Look upExchange.htm; for Scotland try www.sctbdm.com and for Ireland http://vicki.thauvin.net/chance/ireland/bmd.

If your ancestors divorced in England and Wales, Ancestry hosts a UK Civil Divorce Records, 1858–1911 collection.

Scotland

Scottish civil registration was begun in 1855 by the General Register Office for Scotland, now part of the National Records of Scotland (see www.gro-scotland.gov.uk). For a background to its establishment, consult The Scottish Way of Birth and Death (www.gla.ac.uk/schools/socialpolitical/research/economicsocialhistory/historymedicine/scottishwayofbirth anddeath).

The records of civil births, marriages and deaths have been digitised and made partially available online at the ScotlandsPeople website. Whilst this currently contains indexes up to 2011, it operates an online closure policy for some of the register images, meaning that full birth record entries for the last 100 years cannot be viewed, nor marriages for the last seventy-five years or deaths for the last fifty. The indexes for the most recent records also carry less detail, but can be used to order up official printed extracts from the NRS.

The records include many minor collections (such as overseas military death registrations) and the Register for Corrected Entries, in which subsequent amendments to BMD records were registered, though this cannot be searched as a database in its own right – a link to the register is highlighted if mentioned in a statutory record and accessible for additional credits. Civil birth and marriage records from 1855–1875 are also indexed on FamilySearch's IGI database (p.19), though not deaths. Whilst Scottish divorce records cannot be consulted online, a useful research guide on divorce is available from the NRS at www.nas.gov.uk/guides/divorce.asp.

If your Scottish ancestor moved to England, consult the Anglo-Scottish Family History Society website (www.anglo-scots.mlfhs.org.uk), which has placed a helpful database online for marriages where at least one of the spouses was Scottish, and noting from where in Scotland he or she originated.

Ireland

Civil registration commenced in Ireland in April 1845, but only for non-Roman Catholic religious marriages and civil marriages performed by the state. It was not until January 1864 that a full system was introduced for all births, marriages and deaths, similar to that in Britain, with copies of all locally registered events going to the national GRO at Dublin. Following Partition in 1921, the GRO in Dublin continued to record information for the south, whilst the newly established GRO in Belfast did likewise for the north.

The majority of civil records indexes for the whole island from 1845 to 1921 are transcribed and freely available at FamilySearch – for the Republic, additional indexes up to 1958 are also available. The same indexes are also available on Ancestry's Irish pages at **www.ancestry.co.uk/cs/uk/Ireland** and through FindmyPast's Worldwide subscription; the latter is particularly useful because you can successfully perform a marriage search using both spouses' surnames in your query. The indexes can be used to order photocopied extracts from the Republic's GRO (**www.groireland.ie**) at €4 per copy, although the GRO has stated that a new replacement site is under development.

For events in the north after Partition, you can apply online for records through the Northern Irish GRO website (**www.groni.gov.uk**). Events before 1922 can be ordered here also, but are considerably more expensive to obtain than those from the south. It is intended in the very near future that a ScotlandsPeople-type website will be made available for Northern Irish-based BMD events.

Some of the early civil records of Irish BMDs have also been indexed on FamilySearch as part of the International Genealogical Index (see p.X) – in some cases offering additional details than those in the BMD indexes from 1845–1958, such as names of fathers in marriage entries – but the certificates (or copies) should still be obtained for full details.

British subjects overseas

If your ancestor moved abroad, check FamilyRelatives for freely hosted indexes of consular and overseas records, as well as Chaplains' returns for overseas regiments, with events recorded as recently as 2005. These too can be ordered from the English-based GRO (see p.15), though via a separate online application form. Many of the indexes are also hosted at FindmyPast and The Genealogist websites, with the latter also having additional records from the General Register Office: Miscellaneous Foreign Returns (1831–1964) collection at TNA (RG 32). This includes vital records as recorded on British and foreign ships, and of British subjects and British colonial and Commonwealth nationals from around the world. Not all overseas events are online – some are held within consular registers at TNA – but the online collections do represent a significant proportion of what exists.

Stillbirths

Anguline Research Archive hosts an interesting dataset called The Historic Stillbirth Register (**http://anguline.co.uk/stillbirths.html**), which contains some 10,000 stillbirths transcribed from parish registers, and other sources, predominantly in England and Wales, from 1551–2005.

Adoption and children

For advice concerning adoption issues, visit Adoption Search Reunion (**www.adoptionsearchreunion.org.uk**), or in Scotland, Birthlink (**www.birthlink.org.uk**). For Northern Ireland consult the adoption guide at **www.nidirect.gov.uk/gro**. You can also register an interest with the UK Birth Adoption Register (**www.ukbirth-adoptionregister.com**), after paying a registration fee.

For British children keen to trace their Canadian birth fathers from the Second World War, visit Canadian Roots UK (**www.canadianrootsuk.org**), whilst the Child Migrants Trust (**www.childmigrantstrust.com**) tries to help reunite children sent by the British Government to Canada, New Zealand, Australia and Rhodesia from the end of the Second World War to the early 1970s with their birth families. Library and Archives Canada also has a Home Children database in its Immigration and Citizenship section, located within its Genealogy and Family History portal (see p.179).

If your ancestor spent time at the Foundling Hospital in London visit **www.foundlingmuseum.org.uk/collections**. A genealogy service is available through **www.quarriers.org.uk** to trace records of Scottish street children who stayed in Quarriers Homes, whilst homeless and destitute boys who were sent to the Mars Training Ship in Dundee can be researched at **www.sonsofthemars.com**. Missing Ancestors (**http://missing-ancestors.com**) also provides resources to help trace children who may have gone missing from your tree. For those who spent time at the Magdalene Laundries in Ireland, visit **www.magdalenelaundries.com** for a research guide on how to trace records, and resources such as the Magdalene Name Project.

Surnames

There are several surname websites seeking to provide explanations of the origins of individual names, but many of them need to be taken with a pinch of salt! If I do a search on my own surname of Paton, the British Surnames site (**www.britishsurnames.co.uk**) tells me that the name is Spanish; the Internet Surname Database (**www.surnamedb.com**) informs me that it comes from one of two possible origins, one being English, the other French. (My Scottish ancestors would be turning in their graves!)

The Guild of One-Name Studies, known affectionately to many as the 'GOONS', is a body of dedicated volunteers who have each undertaken to study a single surname in records from across the English-speaking world. A list of over 2,000 names being studied by the organisation is available at **www.one-name.org/register.html**. For the origins of many forenames and surnames, visit the Medieval Names Archive at **www.s-gabriel.org/ names**.

Church records

In the pre-civil registration period, we need to rely on parochial records for evidence of our ancestors' lives. The state church in England, Wales and Ireland was the Anglican Church, whilst in Scotland it was the Presbyterian-based Church of Scotland.

Bear in mind that our ancestors often moved from parish to parish, and were often more mobile then we give them credit for. To understand which parishes may adjoin the 'home' parish, use the Parish Finder website (**www. parishfinder.co.uk:8080**). There are many sites depicting places of worship across the British Isles, such as the Churches of Britain and Ireland website at **www.churches-uk-ireland.org**.

Parish registers

There is no one single source holding all parish records online. The most comprehensive is perhaps the International Genealogical Index (IGI) at FamilySearch (**https://familysearch.org**). This provides a free index to Church of England baptisms and marriages up to 1837, and often beyond, as well as many returns for Nonconformist churches, with Scottish records also included up to 1854, and some Irish records. The index has been created from registers microfilmed by the Church of Jesus Christ of Latter Day Saints, with each film given a batch number. Using these numbers, IGI searches can also be performed via Hugh Wallis's site at **http://freepages. genealogy.rootsweb.ancestry.com/~hughwallis/IGIBatchNumbers.htm**, though results are displayed at FamilySearch. Once an index entry is found the original record should always be consulted.

FamilySearch has also made material freely available through its United Kingdom and Ireland Historical Record Collections, accessible from the home page of the site. This includes its England Baptisms and England Marriages databases from 1700–1900, as well as separate databases for other

The Comrie family from Fowlis Wester, Perthshire. Author's collection.

parts of the British Isles, including the Crown Dependencies of Man and the Channel Islands (see Chapter 8).

All of the Church of Scotland's surviving parish registers, dating as far back as 1553, have been digitised and made available through the ScotlandsPeople website, with digitised kirk session material, the equivalent of English vestry records, to be made available online in due course. Scottish Roman Catholic Church records are also available on the website – of particular note here is the Bishopric of the Forces collection, which not only covers Scotland, but also provides Catholic records for military bases in England and overseas.

The Church of Scotland was prone to splits and reunions, seemingly thriving on theological disruption routinely from the Reformation. Few records of the dissenting faiths are online as yet, though some have been indexed in FamilySearch's Scottish collections. Another fascinating database for Scottish research, the Survey of Scottish Witchcraft (**www. shc.ed.ac.uk/Research/witches**), has details of nearly 4,000 people tried from 1563–1736 for witchcraft, with evidence for many cases gathered by local kirk sessions.

FreeREG (**www.freereg.org.uk**) also allows for searches of many church baptisms, marriages and burials from across Britain. It provides more details than the IGI, but is not as complete. In Wales, marriage allegations and bonds have been indexed from 1661–1837 by the National Library of Wales and can be searched via its online catalogue (**http://isys.llgc.org.uk**).

The commercial websites offer a great deal of parish register material. FindmyPast's Parish Records Collection 1538–2005, produced in association with the Federation of Family History Societies, includes most of the second edition of the National Burial Index, providing an index to information compiled from various registers by family history societies across England and Wales. The site has also partnered with many local archives in England to digitise and index original registers on the site. The Genealogist also offers English and Welsh holdings; of particular note is its Nonconformist records collection, including events recorded by Presbyterians, Congregationalists, Baptists, Quakers, Methodists, Unitarians and the Russian Orthodox Church, as well as records of clandestine marriages and baptisms performed at the Fleet prison from 1667–1777. The same collection is accessible at **www. bmdregisters.co.uk**.

Ancestry's UK Parish Baptism, Marriage and Burial Records collection contains British records extracted from the 1500s to the 1900s, including many Scottish returns (Episcopalian, Catholic etc). Like FindmyPast, Ancestry has also been digitising many records in partnership with archives across Britain, notably for the Greater London area. It also hosts useful resources such as Pallot's marriage and baptism indexes for England (mainly London and Middlesex) from 1780–1837. The Origins Network hosts additional records for areas across England.

For Northern Ireland, PRONI's guide on church records holdings at **www.proni.gov.uk/guide_to_church_records.pdf** is useful. The National Library of Ireland has a similar guide for its Roman Catholic record holdings at **www.nli.ie/en/parish-register.aspx**, whilst at **www.irishtimes.com/ ancestor/browse/counties/rcmaps** the *Irish Times* hosts an interactive map leading to individual Catholic parishes and the availability of records within each. The main online source for accessing transcriptions of parish material in Ireland, north and south, is the Irish Family History Foundation's RootsIreland site (**www.rootsireland.ie**). This carries transcribed Roman Catholic, Church of Ireland and Presbyterian parish records, and some county-based civil records, with transcriptions costing €5 each to access at the time of writing. Emerald Ancestors (**www.emeraldancestors.com**) has index databases for Northern Irish births (1796–1924), marriages (1823–1922) and deaths (1803–1900), from both church and civil registration records. An ordering service is available for fully transcribed extracts.

Gravestones and burials

Several sites provide access to transcriptions and/or photographs of gravestone inscriptions, including Interment.net (**www.interment.net**), and Gravestone Photos (**www.gravestonephotos.com**). Deceased Online (**www.deceasedonline.com**) is continuing to digitise burial and cremation records from across Britain, and making them available on its pay-per-view site, in many cases with accompanying layer maps. To understand gravestones written in Welsh, John Ball's site offers some handy translations at **www.jlb2011.co.uk/wales/welsh-phrases.htm**.

The Scottish Graveyards Project (**www.scottishgraveyards.org.uk**) is recording and conserving many grave sites across the country, whilst Highland Memorial Inscriptions (**https://sites.google.com/site/highland memorialinscriptions/home**), Find a Grave in Scotland (**www.findagrave inscotland.com**), Memento Mori (**www.memento-mori.co.uk**) and Scottish Monumental Inscriptions (**www.scottish-monumental-inscriptions. com**) can also help. Many of the latter's records can also be found via Deceased Online.

The History from Headstones project (**www.historyfromhead stones.com**) has about 50,000 inscriptions from over 800 graveyards in Northern Ireland, whilst the North of Ireland Family History Society operates a members' look-up scheme for graveyards which it is recording (**www.nifhs.org/lookups.htm**). For Belfast visit **www.belfastcity.gov.uk/ community/burialrecords/burialrecords.aspx**, whilst many other Irish-based parish graveyards are recorded at **www.discovereverafter.com**.

Other resources

The JewishGen and JGSGB UK database (**www.jewishgen.org/ databases/UK**) contains over 220,000 records, including many entries for BMD events. A handful of marriage contracts written in Aramaic can also be found at **http://jnul.huji.ac.il/dl/ketubbot/html/UnitedKingdom.htm**, whilst the United Synagogue site (**www.theus.org.uk**) has two useful databases, the first containing over 11,000 Jewish marriage records from 1880–1894, the other containing burial records from fourteen southern English-based cemeteries. For Jewish research in Ireland visit **www. jewishireland.org**, and for Scotland visit **www.sjac.org.uk**. The Knowles Collection blog may also assist at **http://knowlescollection.blogspot. co.uk**, which also carries a link to its main collection as hosted on FamilySearch. For Holocaust research, visit Yad Vashem at **www.yad vashem.org** and the Holocaust Survivor Children Missing Identity Project at **www.missing-identity.net**. (See p. 176 for additional resources)

The Quaker Family History Society (**www.qfhs.co.uk**) provides links to Meetings records from across Britain, whilst the Library of the Religious Society of Friends has an online catalogue for its holdings (**www.quaker. org.uk/search-catalogue**). The Genealogist website has made available records concerning Quakers in its Nonconformist collection, whilst the Yorkshire Quaker Heritage Project has also compiled a list of useful sources from across Britain (**www.hull.ac.uk/oldlib/archives/quaker/archon. htm**). The University of Leeds Library's Special Collections page has a further guide to Quaker records in North and West Yorkshire at **http://library. leeds.ac.uk/special-collections-search**. For Ireland, visit **www. quakers-in-ireland.ie**.

A gateway site for many archives and repositories relating to the Roman Catholic Church can be found at **www.catholic-history.org.uk**, and the catalogue for the Catholic National Library at **www.catholic-library.org.uk**. The Catholic Encyclopaedia may also assist at **www.newadvent.org/cathen /01729a.htm**. For Scotland, consult the Scottish Catholic Archives (**www. scottishcatholicarchives.org.uk**).

Censuses

A decennial census has been recorded in Britain from 1801, though the 1841 census was the first to be genealogically useful in listing names of those present in each household on census night, effectively providing a snapshot of life once every ten years. Most of the main genealogical vendors offer

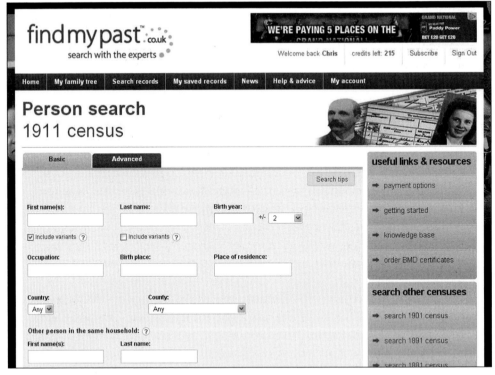

FindmyPast is one of many vendors offering access to the British decennial censuses.

access to digitised copies of the original returns for England and Wales – from 1841–1901 the records are presented as single page enumerators' returns, for 1911 as multi-page household schedules (in most cases filled in by the head of the household), with additional pages of information.

The Genealogist, as is common with many service providers, outsourced its indexing overseas, but soon after introduced a popular volunteer transcription project at **www.ukindexer.co.uk,** allowing users to gain free credits for use on its website by correcting some of the many errors found in the transcribed returns. Ancestry has transcription errors on its site for similar reasons, but invites users to submit corrections through a facility on its site. On GenesReunited, a useful feature is the ability to consult a map for the census location returned on a particular search. The Origins Network also hosts the 1841, 1861 and 1871 returns, whilst the National Archives Digital Microfilms site (see p.11) hosts the returns for the 1851 Ecclesiastical Census of England and Wales, which was carried out on the same weekend as the decennial census. (The Scottish equivalent has largely not survived.)

Scottish census returns from 1841–1911 have been digitised and the images made exclusively available at ScotlandsPeople, although incomplete transcripts for 1841–1901 returns are also available on FindmyPast, Ancestry and FamilySearch. ScotlandsPeople also carries a transcript of the 1881 census (created by the LDS Church) which is cheaper to view than the digitised equivalent. Unlike the rest of the British Isles, the original household schedules for the 1911 census have not survived; as such, the information from them has been made accessible via two-page-long enumerators' returns. Transcripts for many census records from the Borders from 1841–1861 are freely available at **www.maxwellancestry.com**. For an interesting insight into the numbers of Gaelic speakers recorded in Scotland in 1891 (the first year to ask) visit **www.linguae-celticae.org/GLP_English.htm**.

FreeCEN (**www.freecen.org.uk**) is a volunteer-run project painstakingly transcribing records from 1841 to 1891. Its English returns are more complete for the latter censuses; there is little available for Wales, and Scottish coverage tends to favour 1841 and 1851. FamilySearch also hosts very basic indexes to the English and Welsh returns, whilst the Workhouse website (**www.work houses.org**) carries free transcriptions for poor law institutions in the 1881 census.

Census Finder (**www.censusfinder.com**) provides details of many locally hosted transcription projects, including some pre-1841 returns which contain genealogically useful material. The site also provides links to returns for directories, freeholder records, militia lists and other census substitutes for the pre-1801 period.

Although part of the UK, the first successful Irish census was recorded in 1821 (a previous effort from 1813 was never presented to Parliament), but with genealogically useful information from the outset. Unfortunately, for various depressing reasons, only the 1901 and 1911 returns have survived in their entirety. These have been digitised and made freely available by the National Archives of Ireland at **www.genealogy.nationalarchives.ie**. Another complete census, but applying to the Republic of Ireland only, is the 1922 Free State Army census. This is available at **www.military archives.ie**, and worth consulting for those from Northern Ireland who fought for the Irish army during the civil war.

Copies of some Irish census information have survived from 1841 and 1851, which were used to provide evidence for people wishing to claim a state pension from 1908, and indexes can be accessed at both Ancestry and Ireland Genealogy (**www.ireland-genealogy.com**). Some other early census fragments have also survived, which will in due course be made available on the NAI genealogy platform – for details on these consult the sister title to this book, *Tracing Your Irish Family History on the Internet*. If your Irish ancestor was in Britain when the censuses were recorded, check the North of Ireland Family History Society's strays site (**www.nifhs.org/straysA.htm**).

Although most Irish censuses have been lost, several substitutes exist. The most useful is Griffith's Valuation, a land valuation taken in the mid-nineteenth century across the island, which is freely available at **www.ask aboutireland.ie** (the annual Valuation Revision Books following this exercise for Northern Ireland can be freely consulted at PRONI up to 1930). Also online is an earlier census for the island from 1659, known as Pender's Census, at **http://clanmaclochlainn.com/1659cen.htm**. The PRONI website also includes surviving fragments of the 1740 and the 1766 religious census returns in its *Names Search* database.

Statistical information from the censuses can be extremely enlightening. A Vision of Britain Through Time (**www.visionofbritain.org.uk**) hosts reports for the censuses from 1801–1971, as does Histpop at **www.histpop. org**. For the Republic of Ireland, the equivalent reports from 1926–2011 are available at **www.cso.ie/en/census**. The Genealogist site also hosts a Surname Concentration Maps facility, which plots the frequency of surnames in each English and Welsh county as noted in the censuses from 1841–1901 (ScotlandsPeople also allows a similar facility by displaying Scottish census results through its map-based returns screen option). For Ireland, data derived from Robert Matheson's *Special Report on Surnames* in 1890 can be used to plot a surname distribution at **www.ancestryireland .com/data base.php?filename=db_mathesons**.

Probate and Confirmation
Wills and inventories can usefully provide information on how your ancestors once lived, but the systems for probate vary considerably across the UK, being proved or confirmed in a variety of different courts.

England and Wales
Probate for English and Welsh wills was granted by various courts of the hierarchical Church of England up to 1858, and can be difficult to locate. The two highest probate courts in the land were the Prerogative Court of Canterbury (PCC), for the south of England and Wales, and the Prerogative Court of York (PCY) for northern England. A useful guide to the hierarchy below these courts is available in a National Archives guide at **www. nationalarchives.gov.uk/records/looking-for-person/willbefore1858**.

htm. The facility also hosts the complete collection of PCC wills from 1384–1858, with records searchable by first and last names, place, occupation and date of probate. A digital copy can then be purchased. The Genealogist also hosts the collection, with its images of considerably better resolution.

The National Wills Index (**www.nationalwillsindex.com**) from the Origins Network is a project in collaboration with the British Record Society, the York-based Borthwick Institute for Archives, the Genealogical Society of Utah and additional partners. It aims to provide a unique single access point for all surviving pre-1858 wills, including the creation of new indexes and the digitisation of many surviving records. The Borthwick Institute has already commenced the digitisation of many of its records, including records for wills granted probate through the Prerogative Court of York. The site also offers free-to-view British Isles probate jurisdiction maps at **www.origins. net/NationalWills/search/maps/index.aspx**.

The National Wills Index on Origins.net.

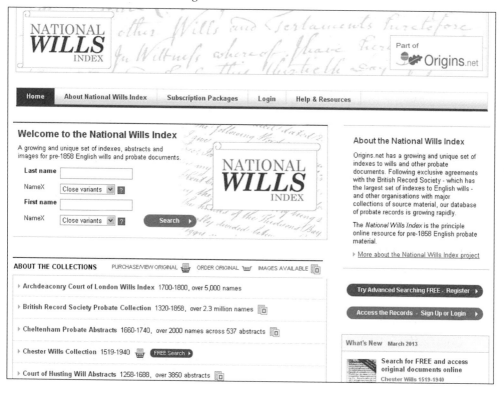

Over 190,000 wills and letters of administration proven in the lower Welsh ecclesiastical courts prior to 1858 have been digitised and made available by the National Library of Wales at **http://tinyurl.com/yl3s9t9**. The index is free, and digital copies can be viewed on the site, though you need to purchase to download a copy.

From 1858, the Probate Service (**www.justice.gov.uk/courts/probate**) has run the show, part of the Family Division of the High Court. The National Probate Calendar (Index of Wills and Administrations) 1858–1966, providing summaries of documents that have gone through the civil courts, is available on Ancestry, and lists the value of estates, details on the deceased and appointed executors, and more. The Treasury's Bona Vacantia site (**www. bonavacantia.gov.uk**), used by so-called 'heir hunters', contains a database of unclaimed estates which can be searched by name, place and date of death.

Another useful online resource for English and Welsh probate is the index to Death Duty Registers 1796–1903, published at FindmyPast. As well as providing information from the original National Archives register, which recorded the legacy duty paid on any monetary sums bequeathed in an estate, the database can also help you to identify where the original will or administration documents may have been granted probate. Digitised images from the registers from 1796–1811 are available from the National Archives website.

Scotland

Prior to the Scottish Reformation, the church dealt with the 'confirmation' of wills (the equivalent of 'probate'), but the role was given to civil Commissary Courts from 1564 to the 1820s, and thereafter to the Sheriff Courts. All records that have undergone confirmation from 1513–1925 are hosted at the ScotlandsPeople website. Scottish First World War soldiers' wills are expected to join them in the near future.

Ireland

A great many probate documents were destroyed during the Irish Civil War, but many copies survived within district probate offices, as well as probate calendars providing summaries of all estates passed through the courts. The PRONI website hosts a Will Calendars database providing free summaries of all such entries for the north of Ireland from 1858–1943, and any copies of wills from 1858–1900 if they have survived. The National Archive of Ireland also hosts the digitised printed calendars for the Republic from

1923–1982, which are fully name searchable and accessible through the site's catalogue. Earlier calendars from 1858–1922 have been made available on the NAI's genealogy records platform. (See p.6)

Prior to 1858 PRONI offers a Name Search database with a surviving index to earlier wills and administration papers. FamilyRelatives has an excellent collection of Irish wills indexes from 1536–1857, whilst the Origins Network hosts an index from 1484–1858.

Directories

Street and trade directories can be useful in establishing the locations of people prior to the nineteenth-century censuses, and indeed, between each of the census years and beyond.

The Historical Directories website from the University of Leicester at **www.historicaldirectories.org** hosts several English and Welsh editions from 1750–1919, though mostly from 1850 onwards. The site does not hold complete sets for each county; Durham has twelve editions between 1801 and 1914, for example, and there are just fifty-four for the whole of Wales. English Trade Directories of the 19th Century (**http://tinyurl.com/4pyhmr**) is also worth consulting, containing a searchable database for sixteen counties, mainly from 1830.

Ancestry has its UK and US Directories 1680–1830 database, compilation of biographical extracts from various directories, including over 140 from England, (though virtually nothing for Wales), whilst its UK City and County Directories 1600–1900 collection provides an impressive array of fully searchable digitised books for the whole of Britain. It also offers the British Phone Books 1880–1984 collection, as sourced from the archives of British Telecom, containing some 1,780 telephone directories.

The Genealogist carries a large collection of directories through its Directories Search category. The most comprehensive collection is for London, with over eighty editions from 1677–1940. Whilst mainly useful for England, there are some holdings for both Wales and Scotland. FamilyRelatives also has various directories from the 1830s and a selection of medical registers and directories from 1853-1943.

Scotland is blessed with a joint project between the National Library of Scotland and the Internet Archive, which has seen many Post Office Directories scanned. The NLS website has a dedicated platform at **http://digital.nls.uk/directories** hosting some 700 editions from 1773–1911; the Internet Archive goes beyond 1911, with over a thousand directories freely available at **htttp://archive.org/details/nationallibraryofscotland**.

The excellent Street Directories section of the PRONI website has many Ulster directories from 1819–1900, whilst additional holdings from 1805–1913 are found at **www.lennonwylie.co.uk**. Various county offerings from 1862 are available at **www.libraryireland.com/Genealogy.php**, whilst The Ulster Towns Directory 1910 is online at **www.libraryireland.com/Ulster Directory1910/Contents.php**. Additional Irish directories are available at **www.failteromhat.com** and on the Origins Network, most notably a major collection of Dublin directories that will eventually see coverage from 1636–1900 when complete.

To trace people in more recent times, visit **www.192.com**, FindMyPast and **www.the ukelectoralroll.co.uk**, where information can be sourced from contemporary electoral registers and directories. Further local directory sites are listed in chapters 4–8.

Maps and Gazetteers

The examination of the built environment where our ancestors once lived can help to contextualise their stories. Changes in landscape can be plotted across time, allowing us to note the development of lines of communication such as canals, roads and railways, as well as the effects of land enclosure and the development of social housing.

Maps

The best gateway site for the discussion of maps from around the world is that run by retired British Library map librarian Tony Campbell at **www. maphistory.info**, though the site does not contain any images. The British Library also has an impressive introduction to the subject at **www.bl.uk/ reshelp/findhelprestype/maps/index.html**.

Several sites provide current maps, including Streetmap (**www.street map.co.uk**), Bing (**www.bing.com/maps**) and Google Maps (**http:// maps.google.co.uk**). The latter is particularly useful, in that in addition to the main map for an area and a satellite overview for the location, ground level photographs ('street view'), can also be viewed – right clicking on these also allows for 3D viewing (though you will need the appropriate glasses!). A historic aerial perspective is obtainable from both **www.oldaerial photos. com** and **http://aerial.rcahms.gov.uk**.

Britain was organised into a series of historic counties up to 1974 and a map showing their locations is at **http://abcounties.com/counties**. The most detailed nineteenth and twentieth century maps are those produced by the Ordnance Survey. The present collection can be viewed at the Get-a-

Map service at www.getamap.ordnancesurveyleisure.co.uk, whilst historic examples are available from several sources. Old Maps (www.old-maps.co.uk) carries the earliest County Series maps at 1:10 560 scale. A Vision of Britain Through Time (www.visionofbritain.org.uk/maps) carries the First Series of the OS for England and Wales from 1805–69, maps from the Revised Series from 1902–05, and several Britain-wide collections. In addition are various other maps series at different scales as recent as 1948, including county boundary maps, sanitary district maps showing civil parishes, and more.

Pre-dating the OS series are a set of English county maps from 1787 by John Cary, available at http://homepage.ntlworld.com/tomals/index11.html. Mapseeker (www.mapseeker.co.uk) also carries older colour maps for some of the larger towns, cities and counties across the country, with the site also listing the sources from whence they were obtained, and a search tool for towns and villages. GENMAPS (http://freepages.genealogy.roots web.ancestry.com/~genmaps/index.html) has an extensive old maps collection for Britain which is free to consult, whilst Baedeker's Old Guide Books (http://contueor.com/baedeker/index.htm) hosts many town plans on its site from 1910 for the whole island.

The National Library of Scotland's dedicated maps site at http://maps.nls.uk has over 48,000 digitised maps, including town plans from 1580 onwards, Timothy Pont's maps from the late sixteenth century and OS returns from the mid-nineteenth to early twentieth century. For a set of Ordnance Survey town plans from 1847-1895, visit http://sites.scran.ac.uk/townplans/townplans.html. The ScotlandsPlaces site (www.scotlandsplaces.gov.uk) also carries Ordnance Survey Name Books.

Tom's Big Chest of Old Welsh Maps (http://homepage.ntlworld.com/tomals/Welsh-Maps-of-Samuel-Lewis,1833.htm) contains Samuel Lewis's maps for the country from 1833, whilst John Ball's Welsh Family History Archive provides additional maps and gazetteer resources at www.jlb2011.co.uk/index.html, including a glossary on how to interpret Welsh place names, and a Sounds of Wales site, where you can hear the pronunciation of over 220 Welsh place names.

The Ordnance Survey of Northern Ireland at https://maps.osni.gov.uk carries both historic and current maps for the country, and the modern Irish Ordnance Survey for the south is available at www.osi.ie. Historic Irish townland maps are at www.pasthomes.com, and www.ulsterancestry.com/free-ulster-maps.html, whilst the Down Survey of 1656-1658 at http://downsurvey.tcd.ie has maps from Ireland's earliest land survey.

Several additional Irish maps are available at **www.failteromhat.com**, including a map of the Irish Free State and a road map of the island from 1877. Geograph Ireland (**www.geograph.ie**) is also trying to photograph every square kilometre of the island, with the results accessible via an interactive map. For Irish poor law union maps visit **www.movinghere. org.uk/deliveryfiles/PRO/MFQ1 _925/0/1.pdf** (also **/2.pdf** and **/3.pdf**).

Gazetteers

The Gazetteer of British Place Names (**www.gazetteer.co.uk**) contains information on the development of the administrative boundaries of England, as well as some historic boundary maps, whilst A Vision of Britain Through Time (**www.visionofbritain.org.uk**) carries descriptive entries from John Marius Wilson's *Imperial Gazetteer of England and Wales* (1870–72) and John Bartholomew's *Gazetteer of the British Isles* (1887), as well as many contemporary letters and documents from writers such as Daniel Defoe.

Several gazetteers are also hosted on British History Online (**www. british-history.ac.uk**), including Samuel Lewis's *Topographical Directory of England* from 1848, and various descriptive volumes for most counties as recorded by the Victoria County History series. A useful Scottish equivalent for the latter is the *Statistical Accounts of Scotland* collections, drawn up from 1791–99 and 1834–45. These have been digitised and made available to view by the University of Edinburgh (**www.edina.ac.uk/stat-acc-scot**), by Google Books (**http://books.google.com**). The National Library of Scotland hosts twenty nineteenth-century gazetteers on its Digital Gallery site at **http://digitalgallery.cfm** (also accessible at the Internet Archive at **www. archive.org/details/scottishgazetteers**). An excellent contemporary gazetteer is Undiscovered Scotland (**www.undiscoveredscotland.co.uk**), whilst a National Gazetteer for Wales is available at **http://homepage.ntlworld. com/geogdata/ngw/places.htm**.

The three volume *Parliamentary Gazetteer of Ireland* from 1844–46 is available on Google Books at **http://tinyurl.com/topographyvol1, http:// tinyurl.com/topographyvol12** and **http://tinyurl.com/topography vol3**), whilst the locations of Irish townlands can be established from databases at both **www.seanruad.com** and **www.ulsterancestry.com**. A useful resource to help with the derivation and translation of Irish locations is the Placenames Database of Ireland (**www.logainm.ie**). For Scottish Gaelic places see **www.ainmean-aite.org** (also accessible at **www.gaelicplace names.org**).

Heritage

For the built landscape, English Heritage (**www.english-heritage. org.uk**) has a wealth of online databases for aerial photos and the National Monuments Record. The Royal Commission on the Ancient and Historical Monuments of Wales (**www.rcahmw.gov.uk**) has a searchable database of its holdings entitled Coflein, whilst the Scottish equivalent, the Royal Commission on the Ancient and Historical Monuments of Scotland (**www.rcahms.gov.uk**), has the equally useful Canmore and Canmap databases. Much of the RCAHMS material is incorporated into the ScotlandsPlaces site (see p.31), which offers both free and subscription-based resources and guides, including boundary change details and tax records from the seventeenth– nineteenth centuries. Ancestry also offers the UK, Land Tax Redemption, 1798 collection (actually for England and Wales), which lists both owners and occupiers of land subject to the tax, whilst Scottish valuation rolls for every tenth year from 1855–1915 are being made available online on ScotlandsPeople.

If you are confident that you can trace your ancestry back to the eleventh century, the Domesday Map project at **http://domesdaymap.co.uk** connects all the placenames mentioned in the work from 1086 to a modern Google map. Information returned includes taxes paid, and the names of feudal lords from both 1066 and 1086. The landholders can also be found listed at **www.domesdaybook.co.uk**.

Newspapers

The British Library receives a copy of every newspaper published in the UK. An online guide to holdings is available at **www.bl.uk/reshelp/findhelp restype/news**, and titles can be searched within the Integrated Catalogue at **http://catalogue.bl.uk**, using the Newspaper Library option in the dropdown menu of the search box. Some titles from the 1800s onwards have been published via the British Library 19th Century Newspaper Collection website, though this can now only be accessed via subscribing institutions. Many libraries offer free access to this as part of their licensed digital collections (you will need to register with your library card). Another British Library release offered by similar means is the digitised Burney Collection, which includes early newspapers from the seventeenth and eighteenth century for London and across Britain, as well as various pamphlets and proclamations.

The British Newspaper Archive

The nineteenth-century collection was also previously accessible to the public via a subscription-based site, but this facility has now been replaced by the British Newspaper Archive (**www.britishnewspaperarchive.co.uk**). As well as incorporating the earlier material from the British Library, the site, operated in partnership with Brightsolid, is seeking to place online some forty million newspaper pages over a ten-year period. At the time of writing much of the content has also been made available through FindmyPast and Genes Reunited, although not including any of its Irish holdings.

Subscription based archives for several national titles printed in England are available online. *The Times* (1785–1985) offers its archive through **www.thetimes.co.uk/tto/archive/**, but can also be viewed for free via subscribing institutions, and through a much better search platform. Both the *Daily Express* and the *Daily Mirror* have twentieth-century archives available at **www.ukpressonline.co.uk**. Public access to the Mirror archive can only be gained up to 1980 (complete access is, however, offered to subscribing institutions), and twenty-first century editions of the *Sunday Express*, *Daily Star* and *Daily Star Sunday* are also available. Two other titles, *The Guardian* and *The Observer*, have also been digitised (1791–2003), and can be viewed at **http://pqasb.pqarchiver.com/guardian**.

Google's News Archive (**http://news.google.com/newspapers**) contains predominantly American and Canadian content, though also has some material from the *Daily Mirror* from 1953. Its greatest British offerings, however, are for three Glaswegian titles – the *Glasgow Herald* (1806–1990), the *Glasgow Advertiser* (1783–1801) and the *Bulletin and Scots Pictorial* (1951–1960). The Scotsman Digital Archive (**http://archive.scotsman.com**) hosts copies of the *Scotsman* newspaper (1817–1950), although free access can be obtained by subscribing to the National Library of Scotland's licensed digital collections via its website. Also for Scotland, an online Guide to Scottish Newspapers Indexes from the National Library of Scotland at **www.nls.uk/collections/ newspapers/indexes/index.cfm** gives information on every Scottish title indexed, the years of coverage, and the locations of the indexes. Its Word on the Street project (**http://digital.nls.uk/broadsides/index.html**) also depicts 1800 broadsheets from across the country from 1650–1910.

A major initiative from the National Library of Wales has seen some two million pages of content from 1844–1910 digitised and made freely available via Welsh Newspapers Online at **http://welshnewspapers.llgc.org.uk** (also **http://papuraunewyddcymru.llgc.org.uk**). An index to the first English-language title from Wales, *The Cambrian*, has also been made available online at **www. swansea.gov.uk/index.cfm?articleid=5673**, covering the period from 1804–1930.

In Ireland, the Irish Newspaper Archives (**www.irishnewsarchive.com**) has a truly impressive range of titles from across the island, including the *Irish Independent* and the *Donegal News*. In addition, another major all-island resource is the *Irish Times* archive site (**www.irishtimes.com/premium/ loginpage**). For the north, Eddie Connolly has extracted many stories and intimations from several Ulster-based newspapers and placed them online at **http://freepages.genealogy.rootsweb.ancestry.com/~econnolly**. Nick Reddan's site at **http://members.iinet.net.au/~nickred/newspaper** is an all-Ireland equivalent.

Ancestry provides some newspaper material, including issues of *The Bristol Times and Mirror* from December 1897, London's *Daily Universal Register* from 1786 and 1787, and other papers covering Lancashire and Staffordshire. It also has a browse-only run of the *Belfast Newsletter* from 1738–1925 and additional Irish titles, as well as a database of information extracted from the *Railway Gazette* from 1860–1930. MyHeritage has a large collection of English newspapers (acquired from World Vital Records). Its most extensive collection is for the *London Daily Mail*, with coverage from 1896–1923, though the availability of other titles is more fragmented, with, for example, the *Daily Post* available for 1729, 1731, 1737–38, 1739 and 1741–44. The Genealogist has several mid-nineteenth-century copies of *The Illustrated London News*, as well as content from *War Illustrated* and *The Great War*. Another useful site carrying over a hundred English and British newspaper titles is the Newspaper Archive (**http://newspaperarchive.com**).

A free and often neglected resource is the *London Gazette*, the official paper of record for the Government from the seventeenth century, carrying notices such as military medal awards, promotions, court appointment, civil honours, personal insolvencies and probate notices. Although most editions are keyword searchable, some editions from the seventeenth and eighteenth century were not scanned using optical character recognition technology, meaning that they must instead be browsed. The paper has sister titles in Edinburgh (from 1699) and Belfast (from 1922); all can be accessed at **www.gazettes-online.co.uk**. Following the Partition of Ireland a separate paper, *Iris Ofigiúil*, was established to replace the all-Ireland *Dublin Gazette*, but its archive can only be searched online from 2002 at **www.irisoifigiuil.ie**.

The Internet Library of Early Journals (**www.bodley.ox.ac.uk/ilej**) allows access to digitised editions of six eighteenth and nineteenth-century periodicals, including the *Gentleman's Magazine* and *Notes and Queries*. JSTOR provides free access to its Early Journal Content for material published prior to 1923 in the United States and prior to 1870 elsewhere (for copyright reasons). The content includes 500,000 articles from more than 200 journals, accessible at **www.jstor.org/action/showAdvancedSearch** – click on the box that states 'Include only content I can access'.

Richard Heaton's Newspaper Collection at **http://tinyurl.com/3aaal9** further provides access to transcripts and extracts from just under 900 fully searchable Georgian and early Victorian regional newspapers, predominantly for Lancashire and the south of England.

Nobility and Gentry

If your blood is of the blue variety, Burke's Peerage and Gentry (**www. burkes-peerage.com**) contains over a million names in its database connected to the British aristocracy. Although subscription-based, there are some free resources available, such as free-to-view versions of Burke's Family Index, Burke's General Armory and Burke's Colonial gentry. Stirnet (**www. stirnet.com**) also provides pedigrees on many families from across the British Isles, whilst the similar but free The Peerage site (**www.the peerage.com**) has many distinguished pedigrees compiled by New Zealand-based Darrel Lundy (an app version is also available for Apple devices). Cracroft's Peerage offers similar holdings at **www.cracroftspeerage .co.uk**, whilst Leigh Rayment's site at **http://leighrayment.com** provides further information on the British peerage, though without any pedigrees.

Debrett's (**www.debretts.com**) has a freely searchable biographical database of the top 25,000 'achievers' in Britain, and useful guides to such subjects as the Royal Family and British orders of chivalry. The official website for the British Monarchy is **www.royal.gov.uk,** which includes details on how to access the Royal Archives, whilst a list of the most important or senior Royal appointments since the fourteenth century can be found at **www. history.ac.uk/publications/office.** The Directory of Royal Genealogical Data (**www.hull.ac.uk/php/cssbct/genealogy/royal/**) contains the pedigrees of the British monarchy and other royal houses connected to it. If your ancestors worked for the royals, FindmyPast carries various collections covering the period from 1526–1924, whilst the Database of Court Officers 1660–1837 may help further at **www.luc.edu/history/fac_resources/bucholz/DCO/ DCO.html**.

The *Oxford Dictionary of National Biography* (**www.oxforddnb.com**) contains over 57,000 biographies on the great and the good, as does *Who's Who* (**www.ukwhoswho.com**). Both are subscription-based sites, though many libraries will provide free access. The *Dictionary of Ulster Biography* (**www.ulsterbiography.co.uk**) is a useful Northern Irish equivalent.

For English and Welsh heraldry, consult the College of Arms site (**www. college-of-arms.gov.uk**) for past editions of its newsletter available in PDF format. The Heraldry Society also has an online presence at **www.the heraldrysociety.com**. North of the border, heraldry matters are regulated by the Court of the Lord Lyon (**www.lyon-court.com**). Coats of arms have been digitised from the *Public Register of All Arms and Bearings* from 1672–1907 and made available at ScotlandsPeople. Many pre-1672 coats of arms, blazons and images can also be consulted at **www.heraldry-scotland.co.uk**.

For Ireland, visit **www.nli.ie/en/intro/heraldry-introduction.aspx** for entries between 1936 and 1980 in the *Registers of Grants of Arms* and an introduction to Irish heraldry, and **www.maproom.org/00/47/index.php** for several plates depicting Irish arms, as recorded in 1905.

If you are interested in obtaining items of silver with your family crest, My Family Silver (**www.myfamilysilver.com**) is well worth consulting. The sites's Crestfinder tool allows you to search through *Fairbairns Book of Crests*, and to search for an item carrying a particular design through the catalogues of some of the world's most famous auctioneering firms, such as Sotheby's and Christies.

Chapter 3

OCCUPATIONAL RECORDS

As well as creating a basic understanding of who our ancestors were and the locations in which they existed, it is also worthwhile pursuing the records of what they did for a living, to help us fully understand the daily struggles of their lives.

Often we will come across a trade name in an old record that completely throws us, but handy sites for enlightenment include Hall Genealogy Website's Old Occupation Names at **http://rmhh.co.uk/occup** and ScotlandsPeople's list of some 1,500 occupations at **http://scotlands people.gov.uk/content/help/index.aspx?r=551&430**. There are many possible trades within which your forebears may have worked, and it would be impossible to list them all. If your ancestor served an apprenticeship the master may have had to pay tax – if so consult Ancestry's UK, Register of Duties Paid for Apprentices' Indentures, 1710–1811 collection. (Additional occupational records on Ancestry can now be found on a dedicated platform at **www.ancestry.co.uk/cs/uk/occupations**). FindmyPast also carries additional apprenticeship collections for Dorset, Lincolnshire, Manchester and Somerset.

The following section concerns some of the more common occupations employing many across the nation.

The Armed Forces
Army
The United Kingdom has engaged in its fair share of wars across the centuries, and it is unlikely that your family does not have a military connection somewhere in its history. One of the best sites covering such history in the British Isles and beyond is the Military History Encyclopaedia on the Web (**www.historyofwar.org**). Equally useful is British Battles (**www.britishbattles.com**) and the Scots at War Trust (**www.scotsatwar. co.uk**).

A list of British Army museums in England and Wales is available from the Army Museums Ogilby Trust (**www.armymuseums.org.uk**), which also contains an extensive bibliography on resources for each regiment, whilst the National Army Museum (at **www.nam.ac.uk**) lists additional information. The Imperial War Museum's Collections and Research site (**www.iwm.org.uk/collections-research**) provides a great deal of information on how to research military ancestors, as well as several comprehensive online catalogues for its holdings. For those wishing to obtain copies of recent service records still held by the Ministry of Defence, the Veterans Agency (**www.veterans-uk.info**) has all the relevant information, as well as a guide to claiming medals. For replacement medals, consult **www.awardmedals.com**. If your ancestor was the recipient of a Victoria Cross, consult Ancestry's UK, Victoria Cross Medals, 1857–2007 collection.

The twentieth century

Possibly the most informative site on the history of the First World War is Chris Baker's exceptional website, The Long, Long Trail (**www.1914-1918. net**). It provides detailed accounts of the various regiments and battalions which fought, and the campaigns engaged in. The site also carries war diaries, despatches, maps and more, and is accompanied by the Great War Forum at **http://1914-1918.invisionzone.com/forums**, which covers just about every war topic that you might wish to discuss. The Western Front Association also has many handy background resources at **www.western frontassociation.com,** and is, at the time of writing, working on the digitisation of some six million Great War soldiers' pension record cards, which it saved from destruction at the Ministry of Defence, with the intention of making them available online – a look-up service is already operating. The records concern all the armed forces (not just army), and include pension applications for both the injured and dependants of all officers and other ranks who died. The University of Oxford has a rich collection of material as submitted by members of the public at **www.oucs.ox.ac.uk/ww1lit/gwa/**, including audio recordings of interviews, diaries, drawings, postcards, paintings, and other useful material that can help you to construct a sense of what it was like to be there. FirstWorldWar.com (**www.firstworldwar.com**) also provides a similarly themed multimedia guide to the war, whilst the BBC's Remembrance site, although no longer updated, still contains a great deal of commemorative material as supplied by the public at **www. bbc.co.uk/remembrance**. Many contemporary documents concerning the First World War can be accessed at **www.gwpda.org**.

About forty per cent of First World War soldiers' service records have survived, and have been digitised by Ancestry.co.uk. Held by TNA in series

WO 363 and WO 364, the company has categorised them on its site as two collections, British Army WW1 Service Records 1914–20 and British Army WW1 Pensions 1914–20. In fact, both contain service records, with the latter for soldiers who were discharged and who subsequently claimed for a pension. (It is worth noting that a very small number of misfiled service records for Boer War veterans are also found within the collection). The same collection is offered by FamilySearch, but only at its family history centres.

The National Library of Scotland provides dozens of monthly army lists for the world wars at both **www.nls.uk/family-history/military-lists** and **http://archive.org/details/nlsarmylists**.

Ancestry hosts the British Army Medal Rolls Index Cards 1914–20 collection of almost five million records, listing soldiers and airmen who were entitled to receive a medal. The same cards are available via The National Archives website, though only black and white copies of the fronts of the cards are supplied here, as opposed to Ancestry's colour scans of both sides (the backs of the cards sometimes reveal additional useful information). On the plus side, the archive's collection is better indexed, and has cards for women and civilian war workers. The Long, Long Trail site (p.39) has a handy page for interpreting the details on these cards – use the keywords 'medal index cards' in the search box.

The author's great-uncle Charles Mackintosh MacFarlane, in the Cameron Highlanders.

For the provision of soldiers' rolls of honour, the main genealogy vendors have all been competing with each other to provide access. Ancestry, along with FindmyPast, FamilyRelatives, and The Genealogist, has database versions of the *National Roll of the Great War*, *Soldiers Died in the Great War* and *De Ruvigny's Roll of Honour*, which can further help to identify soldiers who fought in the campaign. The same databases are also available at **www.military-genealogy.com**, where entries can be searched at 50p per entry, though with a minimum subscription of £5. Forces War Records (**www. forces-war-records.co.uk**) is another subscription site offering a substantial amount of First World War material, as well as for other conflicts. Some Irish First World War soldiers' wills are available free online at **www.genealogy. nationalarchives.ie,** whilst ScotlandsPeople intends to host Scottish wills in the near future.

On casualties, Ancestry offers a database called UK, Silver War Badge Records 1914–20, detailing British and Empire personnel who claimed the badge as a result of injury or illness, with details including rank, regimental number, unit, dates of enlistment and discharge, and reason for discharge. The Genealogist has additional resources in the form of the War Office's 'Weekly Casualty Lists', covering all ranks.

Additional First World War army resources available via the National Archives website include Prisoner of War Interviews and Reports, as recorded by the Committee on the Treatment of British Prisoners of War, service records for the Women's Army Auxiliary Corps, as well as the Victoria Cross registers (in fact from 1895 to 1944) and Selected First World War and Army of Occupation War Diaries, from 1914–22. The International Red Cross (**www.icrc.org**) provides information on how to consult the society's archives for information on POWs, including an online application form – at the time of writing the research service was suspended to allow for digitisation of many of its First World War resources, a project intended for completion in 2014. If your ancestors were civilian prisoners of war, my own Ruhleben Story site at **http://ruhleben.tripod.com** attempts to provide detailed biographical information on many of the 5,500 British and Commonwealth citizens interned on the outskirts of Berlin during the conflict.

For the Second World War, the National Archives has very little army material available, its only significant holding being the Recommendations for Honours and Awards (1935–1990), which also contains details for RAF and RN personnel. Ancestry, however, has the UK Army Roll of Honour 1939–1945, compiled from various War Office sources between 1944 and 1949, and the UK British Army Prisoners of War 1939–1945 collection, with information on well over 100,000 POWs. The Genealogist equally hosts the Army Roll of Honour for World War Two, but also has records from the Miscellaneous Foreign Returns, 1831–1964 (from TNA's RG 32 collection), which has notifications of deaths in Japanese and German POW camps, including names of those executed as prisoners.

A detailed timeline of the war is available at **www.worldwar-2.net,** whilst **www.secondworldwar.co.uk** offers some background information on the key players and some general statistics. General resource sites on the history of the war include a sites from military historian Paul Reed on the battlefields and commemorations of the war at **www.ww2battlefields.info,** whilst Wartime Memories (**www.wartimememories.co.uk**) encourages the public to commemorate their military relatives' stories by making submissions to the site. Britain at War (**www.britain-at-war.org.uk**) is Ron Taylor's comprehensive site on the conflict which includes rolls of honour (including for British civilian war dead across the globe) and many essays on the various battles of the war. Although predominantly about the Second World War, it also covers the previous conflict and additional events such as Suez. The Association of Jewish Ex-Servicemen and Women website (**www.ajex. org.uk**) hosts a roll of honour for all Jewish service personnel to have lost their lives from 1939–60, with further information available at the Jewish Military Museum in London. A useful site providing an overview of the role of women throughout the war is located at **http://caber.open.ac.uk/schools/stanway/index.html,** whilst Northern Ireland's experience is outlined in detail at **www.secondworldwarni. org**. If your ancestor served in what is now the Royal Logistic Corps, it's pay-per-view Digital Library site at **www.rlcarchive.org** has various journals, including many from the Second World War.

Following the war, many people ended up doing National Service, and Alan Parkinson has produced an interesting site on his experience entitled National Service Memoirs (**www.nationalservicememoirs.co.uk**). Since 1945 the UK has also been involved in a series of conflicts and campaigns, ranging from Korea and the Northern Irish Troubles to the Falklands and Iraq; for comprehensive information on these campaigns, and additional resources such as regimental histories and rolls of honour, visit **www. britains-smallwars.com**.

War memorials

The Commonwealth War Graves Commission (CWGC) hosts a database at **www.cwgc.org** of over 1.7 million British and Commonwealth service personnel who died during the two world wars, as well as 67,000 civilians who died between 1939 and 1945. A similar site is Pierre Vandervelden's In Memory (**www.inmemories.com**). Based in Belgium, Pierre has been valiantly photographing the various cemeteries and providing lists of all the Allied casualties within each, making it easy to see which other members of a regiment were buried alongside your ancestor, perhaps following the same military action. The War Graves Photographic Project (**www.twgpp. org**) is also working in tandem with the CWGC to provide images of every memorial from 1914 to the present day, whilst In From the Cold (**www. infromthecold.org**) is a sort of strays website, listing details of some 1,500 further personnel not officially commemorated by the CWGC. The Genealogist has a War Memorials Records database, which lists many British memorials and also provides a Google Maps/StreetView facility to allow virtual visits to relevant sites.

The Imperial War Museum has an inventory showing the locations of memorials across Britain for all wars at **www.ukniwm.org.uk** – at the time of writing it was also working with Brightsolid on its new Lives of the First World War project (see **www.livesofthefirstworldwar.org**). Many First World War memorials are also listed at **www.roll-of-honour.com**, with details for British-based Royal Mail memorials further available at **http:// catalogue.postalheritage.org.uk** (located in the Collections and Catalogue category). The Scottish Military Research Group (**www.scottish militaryresearch.co.uk**) and the Scottish National War Memorial (**www. snwm.org**) can help north of the border.

Military nursing
TNA offers some service records for nurses at **www.nationalarchives. gov.uk/records/army-nurses-service-records.htm**, mainly for the Queen Alexandra's Imperial Military Nursing Service, the Queen Alexandra's Imperial Military Nursing Service (Reserve) and the Territorial Force Nursing Service. FindmyPast has some 2,328 names in its Gillies Archive, a database of names of those who received plastic surgery from 1918–25, whilst also offering additional nurses service records in its Military Nurses 1856–1994 collection. The British Military Nurses site at **www. scarletfinders.co.uk** includes war diaries from the two world wars, as well as nominal rolls for 1939–1940.

Earlier campaigns
FindmyPast has digitised the pre-First World War Chelsea Pension records held at TNA, which lists service records for soldiers pensioned out following their military service, most of whom were 'out-pensioners', i.e. not resident at the Royal Hospital at Chelsea itself. Its database, entitled British Army Service Records 1760–1915, also includes militia service records from 1806–1915, and yeomanry records from the Imperial Yeomanry from 1899–1902, who served in the South African War. The vendor also has a separate database for British soldiers discharged to pension from the Royal Hospital Kilmainham in Dublin from 1783–1822.

John Henry Fry's service record from 1888; Barnstaple-born Fry served for just three days before being discharged. (Crown copyright WO972843/23 reproduced courtesy of The National Archives and findmypast.co.uk)

A series of guides at **www.nationalarchives.gov.uk/records/looking-for-person/default.htm** explains where to direct research efforts for both lower ranks and officers. The latter are fairly well recorded in annual guides such as Hart's Army List (established in 1839). A good selection including this and earlier lists dating back to 1798 is available at the FamilyRelatives site, providing information on an officer's career up to the date of each publication, as well as at **http://archive.org/details/nlsarmylists**. The Internet Archive also provides a useful regimental guide from 1901 at **www. archive.org/details/cu31924030726503**, entitled *The Regimental Records of the British Army: a Historical Resume Chronologically Arranged of Titles, Campaigns, Honours, Uniforms, Facings, Badges, Nicknames etc.* Many nineteenth-century editions of Hart's Army Lists are freely available from the National Library of Scotland (see p.7).

There are many sites dedicated to earlier campaigns – information on soldiers from all ranks involved in the Boer War is extensively recorded at **www.roll-of-honour.com/Boer**, with lists of medals awarded, the wounded, participating soldiers, POWs etc, and at **www.angloboerwar.com**.

For the Napoleonic wars, the Peninsula Medal Roll is available at FindmyPast (1793–1814) and the Waterloo Medal Roll for 1815, whilst a roll call of mainly officers present at Waterloo is available at FamilyRelatives (some NCOs are also listed). The Original Record website also carries many records for individual regiments.

For the history of the seventeenth-century Civil Wars in Britain visit **www.british-civil-wars.co.uk**, and if you can connect back to the Hundred Years War visit **www.icmacentre.ac.uk/soldier/database/index.php** for muster rolls, protection rolls and garrison rolls containing over 200,000 names between 1369 and 1453.

Finally, two other sites worth visiting are that of the Army Children Archive (**www.archhistory.co.uk**), which chronicles how children raised in military families coped in their day-to-day existence, and **www.achart.ca**, on the history of the Royal Hibernian Military School and the Duke of York's School.

Royal Air Force

Taking to the air, the Royal Air Force began as the Royal Flying Corps, the history of which is outlined from 1914–18 at **www.airwar1.org.uk**, with the site including some pilots' accounts of hostilities as well as information on the planes used. The Aerodrome (**www.theaerodrome.com**) is a site with a much wider remit, containing information on aces and aircraft from the various nations involved. Ancestry hosts the Great Britain, Royal Aero Club Aviators' Certificates 1910–1950 collection, which contains 28,000 index cards for pilots issued with licenses to fly. This includes the names and details of many who joined the RFC and the Royal Naval Air Service, as well as thirty-three out of thirty-four surviving photo albums containing images of airmen. Additional RAC resources can be found at **http://raec.sds.websds.net**. TNA also has the digitised service records of RAF officers as well as members of the Women's Royal Air Force, who served during the First World War. A Roll of Honour for airmen who have died whilst serving with the Fleet Air Arm can be searched at **www.fleetairarm.com/fleet-air-arm-roll-of-honour.aspx**, mainly for the Second World War and onwards.

The RAF Museum (**www.rafmuseum.org.uk**) has many useful resources, including downloadable copies in PDF format of RAF Historical Society journals, details on the museum's resources, and online exhibitions such as Lest We Forget, which also includes a virtual Book of Remembrance. The museum's Navigator site (**http://navigator.rafmuseum.org**) has more detailed information on the collections, including many images. The museum is at the time of writing digitising 300,000 First World War personnel records as part of a new permanent exhibition exploring the 1914–18 conflict. FindmyPast has a 1918 RAF muster roll, detailing the names of 181,000 servicemen who signed up to the service upon its creation in April 1918. For a list of RAF squadron associations, and their contact details, visit **www.associations.rafinfo.org.uk/squadron.htm**, whilst a series of RAF lists from the 1920s can be consulted at FamilyRelatives, with information on all ranks from Air Marshal to Pilot Officer. Further Air Force lists for 1919, the late 1930s and most of the Second World War are available from the National Library of Scotland (see p.8).

For the Battle of Britain, consult **www.raf.mod.uk/history/BattleofBritainRollofHonour.cfm** to view a Roll of Honour for the conflict, and **www.raf.mod.uk/history/battleofbritain70thanniversary.cfm** for a set of daily reports pertaining to sorties between July and October 1940. Air Ministry combat reports are available for the Second World War via the TNA website at **www.nationalarchives.gov.uk/records/combat-reports-ww2.htm**, as are Air Ministry operations records books at **www.nationalarchives.gov.uk/records/raf-operations-record-books.htm**. For downed aircraft in Britain, visit Jim Kimpton's Treetectives Air Crash Project at **http://jimkimpton.co.uk/treetectives/aircraft/aircrash.htm**.

Many abbreviations found in RAF service records, and some RAF slang, can be decoded using **www.lancaster-archive.com/bc_abbreviations.htm**.

Royal Navy

For the senior service, the National Museum of the Royal Navy website (**www.nmrn.org.uk**) has curator's highlights, videos, news and more. The Naval History site (**www.naval-history.net**) has an extensive collection of resources available on the history of ships and personnel, including many rolls of honour and useful resources for the Navy's story from the First World War to the Falklands.

TNA offers the Registers of Seamen's Services from 1853–1923, Royal Naval Officers' Service Records from 1756–1917, wills of Royal Naval Seamen from 1786–1882, Women's Royal Naval Service Records from 1917–1919, and also Royal Naval Division Service Records from 1914–19, detailing the reservist seamen who fought alongside the army in the trenches during the war (a database of First World War Royal Naval Division casualties is also available from both FindmyPast and Ancestry). Earlier naval records exist on the site in the form of logs from Royal Naval exploration voyages from 1757–1861. The site also has two collections for those with Royal Marines in their trees – Royal Marines Service Records from 1842–1936 and Royal Marines: Selected Plymouth Attestations from 1805–1848. Additional Admiralty records are freely available from the archive's Digital Microfilms facility, including resources for seamen's medals and wills.

For earlier records of the navy prior to the twentieth century, the Naval Biographical database (**www.navylist.org**) contains entries of many officers from 1660 to 1870, but only in the form of an index, from which you can purchase a full report on the officer in question, after agreeing to a price from a supplied estimate, whilst a similar database of Commissioned Sea Officers from 1660–1815 is available at Family Relatives.com. Several Royal Naval lists can be viewed for free at the Internet Archive (**http://archive.org/details/nlsnavylists**), containing details on officers, whilst The Genealogist also has some lists from 1822–1944 available. Paul Benyon has extracted many names from Navy lists from 1844–1879 and placed them online at **www.pbenyon1.plus.com/Nbd/Index.html**, with all ranks listed including carpenters, chaplains and more. TNA has a useful guide for researching ex-sailors who became Greenwich Pensioners at **www. national archives.gov.uk/records/research-guides/royal-navy-rating-pension. htm**.

Ancestry has two useful naval medical collections, Surgeon Superintendents' Journals of Convict Ships, 1858–1867, and UK Royal Navy Medical Journals, 1817–1857.

To learn about life in the navy in the early nineteenth century, and the battles of Trafalgar and the Nile, visit **www.nelsonsnavy.co.uk/ broadside.html,** whilst an unusual site at **http://home.planet.nl/~pdavis** allows you to download a simulator of a three and two-masted square-rigged sailing ship from the period, HMS *Surprise.* TNA has a database listing everyone who served at Trafalgar at **www.nationalarchives.gov.uk/ trafalgarancestors,** with service details and additional biographical notes where known, whilst The Age of Nelson website (**www.ageofnelson.org**) might also help.

If your connection is with the silent service, the Royal Naval Submarine Museum website (**www.submarine-museum.co.uk**) contains many photographic collections, an index of submarine losses, and a history of the service from its creation in 1901, as well as several online exhibitions.

A list of British coastguards recorded in the censuses from 1841–1901 can be found at **www.genuki.org.uk/big/Coastguards,** whilst for Irish coastguards visit the excellent Coastguards of Yesteryear site (**www.coast guardsofyesteryear.org**). Resources on Customs officials and their history can be found at **www.hm-waterguard.org.uk/People.htm.**

The National Archives database listing all those who fought at Trafalgar.

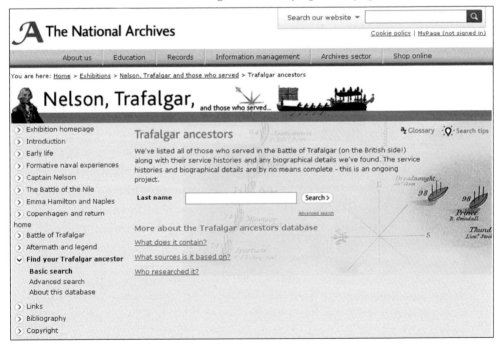

Merchant seamen

Shipping records for merchant seamen are held at archives across the British Isles and in many overseas countries such as Canada, which traded heavily with the UK. Increasingly information on both the crews and the ships involved is finding its way on to the net.

The National Maritime Museum at Greenwich has useful guides on how to research maritime ancestors at **www.rmg.co.uk/national-maritime-museum,** along with details of its holdings. TNA's Board of Trade records are available through the archive's online collection, with several datasets accessible at **www.nationalarchives.gov.uk/records/merchant-navy.htm,** including Merchant Seamen's Campaign Medal Records 1914–1918, Merchant Seamen's Campaign Medal Records 1914–1918, and Merchant Shipping Movement Cards 1939–1945.

A list of convoy movements in the Second World War can be explored at **www.convoyweb.org.uk,** whilst for merchant seamen interned in Germany as prisoners of war in the First World War visit both **http://spw-surrey. com/mt9** and **http://ruhleben.tripod.com.** Others were confined at Kazerne Holzminden (**www.facesofholzminden.com**), whilst in the Second World War many merchant seamen were interned at 'Milag', the Marine Internment Lager (**www.milag.org**).

The Mariners site at **www.mariners-l.co.uk** has many resources including guides on how to research merchant navy ancestors, fishermen, shipping companies and more. Lloyd's Captains' Registers, which give details on captains and mates serving on vessels whose details were transmitted to Lloyds, have been indexed by the Guildhall Library and made available at **www.history.ac.uk/gh/capintro.htm** for the period from 1851–1911. Whilst many entries will need to be consulted at the library, some lists from 1800 are available at Google Books. FindmyPast hosts a Crew Lists 1861–1913 database, as well as a Merchant Navy Seamen 1835–1941 collection – if your ancestor worked for the White Star Line, the vendor also offers White Star Line Officers' Books 1868–1934. Not to be outdone, Ancestry has equally impressive offerings in the form of its Glasgow Crew Lists 1863–1901, and the UK and Ireland, Masters and Mates Certificates, 1850–1927 database, detailing when certificates of competency were obtained. For the north-west of England, the Through Mighty Seas project is well worth consulting at **http://tinyurl. com/lqxqpdp.**

There are several dedicated sites for Welsh mariner crew lists, including **www.welshmariners.org.uk/search.php,** and **www.swanseamariners. org.uk,** with additional resources listed at **www.morol.eu/The%20 Maritime%20Archive%20of%20Wales.htm.** Almost 270,000 Irish mariners listed as working between 1918 and 1921 are indexed on the Irish Mariners website (**www.irishmariners.ie**), sourced from an index to the CR10 series of index cards held in Southampton Civic Archives. Eddie's Extracts at **http:// freepages.genealogy.rootsweb.ancestry.com/~econnolly/#** indexes deaths from all over Ireland, the Shetland Islands and the Orkney Islands in the late nineteenth and early twentieth century – and offers Mercantile Navy Lists from 1849–50. The Whalers Heritage Project has many pages on the history of whaling, including some crew lists from Britain, at **http:// explorenorth.com/whalers/index.html**.

The Maritime History Archive (**www.mun.ca/mha**) is focussed on Newfoundland, but has lots of British resources including a crew agreements database for 1863–1938 and an online catalogue. For maritime news from 1740–1837, including details of casualties and vessel movements, visit **www. cityoflondon.gov.uk/lloydslist**. Going further back, a list of ships in the service of the East India Company is available at **www.eicships.info**, with information on the names of ship owners and captains included.

Workers' rights

The struggle for employees' rights was long fought, and greatly entangled with the fight for democracy itself. The Chartist Ancestors website (**www.chartists.net**) explores the history of the mid-nineteenth-century Chartist movement, and includes lists of names, trials, uprisings and more, whilst the Working Class Movement Library (**www.wcml.org.uk**) covers many of the great strikes and campaigns, and lists holding within its archives at Salford. The Union History website (**www.unionhistory.info**) provides a trade union history timeline covering many industries over the last two centuries, as well as specialist sections on the General Strike of 1926, the Match Girls strike of 1888, the Workers at War project and more. The Trade Union Ancestors site has similar offerings at **www.union ancestors.co.uk**.

Women were every bit as involved in the struggles for rights. TNA has a comprehensive site detailing the Suffragette movement at **www.national archives.gov.uk/education/britain1906to1918/**, whilst an online exhibition using a series of case studies to demonstrate how women moved 'from the kitchen table to the conference table' is available at **www.co-op.ac.uk/ politicalwomen/default.html**.

Mining

On the mining front, the Coalmining History Resource Centre (**www.**

cmhrc.co.uk/site/home) includes the *Royal Commission of Inquiry into Children's Employment 1842*, a national database of mining deaths in Great Britain, and maps identifying the locations of mines and other resources. The University of Sunderland has several north-east-based mining resources accessible from **http://library.sunderland.ac.uk/resources/special-collections**, including the NEEMARC Collection and Durham Miners' Association Minute Books. The Durham Mining Museum (**www.dmm.org.uk/mindex.htm**) also carries a range of material, not just for Durham, but for surrounding counties, including accident reports, government reports, maps, a who's who, and more.

The history of women in the mines, including a list of women's deaths in the pits from 1851–1919 is provided by Leah Ryan and Ian Winstanley at **http://tinyurl.com/y6bgv77**, whilst Bill Riley's account of working life in the pits is online at **www.dmm.org.uk/pitwork/html/index.htm**. For the history of working men's clubs visit **www.clubhistorians.co.uk**.

An overview of Welsh mining is provided at the Museum Wales site (**www.museumwales.ac.uk/en/bigpit**), and at the Welsh Mines Society (**www.welshmines.org**), with a list of mines in the Peak District in 1896 located at **www.pdmhs.com/MinesIndex1896Wales.asp**. For Scotland, the excellent Scottish Mining Website (**www.scottishmining.co.uk**) provides much useful context, as does The Hoods – History of a Coalmining Community at **www.hoodfamily.info/index.html**. The story of Irish mines can be found via **www.mhti.com**.

Communications

If your ancestors worked on the trains, the Railway Archive (**www.railwaysarchive.co.uk**) is a free online archive charting the development of Britain's railways, and includes accident reports and maps and other resources. Network Rail has its own virtual archive at **www.networkrail.co.uk/virtualarchive/**, covering topics on stations, people, companies, tunnels and bridges/viaducts. Ancestry has an impressive database of UK Railway Employment Records 1833–1963, and Railscot's A History of Britain's Railways (**www.railbrit.co.uk**) also provides a concise history. A description of archival holdings at the National Railways Museum at York and Shildon is available at **www.nrm.org.uk,** whilst the Railway Ancestors Family History Service lists various periodicals of interest at **www.railwayancestors.org.uk**. The National Railway Museum at York has a database listing 20,000 railway workers who died in the First World War at **www.nrm.org.uk/RailwayStories/worldwarone.aspx**.

The Railway and Canal Historical Society (**www.rchs.org.uk**) also has detailed bibliographies of published literature relating to transport history from 2002–07. If you had ancestors living or working on Britain's canals, visit **www.canalmuseum.org.uk/collection/family-history.htm** for a useful guide on how to research their stories, and **www.virtualwaterways.co.uk** for the Virtual Waterways Archive Catalogue.

For those involved in the postal industry, Ancestry has its British Postal Service Appointment Books 1737–1969 collection. For the history and holdings of the British Postal Museum and Archive, as well as a downloadable guide on how to research postal family history, visit **www.postalheritage.org.uk**.

The Church

If your ancestor had a direct line to God, there are many useful online databases and sites to consult. The Church of England has a fully searchable archive catalogue at its Lambeth Palace site (**www.lambethpalace library.org**), whilst a useful, though incomplete, site for researching Anglican ministers is the Clergy of the Church of England Database (**www.theclergydatabase.org.uk**), which contains information on members from 1540–1835. An important study detailing biographies of many Anglican cathedral-based clergy is the *Fasti Ecclesiae Anglicanae*, as drawn up by John Le Neve in 1716, and subsequently revised in 1854. These can be consulted at **www.british-history.ac.uk/catalogue.aspx?type=1&gid=157**. Copies of the original editions by Le Neve are available to read and download from the Internet Archive, which also has Crockford's Clerical Directories from 1861 and 1868. Additional information on ministers recorded in Crockfords between 1858 and 1968 can be found at **www.crockford.org.uk**, though this is a subscription-based site with only a few limited free resources. FindmyPast has also provided access to Kelly's Clergy List from 1896. In Ireland, the Representative Church Body Library has a digitised edition of the first-ever Anglican-based Irish Church Directory from 1862 at **http:// tinyurl.com/8uj7z3x**.

Biographies of Church of Scotland ministers are available in the *Fasti Ecclesiae Scoticanae* collection, available on both Ancestry and the Internet Archive (the latter for free). A database version also exists via FamilySearch's Community Trees site at **http://histfam.familysearch.org**. Entries for ministers in the United Presbyterian Church from 1733–1900 can also be found at **http://tinyurl.com/2dgrlzv**, whilst for Scottish Episcopal Clergy visit Google Books at **http://tinyurl.com/2cch5pn**.

For Nonconformist ancestors, the University of Manchester holds Methodist resources at **www.library.manchester.ac.uk/search resources/ guidetospecialcollections/methodist/**, including an online virtual library, whilst the Wesley Historical Society has a Dictionary of Methodism in Britain and Ireland at **http://dmbi.wesleyhistoricalsociety.org.uk**. The Society of Friends has a library catalogue at **www.quaker. org.uk/library**. Doctor William's Library and Congregational Library (**www.dwlib.co.uk./index.html**) has an online catalogue listing materials relating to English Nonconformist Protestant and Congregationalist history. The two churches merged to form the United Reform Church, which has a limited site at **www.urc.org.uk**. The Surman Index of Congregational ministers from the mid-seventeenth century to 1972 is also available online at **http://surman.english.qmul.ac.uk**, whilst resources for the Unitarian Church are available at **www.unitarianhistory.org.uk**. A further resource for Unitarian ministers is the Dictionary of Unitarian and Unitarian Biography at **www25.uua.org/uuhs/duub**. The Salvation Army's International Heritage Centre in London has many historical resources at **www.salvation army.org.uk/uki/heritage**.

For Roman Catholics, the Catholic Record Society site (**www.catholic- history.org.uk**) contains an index of articles for both its 'Recusant History' series and its 'Records Series', as well as details of other published monographs. The site also provides links to various Catholic history societies across England, including the Catholic Family History Society at **www. catholic-history.org.uk/cfhs/index.htm**. For Scotland visit **www.scottish catholicarchives.org.uk**.

The main repository for records concerning missionaries is the Mundus website (**www.mundus.ac.uk**), which lists over 400 separate collections. The University of Southern California's Internet Mission Photography Archive (**http://digitallibrary.usc.edu/cdm/landingpage/collection/p15799coll12 3**) is well worth consulting, as are the catalogues of holdings for the School of Oriental and African Studies, accessible at **www.soas.ac.uk/library/**.

Law and Order

Details of many UK laws from 1267 to the present day are available at **www. legislation.gov.uk**. Scotland's legal system is different to that in England – for an overview visit the Scottish Legal History Research Guide site at **www.law. georgetown.edu/library/research/guides/scottishlegal history.cfm**.

If your ancestor was called to the bar in London, the Calendars of Inner Temple Records from 1505–1845 are now online at **www.innertemple.org. uk/history/caldendars-of-inner-temple-records-1505-1845**.

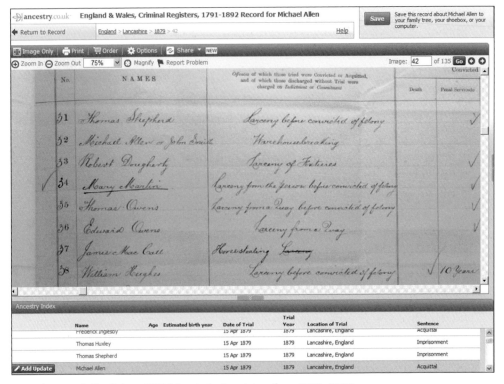

Ancestry's English and Welsh criminal registers from 1791–1888.

An admissions database is also accessible at **www.innertemplearchives. org.uk/index.asp**. If trained as solicitors' apprentices, consult Ancestry's UK, Articles of Clerkship, 1756–1874 set.

For policemen in the family tree, the relevant local force's archive can be identified through a guide from Ian Bridgeman and Clive Emsley at **www. open. ac.uk/Arts/history/policing/police-archives-guide/index.html,** though as it was written in 2006 some contact details may be out of date. The Police History Society has additional details at **www.policehistorysociety.co.uk,** with links to many genealogically useful sites such as the Police Roll of Honour (also accessible at **www.policememorial.org.uk**) and various museums across the country. The Open University has many holdings listed on its Police Collections page (**www.open.ac.uk/library/library-resources /police-collections**). Amongst many useful resources for Ireland are **http:// irishconstabulary.com** and **www.royalulsterconstabulary.org**.

For criminal ancestors Ancestry has digitised 279 English and Welsh criminal registers from 1791–1882 as part of its World Archives Project. The registers were sourced from the HO26 and HO27 collections at TNA and provide information about the individuals charged, their trial and sentence, if convicted, or any other outcome. The Old Bailey (**www.oldbaileyonline. org**) has also made documents freely available from almost 200,000 trials carried out at the London court from 1674–1913, as well as an *Ordinary of Newgate's Accounts*, which provides information on the lives and deaths of convicts at Tyburn from 1692–1772. The stories of some of the most notable executions in Britain during the eighteenth and nineteenth century are also available via the Newgate calendar at **www.exclassics.com/newgate/ ngintro.htm**. State-sponsored death is also dealt with at **www.capital punishmentuk.org,** which not only provides a list of those executed across the British Isles, but also a history of the death penalty itself.

For details on prisoners in other British prisons, consult **www.black sheepancestors.com/uk**. The Victorian Crime and Punishment site at **http://vcp.e2bn.org** provides a searchable database of prisoners from the nineteenth century as well as individual case studies. The National Library of Wales' Crime and Punishment database at **www.llgc.org.uk/sesiwn_ fawr/index_s.htm** further features records extracted from the gaol files of the Court of Great Sessions in Wales from 1730–1830.

Theatrical

If your ancestor once trod the boards for a living then the Theatre Database (**www.theatredatabase.com**) may be of use, charting performances and performers from ancient times to the twentieth century. *The Stage* magazine (**www.thestage.co.uk**) has an online subscription-based archive covering 125 years of theatrical history, with a twenty-four-hour pass costing £5, whilst Footlight Notes (**http://footlightnotes.tripod.com**) is an online magazine specifically covering performance history. The East London Theatre Archive is another impressive database available at **www.elta-project.org**. Bristol University's Theatre Collection has catalogues of holdings at **www.bristol. ac.uk/theatrecollection**.

Alternatively, your forebears may have been travelling performers. The University of Sheffield's National Fairground Archive (**www.nfa.dept. shef.ac.uk**) includes a history of fairgrounds, articles, galleries, and a guide to using the Sheffield-based archive itself, whilst the Circus Historical Society site (**www.circushistory.org**) includes many genealogical resources, such as route books, censuses and directories. The UK Fairground Ancestors site (**www.members.shaw.ca/pauline777/TravellersUK.html**) includes biographies of some of the more prominent fairground families.

On the musical front, the Arts and Humanities Research Council has a database of musical concert programmes in the UK and Ireland at **www. concertprogrammes.org.uk**. For the music hall scene, visit the British Music Hall Society at **www.britishmusichallsociety.com**.

Medical

Accessing medical records can often be tricky, with individual local authorities operating different closure periods. TNA's Hospital Records Database (**www.nationalarchives.gov.uk/hospitalrecords**) can help locate many records held in archives across the country. If this does not list your hospital, try the website of your local county records office or university archive. For the location of asylums in 1844 visit the Index of English and Welsh Lunatic Asylums and Mental Hospitals at **http://studymore. org.uk/4_13_ta.htm**.

In 1948 the principal provider of today's health care arrived in the form of the National Health Service. The BBC has a history of the service at **www.bbc.co.uk/archive/nhs**, whilst for Scotland, consult **www.60yearsof nhsscotland.co.uk**.

Several medical directories and gazetteers are available on both Ancestry and FamilyRelatives. The catalogue for the Royal College of Surgeons in England (established in 1800) can be consulted at **www.rcseng.ac.uk/ library**, whilst the Scottish equivalent, the Royal College of Surgeons of Edinburgh (established 1505) has a similar site at **www.rcsed.ac.uk/ museum-library.aspx**, and a catalogue of holdings from its Sibbald Library available at **http://archives.rcpe.ac.uk/calmView**. For surgeons and physicians, licenses to practice issued by the Archbishop of Canterbury between 1580 and 1775 are indexed at **www.lambethpalacelibrary.org/ files/Medical_Licences.pdf**. The Royal College of Physicians' library has an online catalogue at **www.rcplondon.ac.uk/resources/library**, as does its Scottish equivalent (**www.rcpe.ac.uk/library/index.php**), with a history of the establishment. The Ulster Medical Society Archives (**www.ums.ac.uk**) has transcripts of various histories of medicine in Ulster from 1934 and 1967, whilst the ScotlandsPlaces site (**www.scotlands places.gov.uk**) carries Medical Officers of Health Reports for Scotland from 1895. To research midwives visit **www.rcm.org.uk**.

Information concerning St John's Ambulance's history and archive can be found at **www.sja.org.uk**, whilst resources for the British Red Cross can be found at **www.redcross.org.uk/About-us/Who-we-are/Museum-and-archives**. If your ancestor was in the Royal Voluntary Service visit **www.royalvoluntaryservice.org.uk/about-us/our-history**.

Business

The locations of many records for business can be sourced from the National Register of Archives, and its Scottish equivalent, the National Register of Archives for Scotland (see p.7 for both). The *London Gazette*, and its Belfast and Edinburgh counterparts (see p.36), is always worth examining for notices of appointments of partners, mergers, dissolutions, retirements and even bankruptcies. Many business records will also be sourced locally in local authority and university based archives.

For historical resources concerning occupational pensions, visit the Pensions Archive Trust site at **www.pensionsarchive.org**.

The Poor

Not everyone was able to work at all times, and for those who became destitute the workhouse (poorhouse in Scotland) often beckoned. For details of the poor relief systems employed across the British Isles, and its institutions, visit Peter Higginbotham's Workhouses site (**www.work houses.org.uk**), which also now holds a virtual museum of relevant artefacts. The National Archives has a guide to the various poor law records it holds at **www.nationalarchives.gov.uk/records/research-guides/poor-**

The National Register of Archives database.

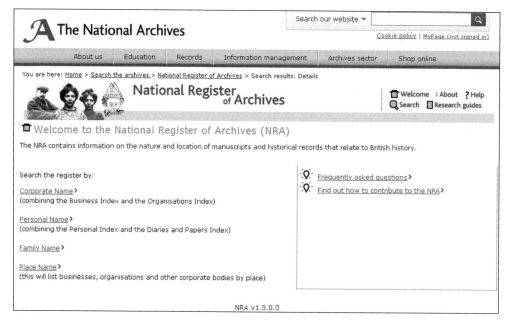

laws.htm, whilst the National Records of Scotland's guide can be found at **www.nas.gov.uk/guides/poor.asp**. Scottish-based genealogist Kirsty Wilkinson has compiled an exceptionally useful list detailing which poor law records still exist across Scotland, accessible as a downloadable PDF file from her site at **www.myainfolk.com**. In Dublin, the National Archives has a guide at **www.nationalarchives.ie/research/research-guides-and-articles/ guide-to-the-records-of-the-poor-law/**.

For nineteenth-century lists of Irish people deported from Britain to Ireland by poor law authorities, visit the House of Commons Parliamentary Papers site at **http://parlipapers.chadwyck.co.uk** (further details are available in *Tracing Your Irish Family History on the Internet*).

Chapter 4

ENGLAND

As well as general resources for England, there are a great many locally-based websites that can assist your research, including archives, libraries, family history societies, and locally created history and genealogy resource sites. The following chapter lists several useful examples from each county.

Bedfordshire

Bedfordshire Libraries hosts a useful family history section at **http://library. culturalservices.net/cgi-bin/vlib.sh,** with gazetteer descriptions from 1586 and 1866–69 also available at **www.genoot.com/eng/bdf/index.html**. The East Anglian Film Archive (**www.eafa.org.uk/default.aspx**) has 200 hours of material accessible for free, with some relating to Bedfordshire. The whole collection is searchable through the site's catalogue.

Hugh Winters' Bedfordshire Surnames List (**http://homepages.ihug.co. nz/~hughw/bedf.html**) contains contact details for researchers with specific surname interests, whilst a Look up Exchange site exists at **http://williams gwynfa.tripod.com/bedfordshirelookupexchange**.

Many marriages in Bedford Registration District from 1837–1901 have been transcribed and made available at **www.sgibbs1.freeserve.co.uk/ ParishRegistersPage.htm**. A site for the Anglican parish church of All Saints in Renhold is hosted at **www.all-saints-church-renhold.org,** which includes a list of the clergy from 1229, a village map, and baptismal, marriage and burials registers transcriptions from 1602–1812, as well as banns from 1754–1812. The history of Ampthill is recorded at **www.ampthill.info/ page10.htm**, whilst for Turvey a useful site is **www.turveybeds.com,** which includes a list of inhabitants from the village in 1551 and transcripts from several nineteenth-century post office directories.

Great Barford parish register transcriptions from 1813 are available at Steve Gibb's website at **www.sgibbs1.freeserve.co.uk/gtbarford,** as well as several census returns and electoral register lists, whilst at **www.leighton-linslade.com** you can access information on the town of Leighton-Linslade and the villages of Billington, Eggington, Heath and Reach, and Stanbridge – the site also contains an index to events in the area during the 1860s, as recorded in the *Leighton Buzzard Observer*.

A gaol register index database from 1801–1901 has been placed at **http://apps.bedfordshire.gov.uk/grd** by the county archive, with details of 35,000 cases, providing the criminal's name, age, colour of hair, height, crime committed, trial dates, and details of punishment if convicted. If your ancestors were more law-abiding, you may find them in local poll books for 1722 and 1784 at **http://abacus.rabancourt.co.uk,** both transcribed by Dr John Dawson.

For the history of Bedfordshire's lace industry visit **www.sandbenders. demon.co.uk/bobbinlace/history.htm**.

Berkshire

The Royal County of Berkshire website (**www.berkshirehistory.com**) contains many useful articles and resources on the area's history, such as a study of the Great Riot of 1327 in Abingdon, as well as information on folklore, historic buildings and more. Pigot's Directory for the county in 1830 is transcribed and available at **http://tinyurl.com/ydh64f3**. Local civil records indexes can be accessed at **www.BerkshireBMD.org.uk**.

An index to Bishop's Transcripts for Appleford (1563–1835) and parish registers for the baptismal register from Lambourne (1560–1837) have both been made available at **www.pbenyon1.plus.com/PR_Index.html,** whilst register transcriptions for Cumnor are available at **www.bodley.ox.ac.uk/ external/cumnor,** which also includes monumental inscriptions for St Michael's Churchyard and a 'Who Was Who' for the parish for the period 1450–1900. Further Bishops' Transcripts for Cookham from 1607–1635 can be found at **http://tinyurl.com/y92zdo4**.

The parish of Bucklebury is well served at **http://home.btconnect. com/buckleburyweb/history.htm,** whilst Wraysbury's past is explored at **www.wraysbury.net/history.htm,** with the site providing a handy historic timeline and village photos. For Faringdon, **www.faringdon.org** hosts resources for the village's war memorial, the United Reform Church, the Civil War, Coles Pits and more. Beenham village's history is dealt with at **www.beenhamonline.org/history.htm**. A bibliography of useful resources for Newbury can be found at **www.burrell-wood.org.uk/LHist/index.htm**. One of the more interesting sites from the county is the Hungerford Virtual Museum at **www.hungerfordvirtualmuseum.co.uk,** with many transcribed resources in the Archive section such as lists of quit rents, constables' accounts, maps and plans, and considerably more. The Reading History Trail website at **http://atschool.eduweb.co.uk/radstock/rht** is no longer up and running, but can be retrieved through the Internet Archive's Wayback Machine (see p.2), whilst the Bracknell Forest Society website at **http://thebracknellforestsociety.org.uk** has a history of the area amongst its many resources.

An index for the Windsor and Eton Express newspaper from 1826–1842 is available at **http://tinyurl.com/yz8q3zz**, which contains about 13,000 names. The Wiltshire and Berkshire Canal Trust site at **www.wbct.org.uk/history** has many articles extracted from newspapers as far back as 1800, and documents concerning legislation surrounding the canals.

The University of Reading's Museum of English Rural Life (**www.reading.ac.uk/merl/collections/merl-collections.aspx**) hosts several online databases. These include a useful *Bibliography of British and Irish Rural History* and an online exhibition linked to the museum's *Digitisation of Countryside Images* project, containing a sample of 300 photographs. The university's Research Centre for Evacuee and War Child Studies (ResCEW) also has an online presence at **www.reading.ac.uk/education/partners/ioe-evacuees-archive.aspx**.

If you fancy something to accompany your tea break, read about the history of biscuit making in Reading by Huntley and Palmers at **www.huntleyandpalmers.org.uk**!

Buckinghamshire

The Milton Keynes Heritage Association (**www.mkheritage.co.uk**) is your first stop for research into Buckinghamshire ancestry. It not only acts as a gateway to many useful sites, from the Bletchley Park Trust to the Open University Archive, but also hosts dedicated pages for many organisations across the county, including the Buckingham Canal Society and The Old Stratford Remembered Group.

The Living Archives project (**www.livingarchive.org.uk**) also carries interesting essays on the history of Milton Keynes, including stories about wartime evacuees and the birth of the city. If your ancestor served at Bletchley Park during the Second World War, visit **www.bletchleypark.org.uk** for a Veterans Roll of Honour and catalogued entries from the facility's archive, as well as many stories and videos from those who served there during the conflict.

A Buckinghamshire land-owners list from 1873 can be consulted at **www.burrell-wood.org.uk/LHist/index.htm**, detailing everyone who owned more than an acre of land.

A detailed one-place study site for the parish of Wing in the Vale of Aylesbury is available at **www.wing-ops.org.uk**, including parish record transcriptions and strays, muster rolls, gazetteer entries, directories and even Sun Insurance records. A website containing a database of instances of the surname 'Roads', as well as surnames appearing in one-place studies of the villages of Waddesdon, Grendon Underwood and Wotton Underwood, is available at **http://wc.rootsweb.ancestry.com/cgi-bin/igm.cgi?db= hrohrer** – the site contains both a simple search and advanced search screen which allows you to search for particular vital events. If your ancestor was from Tingewick, you will find a welcome page on resources for the village at **http://freepages.genealogy.rootsweb.ancestry.com/~tingewick/index.htm**. A fantastic collection of church photographs from across the county can also be found at **www.countyviews.com/bucks/church.htm**.

Monumental inscriptions for St Michael's Church in Hornton can be found at **http://met.open.ac.uk/genuki/big/eng/BKM/Horton/MIs. html**, and for the Church of All Saints at Calverton at **www.xor.org.uk/ calverton/crj97/crj_20.htm**.

Cambridgeshire (and Isle of Ely)

The modern East Anglian county of Cambridgeshire is considerably larger today than its historic equivalent, including the Isle of Ely (formerly a county palatine in itself), the old county of Huntingdonshire and the borough of Peterborough (see p.84).

With the assistance of Cambridgeshire Family History Society, Cambridgeshire Council has made its local statutory indexes for births, marriages and deaths from 1837–2002 available online via its CAMDEX service at **www.camdex.org.uk**. Following successful searches, the records can be ordered and paid for online from the Cambridgeshire County Council Registration Service via **www.cambridgeshire.gov.uk/community/bmd/**.

Cambridgeshire FHS (**www.cfhs.org.uk**) provides several useful databases online, including baptisms and burial indexes from 1801–37, a strays index, an index to poor law papers, indexes for the 1841 and 1851 censuses for the county and an 1891 census index for Cambridge St Andrew the Less. The site also offers a Victoria gold rush emigration database listing surname, forename and year of birth of many who emigrated from the county – unfortunately the original database is now missing and so no further details can be given. A look-up exchange for records within the county can also be consulted at **www.cambridgeshirelookupexchange.co.uk**, with various

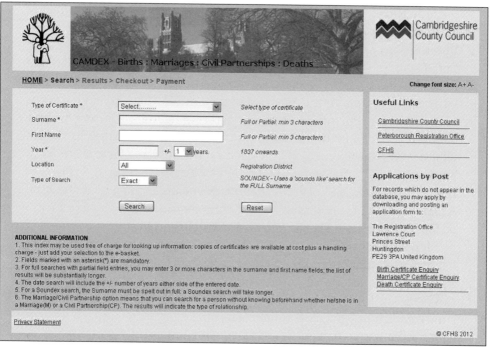

The CAMDEX records database.

volunteers willing to do look-ups for records such as poll books for the county from 1780, 1802 and 1831.

Ancestry and FindmyPast host Cambridgeshire parish register records, as does The Genealogist website in its Parish Records collections, although the records for St Michael's of Cambridge are curiously hidden away within the Directories section, under the title of 1538–1837 Cambridge BMD Directory.

The Cambridgeshire Community Archives Network (**www.ccan.co.uk**) holds many images, documents and historic accounts compiled by members of the public (at the time of writing the site was planning to migrate to a new host platform). If you are looking for famous folk to have come from the county, visit **www.rootsweb.ancestry.com/~engcam/famspple.htm**.

Parish and census indexes for Carlton-cum-Willingham can be found within the history section at **www.carlton-cambridgeshire.org.uk,** whilst monumental inscriptions, census entries and rolls of honour for Foxton can be found in the genealogy section at **www.foxtoncambs.info** – the site's history page has several gazetteer and directory descriptions of the village from 1794, 1851 and 1929. The village of Milton is similarly served at **www.**

miltonvillage.org.uk/opus129.html and Littleport at **http://littleport society.org.uk**. For essays on the history of Little Thetford, visit **www. littlethetford.org**, whilst Steve Odell provides a photographic archive for the villages of Arrington, Croydon, Orwell and Wimpole at **www.steve. odell.dsl.pipex.com**.

The Fenstanton Village site (**www.fenstanton-village.co.uk**) offers a Master Genealogical Index to various vital events and census records, but you must first register with the site, after which you will be emailed a link to a PDF file containing the information. The index is surname-based only, and you will need to purchase a book from the site entitled *Beyond Yesterday – A History of Fenstanton* by Jack Dady (£9.95), after which you are then entitled to ask for unlimited free look-ups for the original documents contained in the index.

Extracts from the *Soham Chronicle* (1787–1899) have been provided at **http://homepage.ntlworld.com/s.walker10/soham_chronicle%20main.htm**, whilst Soham Grammar school's site at **www.sohamgrammar.org.uk** has a roll of honour for former pupils who fell in the two world wars.

If your ancestors came from the Cambridgeshire Fens, **http://contueor. com/wisbech** has links to a variety of resources for parishes in the area (as well as for parts of Norfolk and Lincolnshire). If from the village of Prickwillow you should visit **www.rootsweb.com/~engcam/Prickwillow /Pwillow.htm** for a brief history, a list of inhabitants from 1929 and images from the village war memorial. For Chaterris, there is a genealogy guestbook at **http://resources.rootsweb.com/~guestbook/cgi-bin/public_ guestbook. cgi?gb=3789&action=view** where you can post messages to seek connections with relatives.

Other miscellaneous sites of interest for the county include the Churches of Cambridgeshire site at **www.druidic.org/camchurch/links.htm**, and a site on the history of cholera in Ely at **www.rootsweb.ancestry.com/~eng cam/cholera.htm**. For Cambridge University graduates visit Ancestry. The East Anglian Film Archive also has holdings for the county (see p.X), whilst Gill Blanchard's East Anglian Heritage blog (**http://eastanglianheritage. wordpress.com**) provides news updates on genealogical activities in the region.

Cheshire

One of four English marches counties on the Welsh border, the historic county of Cheshire was reorganised into two separate authorities on 1 April 2009 (Cheshire East, and Cheshire West & Chester). Cheshire Archives and Local Studies (**http://archives.cheshire.gov.uk**) continues to work for both authorities, holding many useful online resources, including historical photos from the county, a catalogue of the archive's holdings, a wills database with over 130,000 wills confirmed from 1492–1940, tithe maps in use during the mid-nineteenth century, and more. Many of the facility's records, including parish registers (established and Nonconformist), bishop's transcripts, workhouse registers and electoral registers have been digitised by FindmyPast and made available as the Cheshire Collection on the site. Bishop's transcripts from 1598–1900 are also on FamilySearch (p.4). To search Tithes Maps for Cheshire visit **http://maps.cheshire.gov.uk/tithemaps**.

Eight directories for the county from 1789–1910 can be found transcribed at **http://cheshiredirectories.manuscripteye.com/index.htm**. Stockport Local Heritage Library details its list of resources at **www.stockport.gov.uk/services/leisureculture/libraries/morelibraryservices/localherielibrary**, whilst a list of Stockport-based Methodists from 1 January 1794 is available at **www.dialsquare.fsnet.co.uk/Methodist.htm**.

A Scrapbook of Cheshire (**www.thornber.org**) contains 959 photographs and commentary on 112 historic sites around the county. The detail for each parish varies, from a simple description of the church at Acton to a genealogical pedigree for the Downes family from the wonderfully named village of Pott Shrigley. Photographs of over 450 churches in the county are located at **www.moston.org/churches.html**.

Indexes for locally-registered civil registration records can be found at **www.cheshirebmd.org.uk,** whilst a look-up exchange exists at **www.rootsweb.ancestry.com/~engchs2**. FamilySearch has made a great deal of material freely available, including bishop's transcripts for the county's churches (1598–1900), Nonconformist records (1671–1900), parish registers (1538–2000), school records (1796–1950) and registers of electors (1842–1900), whilst a separate Cheshire Parish Register Project has transcripts for records from twenty-one parishes at **http://cgi.csc.liv.ac.uk/~cprdb**. Chester wills 1518-1940 are indexed on the Origins Network (p.11).

A look-up service for monumental inscriptions and burial records for Middlewich Cemetery is available at **www.mikewalton.org.uk/mhsweb/mhslook_up.htm**, whilst those for twenty further parishes can also be found at **http://places.wishful-thinking.org.uk/CHS/index.html**. A comprehensive list of all known monumental inscriptions projects that have been carried out in the county is available through the main Family History Society of Cheshire website (**www.fhsc.org.uk**), whilst the society's Crewe-based branch has transcribed two books online at **www.scfhs.org.uk** which detail the heraldic visitations to the county in 1580 and 1613.

Parish resources for Kelsall's two churches (Methodist and Anglican) are at **www.the-dicksons.org/Kelsall/kelsall/parish.htm,** pages concerning the villages of Disley, Lyme Handley, Taxal and Whaley Bridge (Yeardsley cum Whaley) at **www.disley.net,** with resources including census, wills, rolls of honour and strays transcriptions, and a history of Holmes Chapel is available at **http://alancheshire.tripod.com/index-11.html.** St Anne's in Sale is well served by a brilliant website at **www.stannesale.bravehost.com** that contains vestry minutes transcriptions, a roll of honour, war memorial transcriptions, lists of benefactors and considerably more. Tatton manor is explored at **http://tattonpark.cheshirealan.org.uk,** providing information not only on the manorial lords of the Tatton Park estate, but the many staff members who worked there. The county town of Chester is also well explored at **www.chesterwalls.info.**

The history of Cheshire's police is detailed at the county's Museum of Policing site at **www.museumofpolicingincheshire.org.uk.** It includes an online catalogue of the museum's holdings and an online application form for research that can be done by the staff. A register of prisoners held at Chester Gaol from 1810–16 is available at **www.rootsweb.ancestry.com /~engchs/prison.html.** And if you are wondering who might have been responsible for the Dutch courage at the heart of many incidents, visit **http://alancheshire.tripod.com/index-36.html** to explore a list of brewers from the county!

Cornwall

Cornwall Online Parish Clerks (**www.cornwall-opc.org**) provides free access to genealogical information for all parishes within the county. As well as a Resources page with articles on various subjects of local interest, and a map of the county identifying the location of individual parishes, the site also has a detailed parish list, with each parish having its own dedicated website page and 'clerk' to coordinate the research for that location. Some have placed full transcriptions or relevant records online, whilst others elect to do free look-ups instead via e-mail. A consolidated Search Database exists on the site for all uploaded records, and can be searched for parish register and civil registration records, as well as other materials.

The Cornwall Parish Register Index (**www.cornwalleng.com**) also carries a searchable database and a detailed parish map showing the parochial boundaries. A similarly useful resource is the Cornwall Family History Society website (**www.cornwallfhs.com**) which hosts a Location Index, with details on the region's historic parochial infrastructure. The St Keverne Local History

Society site at **www.st-keverne.com/history** hosts various databases for baptisms, marriages and burials, census records, quarter sessions records, old family deeds and leases, and other sets for the parish, whilst Althea Barker's site at **http://freepages.genealogy.rootsweb.com/~althea/index.html** has records for Breage and Godolphin, including bastardy bonds, the 1522 military survey, a 1569 muster roll, and probate records.

The Cornish Database site at **http://webs.lanset.com/azazella/ cornish_database.html** hosts wills abstracts for the county from 1582–1869, manorial records for Ludgvan Lese manor, and has dedicated parish sites for Morvah, Gwithian and Penwith. For West Penwith, Rick and Mary Parsons' site at **http://west-penwith.org.uk** carries many interesting items on the local dialect, Masonic lodges, maps, mines, manors, public houses, Quakers, and more.

For burial records, the Cornish Cemeteries site at **http://freepages. genealogy.rootsweb.ancestry.com/~chrisu/index.htm** carries a guide to cemeteries throughout the county, including photographs and a database of monumental inscriptions. Burials for St Mewan, as well as newspaper transcriptions, maps and the histories of many local families, can be found at **http://freepages.genealogy.rootsweb.ancestry.com/~boneplace/stme wan/contents.html**.

The Cornwall Online Census Project (**http://freepages.genealogy.roots web.ancestry.com/~kayhin/cocp.html**) has transcriptions for the whole county for all censuses from 1841–1901. Kelly's Directory from 1873 for the parish of St Minver is also online at **www.stminveropc.fsworld.co.uk/ Dir_Kelly_1873.htm**, whilst a list of residents in Redruth from the 1910 edition is available at **http://connorsgenealogy.com/Cornwall**.

An interactive gazetteer map of Cornwall is at **www.cornwall-calling. co.uk/map-cornwall-gazetter.htm**, and further gazetteers at **www.old cornwall.org**, as well as old postcards, church histories, glossaries of old Cornish words and a discussion forum. Newspaper transcriptions from the *West Briton and Cornwall Advertiser* from 1836–87 are located at **http:// freepages.genealogy.rootsweb.ancestry.com/~wbritonad**.

The Geevor Tin Mine Museum (**www.geevor.com/index.php?page=38**) lists many mining history resources, whilst the Stone and Quarrymen of the West Country site at **http://freepages.genealogy.rootsweb.ancestry.com/ ~stonemen** names masons, quarrymen, builders, carpenters and other related occupations from both Cornwall and neighbouring Devon.

For Devon and Cornwall police, the force's heritage site at **www.police heritagecentre.co.uk** contains a potted history, an online virtual museum and museum catalogues.

Finally, the Scilly Isles Museum at **www.iosmuseum.org** hosts short family history and archaeology sections which may help.

Cumberland

The Cumbria Family History Society (**www.cumbriafhs.com**) has a free discussion forum which can help those with roots in the historic county of Cumberland. Past Presented (**www.pastpresented.info/index.htm**) carries a diverse range of material from transcriptions of 18th century newspapers, essays on the Great Storms of 1795-96, an Allonby news index, Lucinda's Tour of the Lake District in 1781, views around Millom steelworks from 1968, and several essays about Whitehaven. A guide to Cumbrian manorial records has been produced by the University of Lancaster and can be found at **www.lancs.ac.uk/fass/projects/manorialrecords/index.htm**.

Cumberland Roots (**www.cumberlandroots.co.uk**) hosts records indexes and transcriptions sourced from both parish registers and bishops transcripts for fifteen separate parishes. Further records can be found at **www.edenlinks.co.uk** including parish register entries for Bolton, Brigham, Crosscanonby, Crosthwaite, Dean, Kirklinton, Lampkugh, and Mosser, as well as Land Tax assessments from 1764, whilst the Cumberland and Westmorland Archives site (**www.cumberlandarchives.co.uk**) has further church records, and transcribed materials such as *An Abstract of the Sufferings of the People Called Quakers* from 1650–1666.

Photos of gravestones from across Cumberland are available at **www.stevebulman.f9.co.uk/cumbria/frames_home.html,** along with other historic county-sourced photographs and other resources, such as Jollie's Guide of 1811, lists of shipping which worked out of Cumberland, a Carlisle Index, and biographical entries for many of the county's more famous people. Additional historic photos can be found at the Cumbria Images Collection site at **http://cumbriaimagebank.org.uk/index.php**.

Historic newspaper intimations concerning births, baptisms, marriages and deaths have been made available at **http://cumberlandbirthmarriage deaths.yolasite.com,** whilst the Cumberland and Westmorland Newspaper Transcriptions site (**www.cultrans.com**) carries additional newspaper transcriptions, as well as monumental inscriptions for Egremont Cemetery and several burial grounds in Whitehaven. At **www.cumberlandhistory. co.uk** you can also view a handful of old issues of the *West Cumberland Times* from 1895–1930 and the *Cumberland Lake District Life* magazine from 1970–79.

Derbyshire

The Yesterdays Journey project at **http://homepages.rootsweb.ancestry. com/~spire/Yesterday/index.htm** carries a great deal of useful Derbyshire material, including apprenticeship records, bastardy papers, coroners' records, cemetery records, wills and more. Three other sites effectively carve the county up into projects for their respective regions. The South Derbyshire Genealogy Pages at **http://freepages.genealogy.rootsweb.ancestry.com /~brett/sdindex.htm** contain transcriptions of the 1841 census and 1662 hearth tax assessments for parishes in the region, as well as various nineteenth-century trade directory descriptions for Repton and Grisley. The North West Derbyshire Sources site at **http://freepages.genealogy. rootsweb. ancestry.com/~dusk** provides additional resources for its region, including jury lists and hearth tax assessments.

A transcription of White's 1857 Directory can be accessed at **http:// freepages.history.rootsweb.ancestry.com/~claycross/**, whilst Derbyshire's Parishes 1811 (**www.andrewsgen.com/dby/1811/**) provides a description for each parish in the county that year as noted in David Peter Davies' book *History of Derbyshire*. Kelly's Directory for 1891 can also be accessed at **www. andrewsgen.com/dby/kelly/index.htm**. Several old maps for the county can also be found at **www.andrewsgen.com/dby/maps/index.htm**.

General guides for both Derbyshire and the Peak District exist at **www. buxtononline.net** and **www.derbyshireheritage.co.uk,** whilst over 2,000 photos of locations across the county can be viewed at **www.derby photos.co.uk**.

An account of the Pentrich Rebellion of 1817 is found online at **www. pentrichrebellion.co.uk,** including a list of those who were transported to Australia and a play transcript about the event. Records from 1600–1900 for the greater Wirksworth and Matlock area are available at **www.wirks worth.org.uk**. Records for Wingerworth, Chesterfield and Derby can be found at **www.connorsgenealogy.com/Derbyshire**.

A one-village genealogical study for Rosliston at **www.rootsweb. ancestry.com/~engcrosl** includes photos of gravestones at St Mary's churchyard. For Cromford village, **www.cromfordvillage.co.uk** contains records for the 1670 hearth tax, a comprehensive time line, and a list of names from the local war memorial, whilst Scarliffe is well served by **www.rosie.pterosaur.org.uk,** with census records for 1851–61 and 1891–1901, landowners listed in the poor rate assessment of 1832, and several directories.

Burials for cemeteries in Buxton, Glossop, Hope and Thornsett can be freely consulted at **www.highpeak.gov.uk/hp/council-services/parks-and-open-spaces/cemeteries**, searchable in date, grave or surname order.

Other sites to carry useful genealogical records include **http://freepages. genealogy.rootsweb.ancestry.com/~dlhdby** for Crich, **www.belper-research.com/index.html** for Belper, and **http://webspace.webring. com/people/me/emma4/newhall.html** for Newhall.

Many sites also provide useful parish histories, such as that for Aston at **www.aston-on-trent.co.uk** and Whitewell at **www.wlhg.co.uk/index.htm**. Heanor and District Local History Society (**www.heanorhistory.org.uk**) covers the village and surrounding area, whilst a similar site for Ilkeston exists at **www.ilkestonhistory.org.uk**. Baptist Church baptismal and birth records for several parishes in Derbyshire can also be freely sourced at **http://tinyurl.com/yjfbaur**.

The Midland Railway Study Centre site at **www.midlandrailway studycentre.org.uk** contains an online catalogue for its holdings on the local rail industry and Billy Riley's Pitwork site on his coal mining memories is well worth visiting at **www.dmm.org.uk/pitwork/html/index.htm**.

Devonshire

Devon Libraries' Local Studies Service (**www.devon.gov.uk/localstudies**) hosts a timeline of the county's history, early maps, a historical gazetteer, online catalogues, a search facility indexing names from various sources held by the archive, and more. The Friends of Devon's Archives (**www.foda. org.uk**) also carries five major transcription projects, in the form of Devon and Exeter Oath Rolls 1723, records from the Episcopal Visitations for 1744 and 1779, lists of Devon freeholders from 1711–99, tithes records from 1838, and a Black History Project tracing records on the county's black community as far back as the late sixteenth century. Devon Family History Society and several local records offices are also collaborating on the Devon Wills Project at **http://genuki.cs.ncl.ac.uk/DEV/DevonWillsProject**, to act as a finding aid for all surviving copies of pre-1858 wills, many of which were lost in the Second World War.

Several historical resources for Devon, including a map from 1765 and an entry from Samuel Lewis' 1831 Topographical Dictionary can be found at **www.lerwill-life.org.uk/history/devtales.htm**, whilst nineteenth-century tithes apportionments and information on tithes maps for the county are accessible from **www.devon.gov.uk/tithe_records#maps**.

A Florida-based site at **http://turnertree.net** provides a comprehensive list of churches across the whole county, as well as some post office directory descriptions, Devon newspaper extracts from 1913, biographies on famous Devonians, and soldiers buried in the Devonshire Cemetery at the Somme. For Exeter, **www.exetermemories.co.uk** hosts many articles and lists such as *Exeter's Executed* from 1285–1943, a World War I Roll of Honour, police photos and more. Exeter City Council's Bereavement Services department has also uploaded alphabetical index cards for over 100,000 burials in the city's three municipal cemeteries at **www.exeter.gov.uk/index.aspx? articleid=9156**. Torquay is covered by **http://myweb.tiscali.co.uk/terry leaman/index.html**, with many old photos, several directories from 1822–1911, descriptions of places of worship (all denominations), several war memorials and a roll of honour, whilst additional material can be found at **http://content.swgfl.org.uk/seaside/torbay.htm**. For Dartmoor, over 8,000 images, as well as articles on the area's history, can be found at **www. dartmoorarchive.org**.

An Online Parish Clerks scheme is currently being developed at **http://genuki.cs.ncl.ac.uk/DEV/OPCproject.html#Listing**, with volunteers providing free look-ups for the parishes for which they hold material, whilst at **http://tinyurl.com/ycmvf7u** the Devon Parishes Index provides links to many online resources.

Devonshire-based Chardstock's virtual museum.

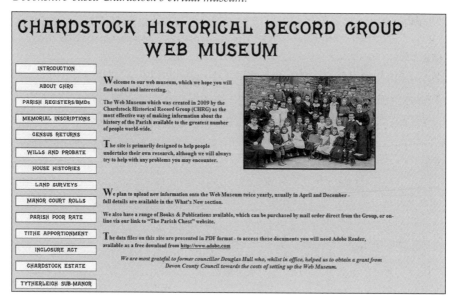

The village of Chardstock, part of Dorset until its relocation into Devonshire in 1896, is particularly well served, with records transcriptions by the website of the Chardstock Historical Record Group Web Museum at **www.chardstockwebmuseum.org**, whilst a vast range of material for Petrockstowe can be found at **www.petrockstowe.co.uk**. For South Hams, **http://homepages.ihug.co.nz/~our4bears/index.html** provides several parish indexes, monumental inscriptions and 1841 census transcripts.

Moreton History Society's Virtual Archive at **www.moretonhampstead .org.uk** has parish records, the religious census from 1851, newspaper cuttings, maps and miscellaneous texts on the parish. Westleigh Parish Council (**www.westleigh-devon.gov.uk/history/history_index.htm**) hosts many local resources including a guide to local manors, christenings and marriages from 1561–1697, hearth tax and muster roll records, and more.

A site for Brixham is located at **www.brixhamheritage.org.uk**, with some indexed resources and a maritime archive. A parish site for Luppitt exists at **www.luppitt.net**, including a forum, maps and photographs, and there's a history for South Molton at **www.northdevonlink.co.uk/south-molton.htm**.

Finally, heading offshore, an interactive multimedia Flash movie presentation on the history of Lundy Island can be viewed at **www.lundy island.co.uk**. For a list of mariners recorded there in the 1881 census visit **www.angelfire.com/de/BobSanders/Lundy81.html**.

Dorset

Dorset has an Online Parish Clerk website at **www.opcdorset.org**, providing extensive coverage for virtually all of the county's parishes, operating in a similar manner to the Cornish equivalent (see p.66). Equally impressive is the Dorset Parish Registers Index at **www.rootsweb.ancestry .com/~engdorse/ PRBT.html** with various databases of records from across the county. The Somerset and Dorset History Society website at **www.sdfhs. org** has online guides to a range of resources publications and services it can offer. The Origins Network website carries a respectable database of over 150,000 marriages for the county from 1538–1856, sourced from registers and bishops' transcripts, which includes some Nonconformist records. For more information on Dorset-based churches, visit Michael Day's excellent site **http://people.bath.ac.uk/lismd/dorset/churches/**, as well as the West Country Churches site at **www.westcountrychurches.co.uk**.

The Blackmore Vale site (**www.westcountrygenealogy.com**) carries resources for Gillingham, Oborne, Pulham, Sherborne, Stalkbridge and

Sturnminster Newton, such as the 1835 Robson's Directory and bishops' transcripts records. The Dorset Index (**http://freepages.genealogy.roots web.ancestry.com/~pbtyc/Dorset.html**) has further records for the Portland area, including monumental inscriptions for Strangers Cemetery and naval and military burials at the Royal Naval Cemetery, and a page helpfully showing a list of towns and villages which have moved in and out of the county across time with successive boundary changes.

For Bere Regis visit **www.bereregis.org/VillageHistory.htm** to find extensive parish register transcriptions, Domesday Book returns, maps, archaeological notes, and more. Tarrant Crawford is covered at **http://home pages.nildram.co.uk/~jimella/trnscrpt.htm#dorset**, with the site hosting the 1841-1861 and 1881 censuses, as well as bishops' transcripts.

A timeline for the history of Bournemouth is at **http://content. swgfl.org.uk/seaside/Bmouth.htm**. A timeline and bibliography for Burton Bradstock exists at **www.burtonbradstock.org.uk/History/History. htm**, which also includes an online photo exhibition, material on the village at war, maps and tithe information, the 1861 census, and more. Poole History Online (**www.poolehistory.org.uk**) has various photographs, documents and data relating to the borough's local history.

On the mapping front, the Dorset Page at **www.thedorsetpage.com** includes Victorian maps, and maps of Dorset hundreds, as well as an additional resource on boundary changes and the Dorset Poll Book from 1807. The village of Belchalwell has a wonderful site at **www.belchalwell. org.uk** which has many maps for the area, including an 1840 tithe map with records of those eligible to pay tithes.

Durham

The historic county of Durham is well served with online indexes to statutory records, and certificates for most of the county can be ordered via **www. durham.gov.uk/pages/Service.aspx?ServiceId=663**. Several local authorities also have similar services – records for Gateshead can be searched at **http://online.gateshead.gov.uk/bmd**, whilst Darlington has a service at **www.darlington.gov.uk/living/register+office/regofficesearch.htm**. For South Tyneside visit **www.southtyneside.info/article/7652/Births-deaths-marriages**, for Sunderland consult **www.sunderland.gov.uk/index.aspx? articleid=1399** and for Middlesbrough, Hartlepool, Stockton-on-Tees and Redcar and Cleveland, you should visit **www.teesvalley-indexes.co.uk**.

Almost four million pay-per-view records, in the form of baptisms, marriages, burials and census material, are hosted at **www.durhamrecords**

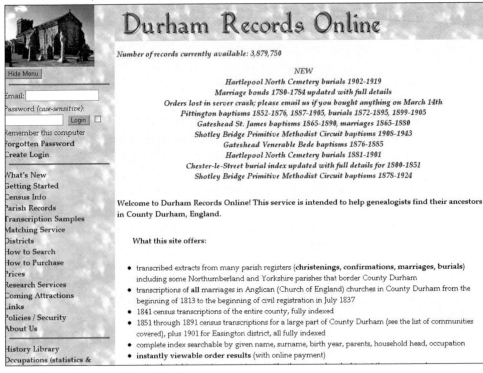

An impressive pay-per-view database resource for Durham-based research.

online.com, which includes complete coverage for Anglican marriages in the county from 1811–1837. The Joiner Marriage Index (**www.joiner marriageindex.co.uk**) carries over 180,000 pre-1837 marriages for Durham, with all but two parishes covered, covering the period from 1521–1837. A look-up exchange also exists at **www.redmire.net/lookup/dur.html** predominantly providing access to census and monumental inscription through volunteers holding the records.

FamilySearch carries bishops' transcripts for records from the Diocese of Durham from 1700–1900, which includes digitised records for Durham, York and Northumberland, as well as marriage bonds and allegations from 1692–1900, and a calendar of marriage bonds and allegations from 1594–1815. At the time of writing the images could only be browsed and not searched by name. A history of Sunderland's Mormon community can be found at **www.sunderlandward.co.uk,** along with a cemetery index.

Durham University Library's North East Inheritance Project (**http:// familyrecords.dur.ac.uk/nei/index.htm**) is a digital image catalogue of over

150,000 probate records from 1527–1857 from the Diocese (and Cathedral) of Durham, which includes material for Durham, Northumberland, Tyne and Wear, Northallerton and some surrounding townships in Yorkshire. The site also hosts several online exhibitions on various subjects from bankers to the twine maker Thomas Robson, and detailed background information on the history and types of probate records.

Durham County Records Office (**www.durhamrecordoffice.org.uk**) hosts over 40,000 historic photos from the county, which are free to access through its online catalogue. Equally useful is the Tomorrow's History site (**www.tomorrows-history.com**), which carries a catalogue and some images for the county, such as a digitised copy of *Bailey's Agriculture of the County of Durham* from 1810, and a great deal of material for Darlington and other towns. An excellent history project for the east of the county is located at **www.east-durham.co.uk,** a site designed to 'capture and preserve photographs, memories of past times and experiences before they are lost and forgotten'. For the story of the Durham Light Infantry, visit **http://durhamlightinfantry.net**. Durham Home Guard records are available online from the National Archives (p.5).

In addition to the Durham Mining Museum website (see p.51), the Durham Miner (**www.durham-miner.org.uk**) includes material on everything from local collieries to brass bands, and also has a handy Miner Mapping facility, which hosts maps for villages and towns across the entire county from the nineteenth century to 2004. Further resources for Durham's coal mining district are also located at **www.durham recordsonline.com/literature/literature_index.php**, with records including a list of inhabitants in Bishopwearmouth in 1567, hearth tax returns for Monkwearmouth in 1666 and 1674, and an electoral and trade register for Greater Seaham from 1833. A database including entries from Slater's 1854 trade directory of Durham is available at **http://tinyurl.com/4pyhmr**.

Silksworth Colliery is dealt with at **www.silksworthheritage.org.uk**, along with other aspects of the area's history, whilst a site commemorating the fallen of Silksworth and Tunstall in the First World War is found at **www.tunsilk.co.uk**. For South Hylton, various resources have been made available at **www.shlhs.com**, including some post-1837 parish register material and various trade directories.

Sunderland's maritime heritage is examined at **www.sunderland maritimeheritage.org.uk**, whilst the Nautical Archaeological Society provides a gateway to Hartlepool-based resources at **http://tinyurl.com/**

nckg7qx. Finally, the *Teesdale Mercury* newspaper from 1854–1954 is digitised and freely available at **www.teesdalemercuryarchive.org.uk**.

Essex

Essex Record Offices's online SEAX catalogue (**http://seax. essexcc.gov.uk**) has complete details for all of the archive's holdings. It allows you to search for information on records held at the parish level, including details of parish records, electoral registers, poor law records, marriage bonds, vehicle registrations and more.

History House (**www.historyhouse.co.uk**), which invites you to 'dip into the history of Essex', is another excellent gateway site with links to resources for each individual town and village in the county, as well as a transcribed version of Daniel Defoe's 1722 work *Tour through the Eastern Counties of England*. For the east of the county you should also visit **www.essex-family-history.co.uk**, which has transcriptions of every possible type of genealogical record you can think of, whilst a sister site at **www.essex-country-life.co.uk** provides resources on farming life in the county and on pastimes.

Essex churches are well recorded and described if you wish to see where your ancestors worshipped. The Essex Churches website at **www.essex churches.info** carries a range of useful resources, including photographs and videos of various properties across the country. These are accessible through a handy gazetteer or via an interactive map. The East Anglian Film Archive has many holdings for the county (see p.59).

There are no major parish and census records sites covering all of Essex, though the Foxearth and District Local History Society site at **www. oxearth.org.uk** has extracts from various newspapers from 1740–1952, and various north Essex census records and indexes. An impressive site for the village of Earls Colne at **http://linux02.lib.cam.ac.uk/earlscolne/** hosts material from 1375–1854, including parish registers, censuses, court records, manorial records, and personal records, with gems such as the diary of seventeenth-century vicar Ralph Josselin. The history of Henham at **www. henhamhistory.org** has parish birth and marriage indexes, as well as wills of parish residents and census indexes, whilst Buckhurst Hill is well catered for at **http://buckhurst-hill-history.btck.co.uk**, with a useful genealogy section including census records, aircraft crew death records and war memorial names. Also on the war memorial front, Chingford's sacrifice in the Great War is commemorated at **www.chingfordwarmemorial.co.uk**, with links on the page to sister sites for Walthamstow, Leytonstone, Forest Gate, Leyton, and Highams Park.

The Camulos site (**www.camulos.com**) covers Colchester, with resources on war memorials listings, local witches, inns, pubs and taverns, King Arthur and more. The names of accused witches and their accomplices from earlier times are also indexed online at **www.hulford.co.uk/towns.html**. An equally varied site is that for Bures Hamlet and Bures St Mary at **www.bures-online.co.uk**, which covers the area's history from 1900–2010, with subjects ranging from the women's land army to local dragon myths! Other useful history sites include an excellent photo resource site for Romford at **www.romford.org**, whilst the Wivenhoe area is very well served by a history forum at **www.wivencyclopedia.org/History/history_home.htm** with various topics and threads discussing the region's past.

On law and order, the history of Essex police, with many past cases explored through an online magazine entitled *History Notebook*, is available at the Essex Police Museum site at **www.essex.police.uk/museum/about-us.php**.

Gloucestershire and Bristol

Gloucestershire Archives has a Genealogical Database at **ww3.gloucester shire.gov.uk/genealogy/Search.aspx**, which allows you to search for wills and administrations from 1541–1858, inventories from 1587–1800, gaol records, overseers' records, and church records. A collection of inquest reports from the *Gloucester Journal* from 1722–1838 have been recorded at **www. genebug.net/glsinquests.htm**.

Monumental inscriptions for several parishes in Gloucestershire, as well as photographs of many churches, can be found at **http://places.wishful-thinking.org.uk/GLS/index.html**. GlosGen (**www.glosgen.co.uk**) has many records of war memorials from across the county, with some additional, though minimal, parish record material. A useful portal site with some further links for the whole county of Gloucestershire can be found at **www.jimella.me.uk/gloucs.cfm**.

The Forest of Dean Family History Pages project (**www.forest-of-dean.net**) includes a database of wills as extracted from probate calendars for the west of the county (1858–1941), e-books, village descriptions, parish records, maps and more. You will need to register with the site, but registration is free. Directory records for the Forest of Dean are also accessible at **http://freepages.genealogy.rootsweb.ancestry.com/~cbennett**.

A site on Ampney Crucis at **www.ampneycrucis.f9.co.uk** offers limited resources, though does contain photos of gravestones from 1875–1950 where the inscriptions are still legible. A site for Condicote at **www.condicote.**

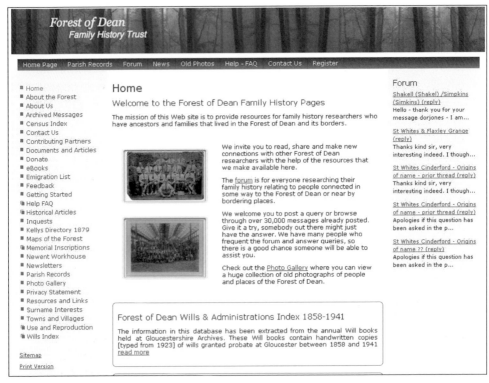

The Forest of Dean Family History project.

webs.com includes war memorial inscriptions from the village as well as a brief history, whilst Cromhall is equally served at **www.cromhall. com/archive/home.php** with war memorial details and a map from 1889. Records for Bitton and surrounding parishes can be located at **www. bittonfamilies.com** and for Longhope at **www.longhopevillage.co.uk**.

Parish register transcriptions for Ashleworth, Boddington, Bromsberrow, Corse, Deerhurst, Elmstone Hardwicke, Forthampton, Hasfield, Lassington, The Leigh, Norton, Oxenton, Staverton, Tewkesbury, Tirley and Tredington are available at **http://freepages.genealogy.rootsweb.ancestry.com/~wrag 44/index.htm**.

The village of Randwick is well served at **www.sandford.plus. com/randwick** with parish registers, bastardy bonds and settlement records, but the links to these from the home page are written in an extremely tiny font, so you may struggle to read them! The Scribes Alcove site (**www. scribes-alcove.co.uk**) has an equally impressive range of material for Berkeley, Hill, Rockhampton, Stone, Oldbury-upon-Severn and Thornbury.

The Thornbury Roots site at **www.thornburyroots.co.uk** contains a history of the village street by street, as well as a searchable monumental inscriptions database, voters lists and more, with access gained via the 'Thornbury Sources' button on the home page, whilst additional resources for the area can also be found via **www.mythornbury.co.uk/thornbury/local_history**. For the civil parish of Winterbourne, parish magazines, school records and the usual birth, marriage and death and census records can be found at **www.frenchaymuseumarchives.co.uk**.

A history of Gloucestershire pubs, including searchable databases for both pubs and breweries in the county, is online at **www.gloucestershirepubs. co.uk/index.htm,** and if you are up for an extensive pub crawl, a similar site for Bristol is located at **http://bristolslostpubs.eu**, which includes a dedicated discussion forum.

The City of Bristol is sandwiched between Gloucestershire and Somerset. Bristol Record Office's site (**www.bristol.gov.uk/page/records-and-archives-0**) includes an online catalogue, a detailed guide to its parish holdings (established church and Nonconformist) and an index to wills from 1781–1858. The local family history society, Bristol and Avon, has some useful resources on its site at **www.bafhs.org.uk,** including the National Burial Index for the area, with the place of abode included (not included on the FindmyPast version), a Bristol Home Children project page and a list of places of worship in the city. Bristol records are included within the Somerset Online Parish Clerks site (**wsom-opc.org.uk**).

Hampshire

Hampshire Genealogy Society (**www.hgs-familyhistory.com**) provides an overview of some of its resources, including a free surname facility for its monumental inscriptions CDs. Hampshire also has an Online Parish Clerk system, hosted at **www.knightroots.co.uk,** the family history site of Southampton-based Linda and Tony Knight. Similar to other county-based OPC sites, it is accessible via the 'Online Transcriptions' tab on the left of the screen. A look-up exchange is also in operation at **http://members. madasafish.com/~dolton/,** with volunteer look-ups available for various birth, marriage, death, census and wills records, as well as rental rolls for the Fleming estates in Hampshire and the Isle of Wight (see p.80). Historic maps for the county dating back to 1575 can be perused via the Old Hampshire Mapped Site at **www.geog.port.ac.uk/webmap/hantsmap/hantsmap**.

More locally, parish records for Botley from 1679–1837 are available at Michael Cooper's page at **http://michaelcooper.org.uk/BOT/bot.htm,**

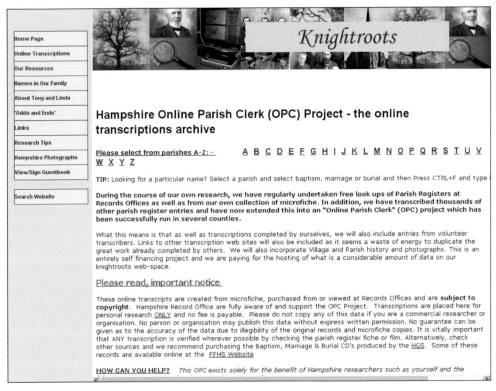

Hampshire's OPC project, accessible via the Knightroots site.

with marriage records handily indexed for both spouses. The village of Froyle's parish records are very comprehensively covered at **www.froyle.com/contents.htm**, with census records included. For Blendworth, Colemore, East Meon, Farringdon, Herriard, Newton Valence and Priors Dean you should visit **http://tinyurl.com/yc84zf7**. If you have connections to Rownhams and North Baddesley then it is well worth visiting **http://homepage.ntlworld.com/sandra.s**, one of the best Hampshire-based genealogy sites around, packed with extracts from directories, parish registers, and other records, including fourteenth-century records of The Order of the Knights Hospitallers of St John of Jerusalem.

Further parish records for St Mary's Crawley (1649–1930), St Catherine's Littleton (1736–1930) and St Stephen's Sparsholt with Lainston (1609–1930) can be found at the Downs Benefice site at **www.downs-benefice.hampshire.org.uk** (bottom right corner for the relevant links), whilst parish and census records for Dursley are located at **www.durley.hampshire. org.uk/parishrecords/contentrecs.htm**. Burials for Blendworth from 1813–1899 can be examined at **http://tinyurl.com/yzxj7pr**, whilst those from the nineteenth and twentieth century for St George's Waterlooville are indexed at **www.stgeorgesnews.org/registers/graveyard.htm**, along with baptisms, weddings and burials from 1997–2010.

For the history of Longparish, East Aston, West Aston, Middleton and Forton, visit **www.longparish.org.uk/history/cover.htm** to find various resources, including subsidy rolls for the area from 1586, the hearth tax from 1665, and more. The Hearth Tax for the hundred of Kingsclere from 1665 is available at **http://kingsclere.org.uk/hearth_tax.html**. Medstead's history is served by **www.medstead.org**, with census records, tithe maps, and a timeline. Alton's past is also explored on the Curtis Museum website at **www.3.hants.gov.uk/museum/curtis-museum/alton-history.htm**.

The south of Hampshire has a long-established maritime heritage. The Port Cities website at **www.plimsoll.org/registersAndRecords** contains a comprehensive examination of the history of Southampton, with pages on the *Titanic*, Southampton at War, various street directories, image galleries, biographies and more. For those with customs connections, **www.customs cowes.co.uk** has a history for both Cowes and the Isle of Wight, including newspaper extracts on Cowes from 1800 onwards, record books, lists of customs prosecutions and customs staff.

The Isle of Wight Record Office (**http://tinyurl.com/ogquxbt**) has a copy of *Speed's Atlas* from 1627, as well as various catalogues in the Collections section relating to several of the archive's holdings, such as court records, estate papers, hospitals and workhouses' records and more. At the bottom of the page, the archive also has links to pages detailing the extent of its collections of cemetery records, censuses, electoral registers, manors, monumental inscriptions, newspapers, trade directories and wills. There are databases available for paupers receiving poor relief (1868–1875), and issued alehouse licenses (1766–1819).

The Isle of Wight Family History Society site (**www.isle-of-wight-fhs.co.uk/bmd/startbmd.htm**) has searchable indexes of locally registered births, marriages and deaths from 1837–2002, as well as other databases such as monumental inscriptions and burials indexes, census strays, a pedigree index, a photo gallery and a church burials index. Wootton Bridge Historical (**www.woottonbridgeiow.co.uk**) provides information on local history for both Wooton Bridge and the Isle of Wight in general, with over 250 written articles and over a thousand images.

A database of island based photographers (1840–1940) is online at **www.iowphotos.info**, along with many historical images of local inhabitants. A guide to the island's many memorials and monuments can be found at **www.isle-of-wight-memorials.org.uk**.

Herefordshire

One of the Welsh Marches border counties, Herefordshire is not so well served online as its counterparts, but does still have some useful material available.

The Herefordshire Through Time project (**http://htt.herefordshire.gov. uk**) has many wonderful sections devoted to subjects such as workhouses, transport, prisons, agriculture and industry. The Transport section alone includes the history of the county's railways, and the work of the navvies who constructed them. The site also provides access to the county's Sites and Monuments Records database, and a Field Names and Landowners database.

Herefordshire Archive Service has a limited online presence at **https://www.herefordshire.gov.uk/archives**, though this does include beginner's guides to subjects such as house history and family history. Bromyard History Society (**http://bromyardhistorysociety.org.uk**) outlines the services and resources which the society can provide, and also has an online parish map for the district (in the Archive section), as well as some local photos.

Herefordshire Family History Society has some useful material at **www. rootsweb.ancestry.com/~ukhfhs/index.html**, including a monumental inscriptions index for the county, and an index to its journal, *Herefordiensis*. A list of marriages for Bishops Frome from 1754–1799 can be found at **http://tinyurl.com/yk9uj2g**. For the 1830 Pigot's Directory of the county visit **http://tinyurl.com/35ukhwl**; for 1840, visit **http://tinyurl.com/36ps dvm**.

Hertfordshire

Hertfordshire Archives and Local Studies website at **www. hertsdirect. org/services/leisculture/heritage1/hals/** has a useful combined online index to several of its collections which is fully searchable by name. Amongst the collections included are an apprentice index for 1599–1903, fatalities from 1827–1933 (coroners' inquest records), marriages from 1538–1837, newspapers and magazines, parish removals from 1688–1882, and settlements from 1679–1865.

A look-up exchange at **http://graham.rootsweb.ancestry.com/herts_ exchange** allows for access to various types of records across the county, whilst a gateway site at **www.hertfordshiregenealogy.co.uk** has some useful but limited resources, such as the names of towns and villages within the counties' various hundreds. The Herts Memories project (**www. hertsmemories.org.uk**) collects old photos and memories from people across the county, and has a useful town and village guide, with links to additional history based resources. The East Anglian Film Archive includes material for the county (see p.59).

Paul Joiner's marriage index at **www.joinermarriageindex.co.uk** holds 111,000 marriage records from 132 parishes in Hertfordshire, from 1516–1837. Paul is also the administrator of the GENUKI page on the county, which can be found on his site at **www.joinermarriageindex.co.uk/ pjoiner/genuki/HRT**. If you are interested in finding where a marriage took place, photographs of various churches from across the county can be found at **http://iananddot.org/chphoto/hertschurches.htm**.

Parish records for Therfield, along with directories and censuses, are located at **www.therfield.net**, including annual census lists from 1803–1807 and 1821, in addition to the main decennial censuses from 1841 onwards. The site also hosts the wonderful Parochial Pedigrees work compiled by the Reverend John Godwin Hale, rector of the parish from 1870–1907. For the village of Redbourne, Chelsea Pensioner names from the 1851 census and militia names from 1758–1786 are amongst the records which can be consulted at **www.redbourn.org.uk/Redbourn/RedbournGenealogy**. Pirton's local history group site at **www.pirtonhistory.org.uk/Default.aspx** hosts a 'searchable relational database' which can be used to find parish and census records, as well as directories, militia lists, wills and monumental inscriptions. Photos and maps are also available.

Monumental inscriptions for Knebworth Cemetery, burial grounds at Almonds Lane and Weston Road in Stevenage, St Mary's Church in Shephall, Stevenage, and further grounds at Welwyn, Woolmer Green and Hitchin can be accessed at **http://homepage.ntlworld.com/jeffery. knaggs/MIs.html**. Additional inscriptions for St James the Great, Thorley, along with various parish register transcriptions, can be found at **http:// friends-stjames. org/Parish_Registers.htm**, whilst records for Three Close Lane graveyard in Berkhamsted can be viewed at **http://tinyurl.com/ yzdx69z**.

Recollections of Rushden, with a pictorial history guide, and timeline of village history, are available at **http://alephzero.tripod.com**, whilst Bishop's

Stortford enjoys a series of history guides to the area at **www.stortford history.co.uk**, covering everything from individual streets to the local leather industry. The Bovingdon village website (**www.bovingdon.org**) includes local history notes, photos and Bovingdon School log book extracts from 1890–1927, whilst a history of Barkley, with a map and some aerial photos, is available at **www.barley-village.co.uk/the_village.htm**.

If there were genealogical website awards given out, one site definitely worthy of nomination is Barbara Chapman's splendid effort, the *Leverstock Green Chronicle*, located at **http://lgchronicle20.homestead.com/index. html**. A detailed labour of love, the project hosts practically every sort of historical record and essay under the sun.

Huntingdonshire

The historic county of Huntingdonshire now forms the western part of modern Cambridgeshire. Confusingly, the north of the old county, containing Peterborough, was also briefly part of Northamptonshire. As such, many records for Huntingdonshire can also be found within both Cambridgeshire and Northamptonshire repositories. Cambridgeshire Archives' catalogue (**www.cambridgeshire.gov.uk/leisure/archives/catalogue**) contains details of all of Huntingdonshire's old parish records and additional resources, whilst the CAMDEX system (see p.62) also carries modern statutory records indexes for Huntingdonshire.

A county look-up exchange exists at **http://aztecrose.tripod.com/ huntingdon/hun.html**, whilst Huntingdonshire Family History Society (**www.huntsfhs.org.uk/MembersPages.html**) has a link to various members' pages, such as Martyn Smith's interesting history of Huntingdonshire cyclist battalions at **www.huntscycles.co.uk**. For records from Fenstanton, visit **www.fenstanton-village.co.uk**. Peterborough Cathedral burials are on Deceased Online (p.12).

A list of mayors of Huntingdon from 1800–1840 exists at GENUKI, but a further list of mayors for the whole county in 1902 is also listed at **www. rootsweb.ancestry.com/~enghun**, with the site also carrying additional resources such as a section on Huntingdon railways and a gazetteer.

Finally, the history of Huntingdonshire Methodism is explored at **www. rootsweb.ancestry.com/~engcam/method.htm**.

Kent

An online parish clerk site for Kent is slowly building momentum at **www.kent-opc.org**, whilst a volunteer based look-up exchange is also in operation at **http://jo42.tripod.com/knt.html**. Kent Genealogy (**http://freepages.genealogy.rootsweb.ancestry.com/~mrawson**) also carries a significant amount of material, including parish register transcriptions, quarter session records, probate records and census and directory entries. Many Kent parish records, including from the Archdeaconry of Canterbury, are on FindmyPast. A detailed parish gazetteer of West Kent is available via **www.nwkfhs.org.uk**, where you will also find free census and monumental inscriptions databases.

Medway Council's archive service has an online database of holdings available through its CityArk site (**http://cityark.medway.gov.uk**) and includes a significant collection of digitised parish registers which can be browsed, and a marriage index for the years 1837–1911. Various other collections are also present, including shipping registers, licensing records and burial records for a limited number of parishes.

Within its Library and Collections section the Kent Archaeological Society website (**www.kentarchaeology.org.uk**) includes a substantial number of monumental inscriptions from across the county, exchequer pipe rolls, 6-inch scale OS maps from 1905–08, wills transcriptions and more. Various essays on the county's history can also be accessed at **www.hereshistory kent.org.uk/index.cfm**, along with an impressive timeline.

A comprehensive collection of records for Folkestone is available at **http://freepages.genealogy.rootsweb.ancestry.com/~folkestonefamilies** though when you first access the homepage you would be as well to turn off your computer's speakers, as what can only be described as a disconcerting blast of noise hits you – various pages on the site are further blessed with bells pealing and all sorts to drive you slowly mad! The resources themselves are limited, though there are some interesting essays and some excellent census material. Bishop's transcripts for Farnborough from 1813–1850 are at **http://tinyurl.com/2u9de2g**, whilst a marriage index for parishes in the mid-Kent area from 1754–1911 can be found at **http://woodchurch ancestry.org.uk/midkentmarriages**. A Dover 'scrapbook' by Kathleen Hollingsbee at **http://doversociety.homestead.com/DoverHistoryScrap book.html** is quite literally that, with a real mixture of anecdotes, resources and images, whilst the history of Dover's hostelries is recorded at **www. dover-kent.com**.

The parish of Northbourne is well provided for at **http://freespace. virgin.net/andrew.parkinson4** with tithe records, poll books, directories, memorial listings and more, whilst the Isle of Sheppey is equally well served at **http://freepages.genealogy.rootsweb.ancestry.com/~penney**. Resources for Staplehurst are at **http://tinyurl.com/yak62lb**, including probate indexes, censuses, parish registers, tithe awards and monumental inscriptions, whilst the Kemsing Heritage Centre (**www.kemsingheritage centre.org.uk**) has some interesting material, such as a list of patients and staff working at the local VAD hospital in the First World War.

Various projects are available for Sittingbourne. The local museum (**www. sittingbourne-museum.co.uk**) provides a general background to the area, as well as a series of monumental inscriptions at **http://tinyurl.com/ ygfytc7** for Borden Churchyard. The Sittingbourne Remembers project (**www.pigstrough.co.uk/ww1/index.html**) has a great deal of historic content commemorating the stories of local Sittingbourne and Milton Regis soldiers who fought in the First World War. Additional war memorial projects for the county include the Kent Fallen site (**www.kentfallen.com**), Faded Genes (**www.fadedgenes.co.uk**) and the Dover War Memorial project (**www.doverwarmemorialproject.org.uk**).

An image of Canterbury Cathedral taken from a magic lantern projection slide, one of many images available online from Kent Photo Archive. (Courtesy of kentphotoarchive.org.uk)

Over 2,000 photographs from Maidstone Museum on aspects of Kent history are online at **www.kentphotoarchive.org.uk**, whilst images of churches from across the county can be viewed at **www.kentchurches.info**, with some accompanying contextual information for each. Additional church images can also be found at **www.roughwood.net/ChurchAlbum/Church Frames.htm**, whilst various old photos and postcards of East Kent towns and villages are at **www.eastkent.freeuk.com**.

Lancashire

The historic County Palatine of Lancashire was the heart of the industrial north, taking in several cities such as Manchester, Liverpool and Lancaster, as well as many towns and villages. A digitised copy of the 1854 publication *The Pictorial History of the County of Lancaster* provides a useful overview of the county's history at **www.archive.org/details/pictorialhistor00unkn goog**.

A useful site for Lancashire resources is online at **www.aboutlancs.com**, whilst an online parish clerk site is available at **www.lan-opc.org.uk**. The latter includes a county map and parish list, with the clerk for each parish contactable by email via a link on the left hand side of each parish page. Indexes for locally-held statutory indexes for the county are available at **www.lancashirebmd.org.uk**.

Lancashire's record office has a useful set of downloadable guides at **www.lancashire.gov.uk/education/record_office** which lists its holdings for Church of England, Nonconformist and Roman Catholic parish records. There is also an online database of county police records from 1840–1925, which includes some borough force records for Rochdale, Southport, Preston and Wigan, and an online catalogue for the whole archive entitled LANCAT. Another handy council site is Lancashire Lantern (**www.lantern.lancashire. gov.uk**), which carries e-resources on a variety of themes, such as an image archive, a pioneers section, and a library catalogue.

The county's cotton weaving industry is explored at **www.spinning theweb.org.uk**, and includes maps, photos, and place descriptions. Also worth reading is **www.cottontimes.co.uk**, and **www.cottontown.org**, which goes into particular depth on Blackburn and Darwen.

Pastfinder

(**www.manchester.gov.uk/info/448/archives_and_local_studies/3651/pa stfinder_catalogue/1**) has a catalogue of over 4,000 collections held within the Greater Manchester area, whilst Manchester and Lancashire Family History Society has a guide on the city's cemeteries at **www.mlfhs.org.uk/**

Infobase/index.htm. The city's library has an online catalogue hosted at https://librarycatalogue.manchester.gov.uk, which also contains a list of its parish record holdings, whilst Manchester UK (www.manchester2002-uk.com) has gazetteers and historical maps of Greater Manchester and Lancashire. The city's parish records can be found on Ancestry (see p.9), and burials for Trafford's cemeteries on Deceased Online (p.12). Parish records from the wider Diocese of Manchester are also on FamilySearch (p.4). Various additional guides and resources can be found at www.manchester-family-history-research.co.uk. A searchable database of publicly contributed memories and resources for Trafford may also be of use at www.trafford.gov.uk/content/tca. Trafford Local Studies Archive catalogue is also available at http://archives.trafford. gov.uk.

Due to water damage to several 1851 census returns for Greater Manchester following a flood, a great deal of information was rescued using sophisticated retrieval techniques by TNA and Manchester and Lancashire FHS. This has since been made available at Ancestry, but free surname and street indexes for the records for Manchester, Chorlton-on-Medlock, Salford, Ashton-under-Lyme and Oldham are available at www.1851-unfilmed.org.uk. Manchester University's First World War Roll of Service is available on the Internet Archive at http://tinyurl.com/bovjlrz.

On the Mersey, the Port Cities Liverpool page at www.portcities.org.uk has essays on slavery, the Blitz and more. Liverpool History Projects at www.liverpoolhistoryprojects.co.uk carries a great deal of Roman Catholic records for the city, a First World War database of Liverpool's Fallen Heroes, information on the Liverpool Irish Regiments, a list of Merseyside immigrants applying for naturalisation from 1879–1912, and its Death in the Pool of Life burial records site, with details on the locations of burial and death records. Various nineteenth-century baptisms, marriages, burials and pauper burials at St Anthony's Liverpool are also found at http://stanthonys-liverpool.com/project/index.php. For a virtual tour of the city in 1825 visit http://liverpool-1825.tripod.com, whilst further material on the city's hinterland can also be examined at www.roydenhistory.co.uk. On the newspaper front, http://jeffmax.pwp.blueyonder.co.uk/abe_max.html carries articles from the *Liverpool Jewish Gazette* from 1968–1970, whilst additional newspaper extracts can be found at www.old-merseytimes.co.uk and www.old-liverpool. co.uk. A list of prisoners and staff from Walton Gaol in 1881 is at www. rootsweb.ancestry.com/~engchs/WAL.html.

Rochdale's www.link4life.org site includes essays on topics such as child labour, coal mining and engineering, as well as several history based e-books and a local studies catalogue. The material is accessed through the Arts and Heritage section, then by visiting the Local Studies link. For Oldham, useful research guides are available at **www.oldham.gov.uk/info/200276/local_studies_and_archives,** whilst an online searchable image guide for Ashton-under-Lyme is located at **www.tameside.gov.uk/localstudies.** A catalogue for Bury Archives is also available at **http://archives.bury.gov.uk.**

Workhouse records for 1871 for Lancaster, Walsden and Preston are to be found at **http://tinyurl.com/yzv57c7,** and a Lancaster convict database for the early nineteenth century at **www.lancastercastle.com/home.php.** Resources for Bolton at **http://tinyurl.com/ybkbbyq** include lists of special constables from 1816–1831, workhouse birth registers, marriage licenses, and more. Cemetery records for Wigan can be consulted at **www.wiganworld. co.uk/stuff.**

There are many other excellent sites for smaller settlements around the county. Parish records and other resources for Todmorden and Walsden are available at **http://todmordenandwalsden.co.uk,** whilst the villages cleared to make way for the Stocks Reservoir in the Dalehead Valley are commemorated at **www.dalehead.org.** Materials for Cronton, Halewood, Huyton, Kirkby, Knowsley village, Prescot, Roby, Tarbock and Whiston can be found at the Knowsley Local History site at **http://history.knowsley.gov.uk.**

Finally, for a dose of a world gone mad, explore the stories of the Pendle Witches at the brilliant **www.pendlewitches.co.uk.**

Leicestershire

There is a Leicestershire online parish clerk site at **www.rootsweb. ancestry.com/~engleiopc,** but many links on the parish pages were found not to be working at the time of writing, the site not having been updated since mid-2008. However, there are some useful resources still available, including maps, photos and census records.

A guide for holdings at Leicestershire's records office is available at **http://tinyurl.com/ykzfyk6,** whilst a gateway site for information on the county's many villages is online at **www.leicestershirevillages.com,** containing links to several locally-based history projects. The site suggests that you will need to register first before use, but you can easily access details on individual villages without doing so.

For images and details of churches across the county, visit **www. leicestershirechurches.co.uk.** The Leicestershire and Rutland Family History Society also provides free church images from the county at its site at **www.lrfhs.org.uk,** and offers a free email look-up service for Methodist register entries from across the county. Baptist records for several parishes, including some monumental inscriptions, can also be freely sourced at **http://tinyurl.com/yjfbaur**.

Many records for Leicestershire are found on Guy Etchells' website at **http://freespace.virgin.net/guy.etchells**, including parish register transcriptions for Muston, Bottesford, Eastwell, Quorndon, Long Clawson, Wartnaby and Hoton, as well as maps, wills and more. Village resources for Redmile, in the county's north east, including marriages, censuses and directories, can be found at **www.redmilearchive.freeuk.com**, whilst Ratcliffe Culey, Sheepy Magna, Sibson, Orton-on-the-Hill and Twycross are all catered for at **www.mdlp.co.uk/resources/lei.htm**, with monumental inscriptions, marriage and poor law records, history notes and picture galleries. Tilton on the Hill is also dealt with at **www.tiltononthehill.org.uk**, but the writing is very faint and hard to read. Bear with it though, as it has a useful parish record database and census transcriptions for the village.

Coalville's history is explored at **www.coalville-heritage.info/home.html**, and includes an interesting pronunciation guide for phrases in the local dialect, whilst Whitwick's past is recorded at **www.whitwick. org.uk/opener.php**. The history of the local tanning and mining industries surrounding Swannington can be read at **www.swannington-heritage.co.uk**.

Lincolnshire

There are several county-wide resources for Lincolnshire. A convict transportation database exists at the county archives site at **http://tinyurl.com/yjzsgbk**, along with an index to consistory court wills and lists of parish registers and bishop's transcripts held at the facility. Cultural Collections (**www.lincstothepast.com**) provides a wider database search facility for over half a million items in various other county-based archives, libraries and museums, whilst lay subsidy rolls for various settlements across the county are hosted at **www.historicalresources.myzen.co.uk/LINC/lincers.html**.

A marriage index from 1837–1911 for seventeen Lincolnshire registration districts is found at **http://mi.lincolnshiremarriages.org.uk**, whilst volunteer-based look-up exchanges exist at both **http://williamsgwynfa.tripod.com** and **www.genealogy-links.co.uk/html/lin.lookup.html**. On the military front, the Lincolnshire Bomber Command Memorial appeal site (**www.lincsbombercommandmemorial.com**) has some accounts from those who served in the war, whilst memorials to RAF stations in the county can be found at **www.raf-lincolnshire.info/memorials.htm**. For newspapers,

Lincolnshire's family history society (www.lincolnshirefhs.org.uk) hosts extracts from various editions from 1780–1929, and provides a handy parish map.

The Wisbech and the Fenlands site (http://contueor.com/wisbech) hosts records for Lincolnshire, Cambridgeshire and Norfolk, with a searchable database of almost 18,000 records. Transcriptions of post-1813 baptismal and marriage registers for several parishes are at http://wparkinson.com/transcriptions.htm, whilst the site's creator Wendy Parkinson has also uploaded over 1,200 church photos from the county at www.wparkinson.com/Churches/Guide.htm, taken by her and Paul Fenwick. The latter has an additional photographs site at www.imagesoflincolnshire.co.uk. Photos of gravestones from many churches in the north and north east of the county can be found at www.rootsweb.ancestry.com/~engggfhg.

Parish records for Frodingham from 1750 to the early 1800s are available at www.genogold.com/html/lincolnshire.html. For Springthorpe, school records, lay subsidy rolls and more can be located at www.springthorpe-village.org.uk/history, whilst Sedgebrook is similarly served at http://freepages.history.rootsweb.ancestry.com/~sedgebrook/, with transcripts of the 1841–1911 censuses, directories, school records, strays and school records. The Metheringham Area Community Leisure Association has an impressive site at www. macla.co.uk containing material for Metheringham, Blankney, Dunston, Nocton, Scopwick and Tanvats, including trade directory extracts and the 1881 census.

Finally, for proof that God may in fact be from Lincolnshire, and seriously interested in genealogy, you should visit the fantastic Axholme Ancestry site at www.red1st.com. Centred on the Isle of Axholme, but also covering a wider area in both Lincolnshire and Yorkshire, the sheer range of digitised resources, databases, manorial rolls, monumental inscriptions and pedigrees is seriously impressive.

London (Greater London including Middlesex)

The former historic county of Middlesex, the second smallest in England, is now in its entirety a part of the Greater London area (which also takes in parts of Essex, Kent, Surrey and Hertfordshire). A list of Middlesex parishes is located at www.angelfire.com/fl/Sumter/Middlesex.html, with an additional list and parish maps available at www.west-middlesex-fhs.org.uk/content/research.aspx.

The major genealogy vendor sites have provided a great deal of resources online concerning the nation's capital. Ancestry reigns supreme on this front,

The London Historical Records Collection hosted on Ancestry.co.uk.

with its partnership agreement with the London Metropolitan Archives and Guildhall Library Manuscripts that has seen many records collections digitised and released at **www.ancestry.co.uk/cs/uk/lma**. This includes birth, marriage and burial registers from 1538–1812, births and baptisms from 1813–1906, marriage registers from 1754–1921, burials from 1813–1980, tax records from 1692–1932, poll books and electoral registers from 1538–1893, and Board of Guardians records for the capital's workhouses. Additional parish records, including those for Westminster, can be found on FindmyPast.

The Origins Network also has several major London-centred collections online, including Boyd's Marriage Index from 1538–1840, St Andrew Holborn Marriage Index 1754–1812, Marriage License Allegations 1694–1850, Archdeaconry Court of London Wills Index 1700–1807, Surrey and South London wills extracts 1470–1856, London Apprenticeship extracts 1442–1850, a London Burials Index for 1538–1853 and a London Consistory Court Depositions Index for 1700–1713.

The AIM25 site at **www.aim25.ac.uk** has a searchable catalogue of over a hundred archives, livery companies, societies and more within the M25 area, whilst a catalogue for all of London's libraries can be found at **http://tinyurl.com/yd63txl**. An online catalogue for London Metropolitan Archives is available at **http://tinyurl.com/yd6c2rc**, and its London Generations database can be accessed at **http://tinyurl.com/cacbngj**. This now comprises detailed research guides for records extant for each of London's boroughs.

The City of Westminster Archive's WESTCAT catalogue (**http://tinyurl.com/yedsqov**) provides some useful indexes, such as St Martin-in-the-Fields Settlement Examinations from 1732–1755, a Survey of London index to street names, and the Motco Project, a database of prints, maps and images of London.

The Institute of Historical Research's Guildhall Library Manuscripts site at **www.history.ac.uk/gh** links to various guides and indexes for business records, livery companies, Lloyd's captains registers, probate inventories from the Peculiar Court of St Paul's Cathedral and marriage licenses from St Katharine-by-the-Tower (1686–1802). The London Metropolitan University's Women's Library website, with a catalogue of holdings, is at **www.lse.ac.uk/library/newsandinformation/womenslibraryatLSE/home.aspx**.

Historical paintings and images of the city, and several virtual exhibitions depicting life in London across time, are available at **http://collage.cityoflondon.gov.uk**. Images from the *Illustrated London News* Picture Library can also be consulted at **www.iln.org.uk** – many editions are also hosted on The Genealogist.

Locating London's Past (**www.locatinglondon.org**) is an interesting project linking data from various digitised records projects and maps from 1746 and 1869–80. If, for example, you wish to locate the sites of all crimes recorded in a particular area, as recorded on the Old Bailey Online site (p.95), you can do so. A similar map project for historic images can be found at **www.visithistoriccities.com**. An interesting project called Bomb Sight (**http://bombsight.org**) is mapping the London Second World War bomb census between 7 October 1940 and 6 June 1941, allowing users to locate where bombs fell but also to discover memories and photographs from the period.

The London School of Economics has also created a site dedicated to Charles Booth's nineteenth-century poverty maps for the city at **http://booth.lse.ac.uk**, with various notebooks and additional resources included. Various nineteenth-century cholera maps of the city drawn up by John Snow

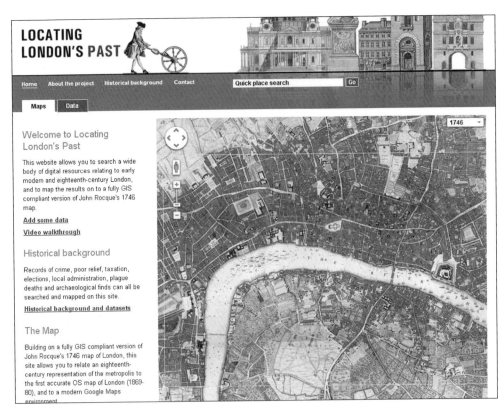

Locating London's Past.

can also be found at **www.ph.ucla.edu/epi/snow.html,** and Greenwood's London map of 1827 at **http://users.bathspa.ac.uk/greenwood.** A Victorian London A-Z is online at **http://homepage.ntlworld.com/hitch/gendocs /lon-str.html,** whilst an aerial survey of the city taken in 1949 can be viewed at **www.oldaerial photos.com.**

London Burials (**www.londonburials.co.uk**) provides an excellent guide to cemetery locations within Greater London, but does not provide any monumental inscriptions; a similar guide for the east of the city is provided by the area's local family history society at **www.eolfhs.org.uk,** a site which also carries a discussion forum and a detailed parish information guide. Deceased Online (p.12) has digitised burial and cremation record images from several London boroughs available. London Remembers (**www.londonremembers.com**) is a useful site attempting to trace memorials in the city, such as plaques and statues.

Lee Jackson's Dictionary of Victorian London (**www.victorian london.org**) provides a detailed guide to life in the capital in the late nineteenth century. The Port Cities London page at **www.portcities. org.uk/london** has a wider reach, examining the city's role from pre-Tudor times to the twentieth century, with resources including a look at the various trades worked at from 1850–1980 and the impact of the Blitz on the Docklands area. A study on the role of bargemen on the Thames is also available at **www.bargemen.co.uk**. For the city's livery companies, visit **www.combs-families.org/combs/records/england/lnd/livery02.htm**.

Essays on Tower Hamlets' history are available at **www.mernick.org.uk/ thhol**, whilst the history of the Isle of Dogs is explored at **www.island history.org.uk**. If you have an interest in Tottenham High Road, visit **www.mickbruff.pwp.blueyonder.co.uk/highroad,** which includes resources such as census returns, directory extracts and monumental inscriptions for All Hallows Church. For a similar site on Brentford High Street in Hounslow, visit **www.bhsproject.co.uk**.

The development of areas such as Barnet, Ealing, Greenwich and Kingston, in relation to the city's transport infrastructure, is dealt with by the London Transport Museum at **www.ltmuseum.co.uk/collections/research,** which also provides a guide to the history of Caribbean recruitment in the transport services. A Roll of Honour for staff of the London Passenger Transport Board who fell in the Second World War is available at **www. eastkent.freeuk.com/misc/lt_deaths_ww2.htm,** whilst the London and North Western Railway Society has an archive catalogue, a staff history research guide and a further roll of honour at **www.lnwrs.org.uk**.

Other notable industry sites include a database of 9,000 photographers and associated trades folk from 1841–1901 at **www.photolondon.org.uk/ default.asp,** a guide to historic Greater London pubs at **http://london publichouse.com,** and a database of entertainers who performed in London's music halls at **www.rhul.ac.uk/drama/Music-hall/index.asp**. Various collections of University of London student records from 1836–1932, as well as the university's military personnel from 1914–1945, are located within the Our Collections section of the Senate House Library website (under Archives and Manuscripts) at **http://tinyurl.com/bex6n2f**.

The Proceedings of the Old Bailey 1674–1913 (**www.oldbaileyonline. org**) carries the proceedings of almost 200,000 trials, plus background history resources on crime and enforcement. Ancestry's Middlesex, England, Convict Transportation Contracts, 1682–1787 collection has 4,299 records of convicts transported to the American colonies and the Caribbean.

The history of the Metropolitan Police, with a timeline, books of remembrance and details on its archives can be explored at **http://content.met.police.uk/Site/history**, whilst a general history of policing in London is at **www.historybytheyard.co.uk**, including the gallantry awards list for the twentieth and twenty-first century. For the Metropolitan Women Police Association story visit **www.metwpa.org.uk**.

On the medical front, the Historic Hospital Admission Records project (**http://hharp.org**) carries resources relating to the early years of three London children's hospitals, namely the Hospital for Sick Children at Great Ormond Street, the Evelina Hospital and the Alexandra Hospital for Children with Hip Disease, with over 100,000 individual admission records from 1852 to 1914. For a series of articles on ragged schools in the capital, visit **www.raggedschoolmuseum.org.uk**.

A website at **www.wbcollyer.org** about Nonconformist minister Dr William Bengo Collyer (1782–1854) of Hanover Chapel, Peckham, contains various register transcripts for the chapel, as well as subscriber lists, London Missionary Society donors and subscribers, and other datasets. Finally for the capital, if your ancestors were members of the true nobility of London, a list of Pearly Kings and Queens can be found at **www.pearlysociety.co.uk**!

Norfolk

The county council's Norfolk Online Access to Heritage platform (**www.noah.norfolk.gov.uk**), aka 'NOAH', allows you to view information and digitised resources from several sources in the county, including the Library Service, the Norfolk Record Office and Norfolk Museums and Archaeology Service. Amongst the holdings are local archive catalogues, newspaper indexes, tithe maps, directories and more – for a full listing use the site's 'Advanced Search' function.

Norfolk Family History Society has a detailed parish guide for the county at **www.norfolkfhs.org.uk**, with links to many online resources (mainly at GENUKI), and very usefully names contiguous parishes for each entry. A county map drawn up in 1797 by William Faden can be explored at **www.fadensmapofnorfolk.co.uk**, whilst several historic maps from the county can be examined at **www.historic-maps.norfolk.gov.uk**.

A Norfolk Baptism Project exists at **http://tinyurl.com/nnf4d9**, providing records from 1813–1880, whilst the Norfolk Transcription Archive at **www.genealogy.doun.org/transcriptions/index.php** has parish register transcriptions, subsidy taxes, muster rolls and census returns. Paddy Apling's excellent site at **http://apling.freeservers.com** has directory information, the 1891 census and many more resources for each of the hundreds within the county, broken down to both parish and village level.

Various newspaper entries from the *Norfolk Chronicle* and other rags can be found at **www.foxearth.org.uk/newspapers.html**. On the photographic front, the Norfolk Broads are well covered at **http://people.netcom.co. uk/j.stringe**, and images of churches from across the county can be viewed at **www.norfolkchurches.co.uk**. The East Anglian Film Archive also has material for the county (see p.59).

The Norfolk Heritage Explorations site (**www.oneninesixzero.co.uk**) covers the history of Mulbarton, Harleston, Happisburgh, Breckles and Reepham, all deliberately chosen as a representative sample of the diverse communities found within the county. The site contains few historic records as such, but carries many recorded memories and images.

A history of Buxton is provided at **www.buxton-norfolk.co.uk/interest. htm**, whilst the settlement of Mattishall is discussed at **www.mattishall-village.co.uk**. Transcriptions of wills, censuses, enclosure maps, directories, and archdeacons' transcripts for Itteringham, and a useful photographic graveyard survey, are available at **www.itteringham.com/history/history. html**. Serving Deopham is **www.deophamhistory.co.uk**, with transcriptions of the 1911 census, directories, gravestones, maps and tithe records for the area. A local history of Merton can be found at **www.merton.ukgo.com**, including information on the two wars and the village's war memorials. For guardians of the poor minutes concerning the poor law union of Erpingham, visit **www.oldshuck.webspace.virgin media.com**.

The interesting **www.salthousehistory.co.uk** site provides some useful material for Salthouse, such as maps and poor prisoners returns from 1815, but also recalls the extraordinary story of a parish register dating back to 1538 which had been buried by a rector in World War Two and was only recently discovered still buried in the ground.

Other useful resources for the county include a list of gamekeepers from Kelly's Directory 1883 at **http://apling.freeservers.com/Jobs/Game keepers.htm**, a database of Norfolk pubs at **www.norfolkpubs.co.uk,** and the wonderful Norfolk Mills site at **www.norfolkmills.co.uk,** which hosts a list of millers' wills from the seventeenth and eighteenth century, names of millers and databases on various types and locations of mills.

Northamptonshire

One of the best Northamptonshire websites is Graham Ward's Miscellenea

Edintone project at **www.edintone.com,** which is packed with resources on the history of the non-established churches in the county, including a virtual library of books. If your ancestor was a clock or watchmaker, you are further in luck, as Graham also provides a useful list of those working in the professions, drawn from several sources. Equally fascinating is the Northamptonshire Black History project (**www.northants-black-history. org.uk**), which includes a brilliant searchable database drawn from newspaper extracts, archive holdings and oral history project material.

If your ancestor was a soldier you should visit **www.northants1841.fsnet. co.uk** to explore the Northampton Independent Soldier Photograph Index. This contains over 3,000 entries from local newspapers written from 1914–20, eighteenth-century militia indexes and a Northampton First World War roll of honour. The site also hosts a wills index from 1854–57, parish removal indexes, strays, Quaker baptisms and marriages, and travellers recorded in baptismal registers from 1751–1812.

There are no major county-wide record transcription projects, but baptisms in Oundle from 1813–1838 can be found at **http://tinyurl.com/yzbxkw7**. The Towcester and District Local Historical Society website at **www.mkheritage. co.uk/tdlhs** also carries several parish register and wills entries.

Rushden and surrounding district are catered for at **www.rushden heritage.co.uk,** with lots of resources on land records, the shoemaking industry, local war memorials, church history and more.

Censuses for Glapthorn can be found at **www.eyemead.com/glap thor.htm,** and for Burton Latimer at **www.burtonlatimer.info,** whilst directories for Cottingham can be accessed at **www.cottinghamhistory. co.uk.** The history of Duston is recalled at **www.duston.org.uk,** with a roll of honour and memorial inscriptions included, and Helmdon is dealt with at **www.helmdon.com,** with a list of obituaries, monumental inscriptions, picture galleries and press cuttings.

Northumberland

The Northumberland Communities site (**http://tinyurl.com/yfs367l**) provides a detailed history for each village and town in the county, accompanied by photos, digitised manuscripts, ordnance survey maps and census information, making it an essential first port of call. Tomorrow's History (**www.tomorrows-history.com**) hosts several Northumberland community history projects.

Newcastle Register Office has placed some limited indexes online at **www.newcastle.gov.uk/your-council/register-office** for statutory births

(1837–1870) and marriages (1837–1900), which can be used to order up copies of the records. For death, extracts from the *Newcastle Evening Chronicle* have been made available at **www.genuki.org.uk/big/eng/NBL/Death Notices** for deaths from 1885–1906, indexed by surname. Northumberland and Durham Family History Society has a list of its records holdings for Northumberland at **www.ndfhs.org.uk,** whilst the county records office website at **www.experiencewoodhorn.com/collections** has an online catalogue, user guides to records and more. A Northumberland look-up exchange exists at **www.redmire.net/lookup/nbl.html** for various sets of records from across the county. FamilySearch (p,4) also hosts a Northumberland Miscellaneous Records 1570–2005 collection.

Durham University Library's North East Inheritance project at **http:// familyrecords.dur.ac.uk/nei/index.htm** carries probate records from 1527–1857 via an online digital image catalogue, with over 150,000 wills and related archive material from across Northumberland, Durham and Tyne and Wear.

The North East Inheritance project, an important resource for northern probate records.

North East Inheritance

Click to access the Probate Catalogue

Durham and Northumberland probate records, 1527-1857

Home

Online exhibitions

Which wills do we hold?

Probate Court

How did a will get proved?

Probate records

History of the collection

About the project

Useful texts

Contact us

Progress

Welcome to Durham University Library's North East Inheritance project, which is funding the creation of an online digital image catalogue of over 150,000 wills and related archives from across County Durham, Tyne and Wear and Northumberland. These will provide an invaluable insight into north-eastern people and communities, their family relationships, trades and lifestyles. The wills date from the 16th Century to the mid-19th Century and many are accompanied by inventories of the goods belonging to the deceased, bonds, accounts, and a variety of associated documents.

Historians, genealogists, students and anyone interested in the history of the region and its people will be able to search the Durham probate records by name, place, occupation or date, and link to a comprehensive set of digital images of the actual wills themselves on the Genealogical Society of Utah's website. The project will also fund the conservation of the most fragile of the archives, and ensure their preservation for future generations. Access to both the catalogue and the digital images will be free and available worldwide. The catalogue will be completed and made available online in 2010.

North East Inheritance is funded by a £274,500 grant from the Heritage Lottery Fund. This grant of £274,500 is matched by contributions from Durham University and by the English Record Collections Society, amounting to a further £141,250.

Steve Bulman's site at **www.stevebulman.f9.co.uk/northumberland** reproduces William Whellan and Co.'s *History of Northumberland* gazetteer from 1855. For Gateshead, a useful site with various old maps, postcards, church images and more is located at **www.picturesofgateshead.co.uk/ index.html**.

Tyneside Family History (**http://tinyurl.com/yh9fukl**) provides a nineteenth-century history of Newcastle and various colliery villages such as Seghill, Cramlington, Killingworth, Burradon, Seaton Burn and Weetslade, with various topics covered including migration, the impact of the Irish, housing, education and work. The Durham Mining Museum project (see p.51) also contains resources for Northumbrian miners and their communities.

FamilySearch carries bishops' transcripts for records from the Diocese of Durham covering the period from 1700–1900, as well as separate Durham diocese databases for marriage bonds and allegations (1692–1900) and calendars of marriage bonds and allegations (1594–1815). Records for Northumberland are included, though the images can only be browsed and not searched by name. There is also a Northumberland Miscellaneous Records 1570–2005 collection containing electoral registers, burial registers, bastardy bonds, court of pleas records and other materials, but this can only be viewed at a Mormon-run Family History Centre.

Finally, the Legacy Tyne and Wear site at **www.legacyarchives.org.uk** looks at the history and heritage of black and ethnic minority communities in the area.

Nottinghamshire
A catalogue of holdings for Nottinghamshire Archives is available at **http:// nawcat.nottinghamshire.gov.uk**, whilst Nottinghamshire Local Studies Library hosts an equivalent at **www.nottinghamcity.gov.uk/libraries**. The county council website also has some interesting online exhibitions at **www. nottinghamshire.gov.uk/learning/history/archives,** focussing on subjects as diverse as Broad Marsh and Narrow Marsh, the Story of Raleigh Cycles, and Nottingham's Afro-Caribbean heritage. In addition it has a searchable catalogue of its holdings and downloadable parish register finding aids for the county. The county's black history is further explored at the Thoroton Society of Nottinghamshire's heritage gateway site at **www.nottsheritage gateway. org.uk,** as well as various other historic topics. The society also has a useful bibliography of county based literature available at **http://tiny url.com/yj7ozum**.

Our Nottinghamshire (**www.ournottinghamshire.org.uk**) is a community history project with essays on various historic topics. An illustrated database of the county's churches can be explored at Heather Faulkes' Old Nottinghamshire site (**www.oldnotts.co.uk**), as well as the history of the Ashfield, Bidsworth and Mansfield areas. Gazetteer descriptions for several parishes in the county from 1855 can be found at **www.stevebulman. f9.co.uk/northumberland/index.html**, whilst a variety of gazetteers and other resources can be found at **www.charliespage.co.uk/pollbookindex. htm**, including *Hodson's Directory* from 1814, a 1754 Poll Book for Nottinghamshire and the names of Sherwood Foresters in the Boer War. Various additional resources can also be found via Axholme Ancestry (**www.red1st.com**).

Nottingham's lace making industry is explored at **www.bbc.co.uk/legacies/ work/england/nottingham/article_1.shtml**, whilst the story of Nottingham lace makers who settled in Calais and then emigrated to Australia in 1848 is detailed by the Australian Society of the Lacemakers of Calais at **www.angelfire.com/ al/aslc**. The Nottstalgia Nottingham Forums (**http://nottstalgia.com/ forums**) also carry discussions on many topics of interest.

Material for Mansfield can be found at **www.pastpresented.ukart. com/lost-mansfield/**, including newspaper extracts, copyhold land survey records from the early seventeenth century and constables' records from the 1730s, whilst additional images and memories from people in the area have been recorded at **www.old-mansfield.org.uk**. For people from across Nottinghamshire who were found recorded in the parish registers of Calverton, Lambley, Oxton, Thurgaton and Tithby there is a marriage strays index at **http://tinyurl.com/ykd322g**, as well as register entries from over twenty parishes, a wills strays index and some marriage licenses.

Guy Etchells' site at **http://freespace.virgin.net/guy.etchells** has parish register transcripts for Lenton, Elton-on-the-Hill, Elston, Bingham and Hickling, as well as *A General View of the Agriculture of the County of Nottingham*, by Robert Lowe, from 1798. Norton Cuckney is covered at **http: //tinyurl.com/yh5bnez**, with various photos, records of baptisms, marriages and burials, and extracts from White's Directory from 1832 and 1864. Parish records for Beeston are also available at **www.beeston-notts.co.uk**, along with an interesting memoir and diary by Sergeant William Jowett of the 7th Royal Fusiliers, published in 1856, which concerns his time at the Crimea. For the village of Bunny, **www.bunnyvillage.org.uk** contains baptisms (1715–1899), marriages (1556–1899) and burials (1715–1899) amongst its offerings.

A one-place study for Normanton-on-Soar is available at **http://free pages.genealogy.rootsweb.ancestry.com/~lesleydonald**, with various records for both the village and adjacent parishes. Ashfield Cemetery Records Online (**www.ashfield-dc.gov.uk/ashfieldcemeteries/intro.php? set=yes**) has records from six local cemeteries, and for Hucknall Huthwaite, **www.huthwaite-online.net/hucknall** contains gazetteer entries and a press archive from 1676–1982.

Finally, a website dedicated to Warsop Vale in the north of the county is online at **www.warsopvale.org**, containing many historic photos and maps for the area throughout its history as a colliery village.

Oxfordshire

A list of Oxfordshire based parishes and villages is located at **www. ontaworld.co.uk/england/oxfordshire/index.html**, with an interactive parish map for the county provided by the Oxfordshire Family History Society at **www.ofhs.org.uk**. This not only helps you to identify parish locations, but also to identify how many records have been recorded by the society for each parish, which can be accessed through its search service. The site also offers monumental inscription indexes, and a wills index naming every person noted within more than 30,000 probate documents, sourced both locally and from the Prerogative Court of Canterbury. Wills and indexes from 1516–1857 are also available on the Origins Network (p.11). For identifying historic locations in the county, Smith's New Map of the County of Oxford (1801) is at **http://mapco.net/oxford/oxford.htm**.

A surname interest list online for Oxfordshire is at **www.oxsil.org.uk**. For a glimpse of Oxfordshire churches visit **www.oxfordshirechurches.info** and **www.flickr.com/photos/oxfordshirechurches/collections/72157606 453865587/**.

Hearth tax returns from 1662 for the hundred of Ploughley are at **www. whipple.org/oxford**, along with transcriptions from Oxford archdeaconry's marriages bonds from 1634–1850. Also within Ploughley, the inhabitants of the parish of Kirtlington in 1723 and 1753 are listed at **www.burrell-wood.org.uk/LHist/Places/Kirtlington/index.htm**, the names having been sourced from local manorial records. For a brief history of Oxford city, visit **www.oxfordcity.co.uk/info/history.html**.

The parish church site for Noke (**http://home.btconnect.com/stgiles _noke**) has register transcriptions, probate records, censuses and hearth tax returns. Headington is catered for at **www.headington.org.uk**, with censuses, directories, maps, school log books, press cuttings and a timeline, whilst Deddington's site at **www.deddington.org.uk** is packed with maps, a workhouse history and more.

Finally for Oxfordshire, an excellent guide to the locations of NHS records from the county, including a list of hospitals, can be found at **www.oxfordshirehealtharchives.nhs.uk**.

Rutland

The smallest of the historic English counties, Rutland only has two towns, Oakham and Uppingham, and today exists as a single unitary authority. Many resources for the county are found in surrounding adjacent counties, in particular Leicestershire. The Leicestershire, Leicester and Rutland Record Office catalogue can be found online at **http://record-office-catalogue. leics.gov.uk/DServe**, whilst a list of the office's parish register holdings, including Rutland, is available at **http://tinyurl. com/yh3sy4r**. The Leicester and Rutland Churches site at **www. leicestershirechurches.co.uk** also covers the county.

The Historic Rutland section of the Rutland Online website at **www. rutnet.co.uk** has various historic resources, including an 1851 census transcription for Uppingham and a useful Towns & Villages guide. A useful guide for researching properties in the town also exists at **www.rutland history.org**, as collated by the local studies group. A feast of transcribed resources for the village of Langham is available at **www.langhamvillage. com**, including maps, manor court rolls, parish registers and censuses.

Finally, a comprehensive site on the county's war memorials is available at **www.users.globalnet.co.uk/~shelvey**, with photographs and transcriptions recorded from some fifty-four war memorials from Ashwell to Wing, as well as individual graves of service personnel where known.

Shropshire

The county of Shropshire (also known as 'Salop') on the Welsh Marches is one of the least populated English counties. The Discovering Shropshire's History site at **www.discovershropshire.org.uk/html** provides a useful gateway to various county-based sites and resources, whilst various maps for the county can be found at **http://freepages.genealogy.rootsweb. ancestry.com/~genmaps/genfiles/COU_Pages/ ENG_pages/sal.htm**.

Shropshire Archives has an online catalogue at **http://archives. shropshire.gov.uk**, whilst a list of parishes and villages in the county is found at **www.ontaworld.co.uk/england/shropshire/index.html**, though at the time of writing only the parish of Acton Burnell can be further explored via a link on the site. Shropshire Family History Society (**www.sfhs.org.uk**) has some useful resources online in the form of a strays index for those appearing in marriages and wills outside of the county, and a monumental inscription surname index. The Joiner Marriage Index at **www.joiner marriageindex.co.uk** carries over 70,000 marriages for 125 Shropshire parishes.

Old Lydbury (**www.old-lydbury.org.uk**) has directories for the village from 1851–1895, and censuses from 1841–1901, with the exception of 1881. Parish registers for Aleveley are available at **www.sheridansweep.free serve.co.uk,** with several lists of people in the village at various periods between 1831 and the 1950s.

Historic Ironbridge can be explored at **www.ironbridge.org.uk,** with the site carrying details on extensive collections held at the local museum, historic photographs and information on the various archaeological projects in the vicinity. The history of Madeley is covered at **www.madeleylocal history.org,** and Broseley at **www.broseley.org.uk,** with the latter including trade directories, tithe maps and more.

For Shropshire's fallen in various British conflicts, a Shropshire War Memorials blog is located at **http://shropshirewarmemorials. blogspot. co.uk**.

Finally for Shropshire, the National Library of Wales' Crime and Punishment database (**www.llgc.org.uk/sesiwn_fawr/index_s.htm**) includes details of some Shropshire felons.

Somerset

If you have ancestors from Somerset you are particularly fortunate, as there is a wealth of online material to help with your research. The county's record office website at **www1.somerset.gov.uk/archives** is a good starting point, with a catalogue of holdings, the Somerset Voices and Exmoor Oral History projects, as well as many digitised maps and pictures. Photos from churches in Somerset can be viewed at **www.westcountrychurches.co.uk.**

The county's best offerings lie, however, within the wealth of sources for parish records. A volunteer-based Online Parish Clerk exists at **http://wsom-opc.org.uk/index.php,** which covers Bristol as well as Somerset, and offers records and links to useful sites for each parish. The South West England Genealogical Indexes site (**www.paulhyb.homecall.co.uk**) is equally useful, with many parish register transcriptions for areas such as Bridgwater and Taunton, but also Somerset trade directories and newspaper records. Taunton is also served at **www.parkhouse.org.uk,** with parish registers, a Somerset Book of Honour (for the First World War), and monumental inscriptions for St Mary Magdalene graveyard in the town. If your ancestors were from the

Weston-Super-Mare area, the local family history society has indexes to baptisms, marriages and burials, as well as images of churches, at **http://wsmfhs.org.uk**. Parish register entries for Blackmore in Wedmore, Burnham-on-Sea, Cheddar, East Brent, East Huntspill, Highbridge, Huntspill, Mark, Pawlett, Brent Knoll, Wedmore, Wookey and Woolavington are available at **www.durtnall.org.uk/Somerset%20Pages.htm,** and for parishes within the hundred of Frome, visit **www.gomezsmart.myzen.co.uk** (also via **http://fromeresearch.org.uk**). For the parish of Nynehead, visit **www.nynehead.org**.

Several Somerset parishes are dealt with at **http://tinyurl.com/yfq4e36,** whilst Paul Kenyon's site (**www.pbenyon1.plus.com**) hosts additional register transcripts and miscellaneous records. For West Somerset, there is again excellent coverage at Martin Southwood's **www.wsom.org.uk/Parreg.html**. The south east is dealt with by West Country Genealogy at **www.westcountrygenealogy.com,** with both parish register and directory listings, and further transcriptions for the south of the county can be found at Sarah Hawkins' excellent **http://freepages.genealogy.rootsweb.ancestry.com/~sarahhawkins**. Records from ten further parishes, including those around Glastonbury, have been placed online at **http://tinyurl.com/yjjjp7b,** mainly from the nineteenth century.

The Winsham Web Museum at **www.winshamwebmuseum.co.uk** is an extremely detailed site with parish records from 1559–1885, burial records for St Stephen's and Winsham cemeteries, and the impressive Winsham Archive, containing many miscellaneous records sets from land sales and other document examples. Kingweston village is covered at **http://kingweston.atspace.com,** and Wedmore is served at **www.tutton.org** with parish records from 1561–1860, and other resources such as the *Wedmore Chronicles* from 1898.

Records for Nailsea can be found at **http://myweb.tiscali.co.uk/ian.sage/Nailsea/nailsea.html,** including war memorial information. Parish entries for Clevedon, along with census material, are online at **www.clevedon-civic-society.org.uk**. For High Littleton and Hallatrow parish records visit **www.highlittletonhistory.org.uk,** and for Timsbury, directories and census records are located at **www.timsbury.net**.

For statutory records in the vicinity of Bath and north-east Somerset, an index can be found at the Bath BMD site (**http://bathbmd.org.uk**), which can be used to order up post-1837 certificates from the local register office. Newspaper extracts from the *Bath Chronicle* are hosted online through a

Georgian Newspaper Project at **www.bathnes.gov.uk/services/libraries-and-archives/archives/georgian-newspaper-project** covering the period from 1770–1800, whilst some further useful resources for Bath, Freshford and Hinton Charterhouse, including images and potted histories, can be found at **www.freshford.com**.

Staffordshire

Images from historic Staffordshire's past can be viewed on the Strolling Through Staffordshire site at **www.thornber.org,** whilst historic maps and essays on a range of historical themes from the county can be viewed at **www.staffspasttrack.org.uk**.

Locally-held statutory birth, marriage and death certificates for Staffordshire can be ordered from the various county-based register offices using the Staffordshire BMD site at **www.staffordshirebmd.org.uk**. An equally useful resource is the Staffordshire and Stoke-on-Trent Archive Service's Staffordshire Name Indexes database at **www.staffsnameindexes .org.uk,** which contains a Calendar of Prisoners at Staffordshire Quarter Sessions Index (1779–1880), a Staffordshire Police Force Registers Index (1842–1920) and a Diocese of Lichfield and Coventry Wills Index (1650–1700), with a database on Workhouse Admissions and Discharges (1834–1900) well underway. A searchable catalogue for all archives and museums in the Black Country can be further consulted at **http://blackcountry history.org,** whilst the Black Country Connections surname interests site at **http://bcconnections.tribalpages.com** can help to make connections. Records of those buried or cremated in seven cemeteries within the modern metropolitan borough of Dudley can be searched freely at **http://tiny url.com/cdqltu4**.

A list of Staffordshire parishes is available at **www.ontaworld.co.uk/ england/staffordshire/index.html** with links to a handful of parish sites providing further information, whilst various parish registers from across the county, in addition to a large Excel file of the Staffordshire Calendar of Prisoners, can be found at **http://uk-transcriptions.accessgenealogy. com/Staffs.htm**. The subscription-based **www.midlandshistoricaldata .org** also offers a great deal of material in the form of censuses, directories, books for Staffordshire and other resources for the Midlands counties.

A catalogue for The Sutherland Papers, a massive archive of papers for the Leveson-Gower family, Marquesses of Stafford and Dukes of Sutherland, for their estates in the county, can be consulted at **www.sutherland collection.org.uk,** and handily includes a personal names index.

For Sedgley, a comprehensive research guide, with various photographs, essays and records, can be viewed at **www.sedgleymanor.com**, and includes additional resources for the county such as the Black Country Dialect Dictionary. The town of Willenhall is covered on two separate sites, with a list of families in 1532, hearth tax records from 1666, several directories and war memorials available at **http://freespace.virgin.net/willen.hall/ Willenhall. html**.

Trade directories, censuses and maps for Whittington are online at **www.whittingtonhistorysociety.org.uk,** whilst records for Hints and Canwell in the south of the county are at **www.hints-village.com**. Wills, parish records, manor court records, quarter sessions records and more for Hollinsclough are at **www.hollinsclough.org.uk/localhistory.htm**. Parish records for the village of Betley (1538–1812) can be consulted at **www. betley.net,** along with wills from 1518 onwards, estate sales, and population data from 1086.

Census indexes, images, and databases on churches and records for Walsall can help at **http://cms.walsall.gov.uk/localhistorycentre,** with the site also hosting an Asian Heritage Project. Walsall's Leather Museum site at **http://cms.walsall.gov.uk/leisure_and_culture/leathermuseum** provides some useful information on a once-important occupation within the area.

The website of Wolverhampton City Archives (**www.wolverhamptonart. org.uk/about-wolverhampton-archives/**) has details of its collections and opening hours should you wish to visit. Images and essays on the history of Wolverhampton can be found at **www. wolverhamptonhistory.org.uk,** whilst war memorials for the city can be found at **www.wolverhampton warmemorials.org.uk**. Memorials for Staffordshire's largest city, Stoke-on-Trent, can also be viewed at **http://tinyurl.com/yfemecn,** whilst various other memorials from across the Midlands, including Staffordshire, are available at **www.midlandsheritage .co.uk/war-memorials**. An interesting site for those who served in the Home Guard in the county from 1940–44 is also worth exploring at **www. staffshomeguard.co.uk**.

On the occupation front, some additional resources include a site on the 1895 Diglake Colliery Disaster at **www.warrinerprimaries.com/Topic/ diglake.htm,** and a report into child labour within Staffordshire potteries at **www.staffs.ac.uk/schools/humanities_and_soc_sciences/census/sc1.htm**

Suffolk

The East Anglian county of Suffolk has produced many famous personalities across the centuries, from the painter John Constable to the Witchfinder

WELCOME, FRIEND! .... YOU HAVE ENTERED THE WEBSITE OF

THE 32ND STAFFORDSHIRE (ALDRIDGE) BATTALION
and of many other units in
THE HOME GUARD ACROSS THE COUNTRY

WELCOME and CONTENTS PAGE

SEARCH - EXPLORE - CONTRIBUTE - BOOKMARK

THIS WEBSITE PROVIDES:

GENERAL INFORMATION
about the Home Guard.

**INFORMATION ABOUT MANY
SPECIFIC HOME GUARD UNITS**
in counties throughout the country
(especially, but not exclusively, the West
Midlands counties of
Shropshire, Staffordshire, Warwickshire and
Worcestershire).

**ONE BATTALION'S DETAILED
STORY**
THE 32ND (ALDRIDGE) BATTALION, SOUTH
STAFFORDSHIRE HOME GUARD
defending
Aldridge, Barr Beacon, Brownhills, Little Aston,
Pelsall, Pheasey, Rushall, Shelfield, Streetly,
Walsall Wood
and nearby areas of central England.

*SEARCH THIS WEBSITE
EXPLORE THIS SITE USING SITE MAP
CONTRIBUTE MATERIAL TO THIS SITE*

Commemorating the South Staffordshire Home Guard.

General Matthew Hopkins. A list of the county's parishes can be found at the Suffolk Parish Registers Index (**www.rootsweb.ancestry.com/~engdorse/ PRSU.html**), with links to some transcribed parish records. Various resources and guides have been made available online by Suffolk Record Office at **www.suffolk.gov.uk/sro**. The East Anglian Film Archive has many holdings for the county (see p.59), whilst images from most of the county's churches are available to view at **www.suffolkchurches.co.uk**.

Stowmarket's history is recorded at **www.stowmarket-history.co.uk**, and includes parish registers, monumental inscriptions and other records. For Woolpit, registers can be found at **http://tinyurl.com/yh3wc4w**, though the year range is not listed, and for Haverhill, visit **www.haverhill-uk.com/pages/genealogy-home-134.htm**. Records for Beaumont Baptist Church and Quay United Reformed Church in Woodbridge can be found at **www.woodbridgechurch.org.uk**.

A guide to researching records for the village of Debenham can be found at **www.debenhamfamilyhistory.org.uk**, as well as information from war memorials, wills indexes and more. The history of Elmswell is recorded at **www.elmswell-history.org.uk**.

On the newspaper front, extracts from the *Suffolk and Essex Free Press*, *Haverhill Echo* and *Suffolk Free Press* are available at **www.foxearth. org.uk/newspapers.html**, whilst details of articles and publications from the Suffolk Record Society are hosted at **www.suffolkrecordssociety.com**, from where copies can be purchased.

Surrey

First recorded as 'Sudrigean' in Saxon times, the historic county of Surrey is located near London in the south-east. As such, many resources for the county are also found within those outlined earlier for Greater London (see p.11).

Exploring Surrey's Past (**www.exploringsurreyspast.org.uk**) is a gateway site offering detailed background to the great and the good, notable and otherwise of the county, as well as a catalogue for several museum, library and archive collections. Surrey History Centre (**www.surreycc.gov.uk/ surreyhistoryservice**) includes guides to the county's parish records, (now accessible on Ancestry), and other resources. The Surrey Plus wills index, which covers Surrey and nine neighbouring counties, is also online at **www.rootsweb.ancestry.com/~engsurry**, with additional wills from the Archdeaconry Court of Surrey wills and Commissary Court available at the Origins Network. An index to *Surrey Advertiser* articles from 1864–67 and 1872 is online at **www.newspaperdetectives.co.uk**, whilst several Hampshire and Surrey titles are indexed at **http://freespace.virgin.net/anglers.rest/surreyhants.htm**. Various parish records collections are available on Ancestry (p.9).

A detailed map for Surrey from 1768 can be found at **www.rootsweb. ancestry.com/~engsurry/maps/roque.html**. For the east of the county, the relevant family history society has several free to use databases at **www. eastsurreyfhs.org.uk/free2view/f2vindex.html**, such as Caterham Asylum wages books, school rolls of honour, Croydon Wesleyan and Congregational parish records, Camberwell apprentices, and more. The Epsom and Ewell History Explorer (**www.epsomandewellhistoryexplorer.org.uk**) has a remarkable collection of essays and photos on a variety of topics from the area, whilst Redhill and Reigate are covered at **www.redhill-reigate-history.co.uk** with maps, photos and resources on the home guard, lists of mayors, and other materials. Census transcriptions for the village of Buckland are online at **www.bucklandsurrey.net**, as well as a history of the local school, and history resources for Leatherhead at **www.leatherhead web.org.uk**.

There are several useful resources for Kingston upon Thames. The local museum at **www.kingston.gov.uk/leisure/museum** contains online guides such as Kingston at War and Kingston's Royal Connections, whilst historical statutory birth and marriage indexes can be accessed at **http://tinyurl. com/yle62n2**.

For Richmond upon Thames, the Local History and Heritage site at **http: //tinyurl.com/yzczmwu** contains guides to people of historical note buried in the borough (separated into two files, A-L and M-Z), Victoria Cross holders, and various timelines. A community archives site at **www.rich mondlibraries.net/rca1/default.asp** contains old photos that can be viewed by both subject and timeline. A downloadable guide to Lambeth's archives holdings can be consulted at **http://tinyurl.com/yj5gu6o**, whilst a database of all resold and reused graves in West Norwood Cemetery is available at **www.lambeth.gov.uk/cemetery**. A list of men from Addlestone who fell in the First World War is online at **www.freewebs.com/addlestone greatwardead**, with detailed biographies of many. For Surrey policemen who died in the same war visit **http://freepages.military.rootsweb. ancestry.com/~thinblueline/page90.html** (the site also caters for Sussex).

In the west of the county, a list of pay-to-view research guides, images of churches and a free-to-view 1837 parish map can be consulted at **www. wsfhs.org**. A one place study for Puttenham at **http://freespace.virgin. net/ar.indexes/puttenham.htm** includes parish records, an index of PCC will entries, bastardy papers, constable records, and several family pedigrees from the area. Records for Wyke, Christmaspie, Willey Green, Pinewood and Flexford (within the parish of Normandy) can be found at **http:// normandyhistorians.co.uk**, and the village of Bisley is well catered for at **www.rootsweb.ancestry.com/~engsurry/bisley**, with parish records, militia musters, lords of the manor, lay subsidies 1585–1649, Nonconformist records and more.

Finally for the county, the Surrey Vintage Vehicle Society hosts an interesting site at **www.svvs.org/help10.shtml**, which can help you to identify vintage cars from old photos.

Sussex

Sussex has an excellent Online Parish Clerks site (**www.sussex-opc.org**)

which includes parish registers databases, protestation returns and poll registers, as well as an interesting project allowing searches for Sussex folk found within the London, Edinburgh and Belfast *Gazettes*. The county's family history society site at **www.sfhg.org.uk** has some equally handy parish resources, back issues of the *Sussex Links* newsletters from 2002–10, a Sussex marriage strays database and more. West Sussex Record Office has a searchable catalogue online at **www.westsussexpast.org.uk/searchonline** which lists its holdings.

The Ye Olde Sussex project (**http://yosp.co.uk**) has several interesting essays on various aspects of the county's past, such as the history of smuggling, gaols, banks, castles, folklore, architecture and more. The Weald of Kent, Surrey and Sussex (**http://weald.org**) carries many pedigrees, images, digitised books and maps, whilst further maps from 1575–1900 can be sourced from **http://tinyurl.com/yjpjh7d**. Sussex Records Society (**www. sussexrecordsociety.org.uk**) hosts twelve records databases including apprentices and masters, lay subsidy rolls 1524–25, the 1747 Window Tax and others. Steve Pickthall has transcribed Kelly's 1867 county directory for

The foremost online repository of Sussex records.]

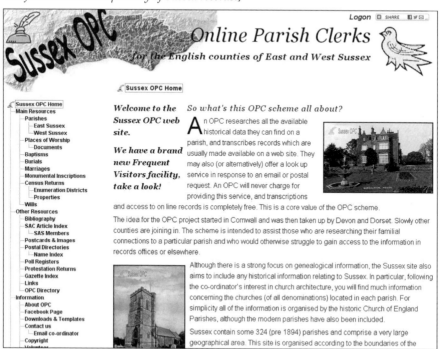

Sussex – the various listings are now incorporated within the GENUKI parish pages at **http://homepages.gold.ac.uk/genuki/SSX/parishes. html**.

The 1066 Genealogy site at **http://tinyurl.com/yjnrfqm** for Hastings and Lewes has census and parish records, but also interesting items such as discussions on Martello towers and more. For Fishbourne, a one-place study at **http://sandh.me.uk/nfops** includes parish registers, census entries and directories, whilst records for Portslade can be consulted at **http://portslade-cofe.blogspot.co.uk/p/parish-registers.html**.

Records for Broadhurst and Worthing can be found at **www.barries genealogy.co.uk**, for Fernhurst at **www.fernhurstsociety.org.uk/genealogy/cen_intro.html** (mainly census material) and for Ringmer at **www.ringmer.info**. A tithe map for Barcombe and Hamsey is available at **www.bandhpast.co.uk**, along with additional maps and the 1841 census. Various burials from Bexhill, Brighton, Halton, Hastings, Salehurst, Shoreham and many other Sussex-based cemeteries can be found at **www. genealogy links.net/uk/england/sussex/cemeteries.htm**. A look-up exchange at **http://homepage.ntlworld.com/w.jowett/sussexlookup.html** provides offers of help for directories, parish records, census entries and more from many other parishes.

Further sites of interest include the Brighton and Hove photographers' studios index at **www.spartacus.schoolnet.co.uk/DSindex.htm**, and the previously mentioned **http://freepages.military.rootsweb.ancestry.com/~thinblueline/page90.html** which commemorates both Sussex and Surrey police men who lost their lives in the First World War.

Warwickshire (and Birmingham)

Warwickshire County Council has searchable indexes to locally registered vital events post-1837 at **www.warwickshire.gov.uk/copycertificates**. The county record office site at **http://tinyurl.com/p5g5fpd** contains an online catalogue entitled Warwickshire's Past Unlocked, which is updated every three months, and a Calendars of Prisoners database listing people held in the county prisons at Warwick, Birmingham and Coventry as they awaited trial at the Courts of Assize and at the Quarter Sessions courts in Warwick between 1800 and 1900. The site also has a Licensed Victuallers database for 1801–28, with information sourced from the calendars of Victuallers' Recognizances held in the county's quarter sessions records, and a Tithe Apportionments database produced in 1836. The archive has partnered with Ancestry and made many other collections available via **www.ancestry. co.uk/warwickshire**, such as parish records, bastardy orders from 1816–39, land tax records from 1773–1830, and more. Windows on Warwickshire (**www.windowsonwarwickshire.org.uk**) carries historic county photos and images.

The excellent Pickard's Pink Pages for Warwickshire (**www.hunimex. com/warwick**) carries free-to-access census, directory, BMD and miscellaneous records for the whole county, such as lists of Warwickshire freeholders, Coventry-based freemen, apprentices, and more – a link is also provided to the Warwickshire Online Parish Clerk site. A 1670 Hearth Tax list is also available at **www.hunimex.com/warwick/census/hearth_ 1670. html**. The subscription based **www.midlandshistoricaldata.org** includes many useful sets of records such as twentieth-century electoral rolls for Birmingham and Warwickshire Poor Law records. For stories from the Industrial Revolution in the West Midlands, including Warwickshire, visit **www.revolutionaryplayers.org.uk/place.stm**.

The Birmingham and Midland Society for Genealogy and Heraldry (**www.bmsgh.org**) has several online research guides for Warwickshire and Birmingham, and a listing of society-held publications in its library. The Nuneaton and North Warwickshire site at **www.nnwfhs.org.uk** includes a parish map from 1871, a photo gallery and downloadable quarterly society journal back issues from 1995–2007.

Specifically for Birmingham, the Archives and Heritage portal at **www. birmingham.gov.uk/archivesandheritage** includes some valuable resources, such as a Black History Collection, maps and lists of famous people from Birmingham. Birmingham Heritage (**www.birminghamheritage.org. uk**) is useful for information on various historic institutions in the city.

Coventry Family History Society has placed some material at **www. covfhs.org.uk**, including transcripts from Lascelle's 1851 directory, a list of canal boats from 1879–1936 (sourced from the Coventry Canal Register of Boats), and a convicts register for 1879 and 1890–97. The city's experience in the Blitz is outlined at **www.familyresearcher.co.uk**.

The University of Warwick's Coventry-based Modern Records Centre at **www2.warwick.ac.uk/services/library/mrc** has online galleries of images themed around subjects as diverse as the Cold War, Trade Unions history and Freedom and Liberty, and carries guides for researching the county's social, economic and political history. (The site is also accessible at **http://modern records.warwick.ac.uk**). For the history of the Midlands in the Industrial Revolution from 1700–1830 visit **www.revolutionaryplayers. org.uk**, which hosts a digital library.

The University of Warwick's Modern Records Centre offers a feast of resources.

Shakespeare's home of Stratford upon Avon is explored at **www.shakespeare.org.uk,** and includes a burials database (1881–1964), a police charge book (1863–1880), workhouse records and even a smallpox census from 1765 (these are directly accessible at **http://databases 2.shakespeare.org.uk**). Wendy Boland's free look-ups site at **http://uk-transcriptions.accessgenealogy.com/Wendy's%20lookups.htm** is useful for those with ancestry in Birdingbury, Newbold on Avon, Dunchurch, Grandborough, Frankton and Preston Bagot, and contains census entries from 1841 and 1891.

Various aspects of Solihill's history are featured at **www.solihull.gov.uk/about/solihullshistory.htm,** whilst the history of Oxhill is explored at **www.oxhill.org.uk,** including some parish and land records. The county's churches can be further explored via the Warwickshire and Coventry Historic Churches Trust at **www.warwickshirechurches.org.uk**.

Finally for the region, the West Midlands Police Museum (**www.west midlandspolicemuseum.co.uk**) has a detailed history of police forces in the region, including those in Birmingham and Coventry.

Westmorland

There are very few standalone resources for Westmorland alone, as the former county is often lumped in with Cumberland (see p. 68) as part of modern Cumbria. Cumberland and Westmorland Archives (**www.cumber landarchives.co.uk**) includes parish registers and an 1873 directory, whilst Westmorland Hearth Tax records from 1674 are available at **http://tiny url.com/ygxpcql**.

A list of relevant county history publications can be consulted at **http:// cumbriafhs.com,** and information on the work behind the Victoria County History for the region is detailed at **www.cumbrialocalhistory. org.uk**.

The Durham Mining Museum project (see p.51) covers Westmorland, and records from the Cumbrian Manorial Records Project from the University of Lancashire can be examined at **www.lancaster.ac.uk/fass/projects/ manorialrecords/index.htm**.

Wiltshire

Wiltshire and Swindon Archive (**http://history.wiltshire.gov.uk**) carries an online catalogue for its holdings, whilst the site's impressive Wiltshire Wills database at **http://history.wiltshire.gov.uk/heritage/** catalogues wills from 1540–1858, as sourced from the Salisbury Diocese. Many have been digitised, and can be consulted upon payment of a fee. As well as Wiltshire, there are some entries for people from Berkshire, Devon and Dorset.

The Wiltshire Web project (**www.wiltshire-web.co.uk/towns_villages.asp**) has a guide to the county's many towns and villages, whilst an Online Parish Clerks site is available at **www.wiltshire-opc.org.uk**. Duncan and Mandy Ball's site of 28,000 photos of churches taken in North Wiltshire is well worth consulting at **http://oodwooc.co.uk**. Window on Wiltshire Heritage (**www. wowheritage.org.uk**) has a virtual display of the county's heritage from twenty-two organisations.

Parish register records from Brinkworth and Dauntsey are available at **www.henly.f9.co.uk/wiltshire.html,** as well as ships' money lists, manorial surveys and resources for neighbouring parishes. Dauntsey parish records are also found at the Moonrakers Wiltshire Genealogy site (**www.moonrakers. org.uk**), as well as for Bishoptone, with the project also containing many pedigree and surname lists. Records for Aldbourne (1790–1849) are at **www.treelines.co.uk/OPC/opcintro.html,** whilst baptisms from bishops' transcripts for Donhead St Mary (1622–1810) have been placed at **www.roughwood.net/VitalRecords/VitalRecords Frames.htm.**

West Grimstead records can be accessed at **www.westgrimstead familyhistory.co.uk,** including bastardy orders, the 1841–1911 censuses, parish records from 1622–1983 (though most twentieth-century records must be applied for by email), Methodist records, a 1918 register of electors and a roll of honour. A list of incumbents for Swindon parish church from 1302–1885 is available at **http://homepages.nildram.co.uk/~jimella/ trnscrpt.htm#wilts,** along with names of people in and around South Marston. If your ancestry lies in Limpley Stoke, visit **www.freshford.com** for various historic images, OS and tithe maps. The site goes into more detail for Bradford on Avon, with records such as poor rates, land tax records, the Duke of Kingston's Survey of 1752 and a rental list from 1550.

Two further interesting resources for the county include **www. wbct.org.uk/history,** which has a history of Wiltshire and Berkshire Canal Trust, newspaper extracts from the *Swindon Advertiser* (1860–1910) and some historic documents and images, and **www.thewardrobe.org.uk,** the site of the Rifles (Berkshire and Wiltshire) Museum, which includes 16,500 documents war diary records for fifteen battalions of Royal Berkshire and Wiltshire Regiments from 1914–19.

Worcestershire

Worcestershire archive service has several online projects and exhibitions at **www.worcestershire.gov.uk/cms/archive-and-archaeology.aspx,** including an interactive map, photographs and schools databases, as well as virtual exhibitions (including a Victorian exhibition and another on Black and Asian History) and a catalogue.

The Worcestershire branch of the Birmingham and Midland Society for Genealogy and Heraldry (**www.worcesterbmsgh.co.uk**) hosts an online parish records research guide. The information provided includes the identification of a parish by its OS reference and the name of the hundred to which it belongs, the local poor law union, and locations of relevant sets of records. The Bromsgrove branch has made the *Bromsgrove Messenger* from 1860–1937 freely available online at **www.bromsgrovebmsgh.co.uk.** For census returns from 1861 and 1891 visit the Worcestershire Ancestors Project at **www.hunimex.com/warwick/wo-a-p.html.**

The subscription-based **www.midlandshistoricaldata.org** site contains several resources for the county, whilst miscellaneous resources for Kidderminster, Kings Norton, Dudley and Worcester are freely available at **http://uk-transcriptions.accessgenealogy.com/Worcs..htm**. Parish records for Berrow, Bredon and Chaceley and surrounding parishes are found at **http://freepages.genealogy.rootsweb.ancestry.com/~wrag44/index.htm**.

Malvern Family History Society hosts a bibliography of local history books and monumental inscriptions for Cradley and Mathon at **www.mfhs.org. uk/Local%20History%20Books%20new.html**. Cradley, part of the parish of Halesowen, is further explored at **www.cradleylinks.co.uk**, with pictures, monumental inscriptions, the 1841 census, probate records and a list of surname interests. Halesowen, in fact a part of Shropshire until 1844, is dealt with at **www.halesowenroots.com**, with parish records, directories, maps, rolls of honour and various local family history sites. Historic maps and images of Worcester are hosted by Worcester City Museums at **www. worcestercitymuseums.org.uk/content/resind.htm**.

For Wythall, a one-place study at **http://freepages.history.rootsweb. ancestry.com/~wythallindex/index.htm** has information on almost 20,000 names from the parish's history. Burial records from 1904–2009 for Holy Trinity church of Amblecote are online at **www.holytrinityamblecote. org.uk**, whilst parish records for Badsey from 1530–1909 are available at **www.badsey.net**, along with photos, maps, various essays on aspects of Badsey's history. Romsley and Hunnington Local History Society has censuses, probate records, burials and graves records for St Kenelm's and a 1910 OS map at **www.rhhs.org.uk**.

On the military front, the regimental site for the Worcestershire Regiment, which dates back to 1694, is located at **www.worcestershireregiment.com** and includes, amongst many things, POW stories and war diaries transcripts from 1944–45.

Yorkshire

Yorkshire is the largest county in England. Due to its size, the county was historically administered as three 'ridings', in the east, north and west. County-based indexes for statutory birth, marriage and death records from 1837–1950 can be found at the Yorkshire BMD site (**www.yorkshire bmd.org.uk**), and can be used to order up certificates from the various registration offices across the county. The Yorkshire Indexers subscription site (**www.yorkshireindexers. co.uk**) costs £10 a year for unlimited access to monumental inscription records, burial records, the 1937 Leeds Register of Electors, and more, as well as a discussion forum (other subscriptions are available). Several oral history projects have been recorded at **www. myyorkshire.org,** which includes many images and stories from the participants. A guide to printed Yorkshire newspaper indexes and their locations can be found via Newsplan (**www.bl.uk/ aboutus/acrossuk/worknat/news/**)

On the military front, the Prince of Wales' Own Regiment of Yorkshire (14th and 15th Regiments of Foot) is explored at **www.pwo-yorkshire. museum,** whilst the names of civilian war dead from the Second World War are included at **www.genuki.org.uk/big/eng/Indexes/NE_WarDead,** alongside entries from Northumberland and Durham.

FamilySearch carries bishops' transcripts from the Diocese of Durham from 1700–1900, which includes records for York, though the database can only be browsed. Images for Marriage Bonds and Allegations from 1667–1819 are available for the home user, however. The history of Yorkshire Quakers is explored at **www.hull.ac.uk/oldlib/archives/quaker/projres. htm** and has lists of meeting houses and more, whilst a University of Leeds project at **www.leeds.ac.uk/library/spcoll/quaker/index.htm** has a searchable database of Quaker records.

The City of York, in the north of the county, is home to the Borthwick Institute for Archives, which has a great many records for the county, and a series of online research guides at **www.york.ac.uk/library/borthwick.** The guides cover various subjects such as churchwardens' accounts, women's history, disability, LGBT history, health archives and more. Its most significant genealogical collection is perhaps the records for the Prerogative Court of York (PCY), the highest probate court in the north of England. These are slowly being indexed with the Exchequer Courts for York and placed online at the Origins Network site, covering 1731–1858 at the time of writing. Other probate sources on the site include the York Medieval Probate Index (1267–1500) and the York Peculiars Probate Index (1383–1883).

York Castle Prison (**www.yorkcastleprison.org.uk**) has an online database of almost 5,000 convicted criminals, debtors and victims, derived mainly from eighteenth-century records, whilst the City of York and District Family History Society at **www.yorkfamilyhistory.org.uk/resources/york-assizes/** has a York Assizes database (1785–1851), and a parish list.

The Yorkshire Dales are well covered at **www.dalesgenealogy.com,** with census returns for many parishes, emigrant ships' lists, school log books, gravestone photos and more. For Coxwold village, head teachers' log books from the 1860s to the 1970s can be found at **http://tinyurl.com/bakdt4g**.

Various resources for Redmire and Castle Bolton can be found at **www.redmire.net**. The genealogy section of a site focussed on Grewelthorpe at **www.grewelthorpe.org.uk** has details of many families from the village, and census records for Gunnerside are online at **www.gunnerside.info**. Knaresborough's history is detailed at **www.knaresborough.co.uk/history**, whilst resources for Kirby Misperton going back to the Domesday Book can be consulted at **www.kirbymisperton.org.uk**. The whole of North Yorkshire is included in the Durham Mining Museum website (see p.51), whilst Bob Sanders offers North Yorkshire census look-ups at **www.glamorganfamily history.co.uk/maritime/WHITIND.html** the site also acts as an excellent gateway to other resources compiled by many volunteers, notably for Whitby, Scarborough and the moors.

In the east of the county, a comprehensive guide to the censuses taken from 1801–2011 is available from the East of Yorkshire Family History Society (**www.eyfhs.org.uk**). The catalogue for the East Riding Archives based at Beverley can be viewed at **www2.eastriding.gov.uk/leisure/archives-family-and-local-history**.

The city of Hull's museum service has a resources catalogue at **www.hullcc.gov.uk/museumcollections**, whilst Hull History Centre has a catalogue at **www.hullhistorycentre.org.uk**. For Hull's maritime history, the crews of the SS *Canada* and SS *New Zealand*, two fishing boats from the city, are currently being examined at the Hull Trawler Challenge (**www.whatsthatpicture.com/hull-trawler-challenge**). Pocklington's local history group (**www.pocklingtonhistory.com**) has many resources in its Archives section, including maps, church records and more.

An online catalogue at **www.archives.wyjs.org.uk** for the West of Yorkshire Archives Service lists various holdings, whilst the archive's Tracks in Time: the Leeds Tithe Map Project (**www.tracksintime.wyjs.org.uk**) explores the urban and rural townships of Leeds from 1838–1861, with apportionment data for the city and digitised tithes maps which can be compared to modern Ordnance Survey resources. The Treasures of West Yorkshire Archive Service (**http://wyorksarchivestreasures.weebly.com**) has many useful resources, including a guide to West Yorkshire textiles mills in its 'Themes' category. Leeds Library and Information Service (**www.leedslocalindex.net**) hosts many databases, including Leeds and Yorkshire-based news cuttings, a local biographical index, parish, Nonconformist and Quaker registers, and various census resources. The Leeds Rifles regimental site at **www.yorkshire volunteers.org.uk/leedsrifles.htm** may also be of interest, whilst a photographic archive for the city is online at **www.leodis.org**.

The Court Rolls of the Manor of Wakefield from 1274–97 can be found at **http://tinyurl.com/yh4cag9**, whilst a timeline for Bradford's history from 1066–1999 is at **www.bradfordtimeline.co.uk**. At the time of writing Bradford Family History Society (**www.bradfordfhs.org.uk**) is working in collaboration with West Yorkshire Archives Service to make the tithe maps for the area, and their apportionments, available online. Huddersfield and District Family History Society (**www.hdfhs.org.uk**) has a list of townships and parish descriptions from an 1834 directory, and many useful resource lists. For the history of Luddism in the area, visit The Luddite Link (**www. ludditelink.org.uk**).

The village of Brotherton website (**www.brotherton.org.uk**) hosts many family pedigrees, as well as some war memorial and census information. For Todmorden and Walsden, **http://todmordenandwalsden.co.uk** has monumental inscriptions, parish records, the censuses from 1841–1901, and parish relief records. From Weaver to Web (**www.calderdale.gov.uk/wtw**) has an online visual archive of Calderdale's history, which also includes resources for Todmorden, as well as Halifax, Brighouse, Elland, Hebden Bridge and Sowerby Bridge. Calverly is explored at **www.calverley.info/**

The Leeds Tithe Map Project.

cal_home.htm, with a vital record and censuses database, war memorial information, directories and a 1770 parish map, as well as holding records for surrounding villages. Materials for Gisburn village, including burial records (1558–2007) can be found at **www.gisburn.org.uk**, whilst a roll of honour for Haworth is just one of the resources at **www.haworth-village.org.uk**.

In the south, Sheffield's family history society site at **www.sheffield fhs.org.uk** offers many resources including censuses, a Sheffield and Hallam Bank register, a released prisoners index from 1858–72, parish records, and many regionally-based research guides. The Sheffield Indexers (**www. sheffieldindexers.com**) host many free-to-access parish records, the 1841 census, school admission registers, directories and institutions, a statutory births, marriages and deaths certificate project, and a discussion forum. Similar resources can also be found at **www.sheffieldrecords online.org.uk**, whilst a Sheffield Cemetery database can be searched at **www.gencem.org**. The biggest peacetime disaster in Victorian Britain was the Sheffield Flood of March 1864, when the Dale Dyke breached, and Mick Hartfield's excellent website, The Great Flood at Sheffield, gives unparalleled coverage of the event at **http://mick-armitage.staff.shef.ac.uk/sheffield/ flood.html**. Many images from the disaster, one of the first to be photographed in Britain, are online at **www.picturesheffield.com**, a site from the Sheffield Library Service which hosts some 50,000 historic images of the city's past.

The effects of the 1864 flood at Rotherham are also covered online at **www.rotherhamweb.co.uk/h/extracts/flood.htm**, with many newspaper reports and other contemporary materials. The wider history of Rotherham is covered at **www.rotherhamunofficial.co.uk**, with the site including borough and town maps. Rotherham Family History Society (**www. rotherhamfhs.co.uk**) has an Anglican parish map, a list of mayors from 1871, a list of feoffees (trustees) of common lands of Rotherham, and a guide to the area's churches.

An indexing project for Barnsley at **www.barnsleyfhs.co.uk** is catering for the locally-held statutory records from 1837 for the region, whilst the archives section at **www.barnsley.gov.uk** has medieval deeds, log books from St Thomas' School in Worsbrough Dale, a database of names drawn from John Burland's *Annals of Barnsley and its Environs 1744–1864*, and a wills and probate database. For Barnsley burials, visit **www.cemeteries. org.uk**.

Information on churches and records in the district surrounding Doncaster can be found at **www.doncasterfhs.co.uk**, whilst research and subject guides for the city are available at **www.doncaster.gov.uk/ localstudies**. For Tickhill resources visit **www.tickhillhistorysociety.org.uk**. A fascinating site entitled the South Yorkshire Historic Environment Characterisation (**www.sytimescapes.org.uk**) shows how the use of land has changed in the region from 1400 to the present day.

Finally, History to Herstory (**www.historytoherstory.org.uk**) celebrates the lives of Yorskhire women from 1100 to the present day.

Chapter 5

WALES

In this chapter we will look at many Welsh offerings on a county basis, but it is first worth flagging up some additional sites specific to Wales that may be of interest.

The brilliant Data Wales (**www.data-wales.co.uk**) is well worth a visit, with some fascinating articles on subjects such as the role of the Welsh in slavery, Welsh surnames, place names, emigration and more. Of particular interest are dedicated pages on specific topics such as the Welsh slate industry and the legacy of industry in the South Wales valleys. Previously providing some excellent resources was Gathering the Jewels (Casglu'r Tlysau) at **www.gtj.org.uk**, which hosted over 30,000 images of letters, books, aerial photos and more from various different archives and museums, within dedicated sections on Art and Culture, Health, Welfare and Charity, Education, Industry and War and Rebellion. Most of this material is now available via **www.peoplescollectionwales.co.uk**.

The Timeline of Genealogically Interesting Dates at **www.rootsweb. ancestry.com/~ukwales2/HelpPagepearls6.html** is a chronological list of world events but with a strong Welsh bias. As well as placing various Welsh developments of interest into their world context, the site also provides links from each entry to a website that can further explore the subject matter described. BBC Wales has a family history site at **www.bbc.co.uk/wales/ history/sites/themes/family.shtml** which includes a useful article on the subject of the Welsh patronymic naming pattern (eg Rhys ap Dafydd, Rhys son of David, and so on).

Anglesey (Ynys Môn)

The island of Anglesey now forms part of Gwynedd. Its record office has a guide to holdings at **www.anglesey.gov.uk/leisure/records-and-archives**, whilst papers for the island's many estates are actually held at Bangor University Library, which has a searchable catalogue online at **www. bangor.ac.uk/library**. A catalogue for holdings in Anglesey Libraries is also available at **www.anglesey.gov.uk/leisure/libraries**. For an index to articles in *Transactions*, the journal of the Anglesey Antiquarian Society and Field Club, visit **www.hanesmon.org.uk/aas/news.php**.

Indexes for locally-registered statutory births, marriages and deaths from 1837 are included in the North Wales BMD site at **www.northwales bmd.org.uk**. A series of Calvinistic and Wesleyan Methodist births and baptismal records can also be found on the GENUKI Anglesey page, from both the Holyhead and Beaumaris circuits.

A gateway site to various heritage resources, including a history, timeline, maritime history and photos of the island's churches, can be found at **www.anglesey.info**. Further historic photos are available at **http://tiny url.com/yjrsoy3** whilst maps of the island from 1579–1720 can be found at **www.anglesey-history.co.uk/maps/index.html**.

Census and church records for Amlwch, as well as trade directories and information on the local copper mine, can be found at **www.amlwchdata. co.uk**, with further information on the mines available at **www.parys mountain.co.uk**. Records for Llanddaniel can be found online at **www. llanddaniel.co.uk**, whilst the *Reports of the Commissioners of Inquiry into the State of Education in Wales* (1847) has a return for Anglesey at **www.llgc. org.uk/index.php?id=776**. A return of landowners from 1873 is at **www. genuki.org.uk/big/wal/GreatLandowners.html**.

Breconshire (Brecknockshire)

Today, most of the historic county of Breconshire is incorporated within the modern local government county of Powys. A description of the county in the 1868 National Gazetteer is available at **www.genuki.com/big/wal/ BRE/Gaz1868.html**. Powys Heritage Online (**http://history. powys.org.uk**) has a great deal of material on Breconshire, including articles on subjects as diverse as canals, railways, roads, workhouses, religion, and land units. For the history of its churches, visit the Brecknockshire Churches Survey pages at **www.cpat.demon.co.uk/projects/longer/churches/brecon/idxbrec. htm**, the results of a survey carried out in 1995/96 by the Clwyd-Powys Archaeological Trust.

Powys County Archive Office library catalogue is available at **www. powys.gov.uk/index.php?id=647&L=0&** and hosts a detailed guide of holdings – follow the links to Local Studies Sources. Powys Family History Society offers various online indexes for members at **www.powysfhs. org.uk**, including a strays index and entries in the National Burial Index.

Census entries for Christ College, Brecon (1871–1911) can be found at **www.jlb2011.co.uk/walespic/churches/wfha-breconcensus.htm**. For the history of Hay-on-Wye, the famous book town, visit **www.hay-on-wye. co.uk/info/hayhistory.htm**.

Caernarfonshire (Carnarvonshire)

Now a part of Gwynedd, a description of historic Caernarfonshire from the 1849 *Topographical Dictionary of Wales* is located at **www.welshicons.org. uk/html/caernarvonshire.php**.

The local indexes to statutory birth, marriage and death indexes for the county are included in the North Wales BMD project (**www.northwales bmd.org.uk**). A list of major holdings at Caernarfon Record Office is online at **http://tinyurl.com/aqq9vp8**, with details of the archive's parish registers online at **www.genuki.com/big/wal/CAE/CAE_PR.html**. The catalogue for Gwynedd Archives, entitled Rhagorol, is at **www.gwynedd.gov.uk/ datrhagorolnet/default.aspx?iaith=en**.

The history of the various communities in Penll n can be found at **www.penllyn.com/1/Hanes/hanes.htm**. A list of traders extracted from directories and censuses (including the 1794 census for Carnarvon), burials

North Wales BMD.

at Llanbeblig (1699–1968) and various biographies, is hosted at www. carnarvontraders.com. Memorial Inscriptions from St Mary's Church in Conway can be found at http://members.tripod.com/~Caryl_Williams /conwy-7.html, and a list of Nonconformist churches in the county at www.penllyn.com/1/Hanes/capeli.html. A detailed site for the village of Rhiw, including old pictures, history, religion, the 1861–91 censuses, diaries, estate papers and more, exists at www.rhiw.com. For the National Gazetteer entry for the county in 1868, visit www.genuki.org.uk/big/wal/CAE/ Gaz1868.html.

Cardiganshire (Ceredigion)

Now part of Dyfed, information on historic Cardiganshire can be found via Dyfed Family History Society (http://dyfedfhs.org.uk), which carries many useful lists, such as a guide to the county's parishes, burial sites (with some online indexes), graduates from Oxford University and school records.

A catalogue of Ceredigion Archives' holdings is available at http:// archifdy-ceredigion.org.uk. A useful miscellany of interesting facts and material relating to several parishes in the county is found at http://home. clara.net/tirbach/HelpPagepearlsCGN.html.

An index to the Cardiganshire Constabulary Register of Criminals (1897– 1933) is available at www.genuki.org.uk/big/wal/CGN/CGNCriminals .html, which can be used to track down original entries on the manuscript which has been digitised and made available at www.llgc.org.uk/index. php?id=criminals.

A useful list of Nonconformist churches and chapels is also available at www.genuki.com/big/wal/CGN/CGNchapels.html. The history of the parish of Llangynfelyn is explored at www.llangynfelyn.org and includes census records, parish registers, chapel records, tithe records, maps of the parish and county, old and contemporary photographs and more.

For the history of mining in the county visit www.spirit-of-the-miners.org.uk, whilst some recent materials on the Cwmystwyth lead mine and the mines at Llanddewibrefi are available at http://people.exeter. ac.uk/pfclaugh/mhinf/contents.htm#wales.

Carmarthenshire

Historic Carmarthenshire is also a part of modern Dyfed. A map of the county in 1885, as drawn up by the Boundary Commissioners for England and Wales, is available at www.londonancestor.com/maps/bc-ycarm-th. htm.

Carmarthen FHS (www.carmarthenshirefhs.info) has a free downloadable parish map for the county – online resources at Dyfed FHS equally apply to Carmarthenshire (see p.126).

The county records office has a useful guide to its various collections at www.carmarthenshire.gov.uk/english/leisure/archives/pages/archives records.aspx. The Friends of Carmarthenshire County Museum current website is at www.friendsofcarmarthenmuseum.co.uk, but a series of articles of interest on all matters local can still be accessed on its old website at www.carmarthenmuseum.org.uk/articles/index.html. For a database of placenames and estate maps from the county visit Carmarthenshire Antiquarian Society at www.carmants.org.uk, whilst a report on its hundreds, parishes and schools is at http://tinyurl.com/yfhgd6n. The report was originally compiled in 1847 and digitised by the National Library of Wales.

A history of Kidwelly, with articles, directory records, the 1901 census, images, maps, rental rolls, and more can be consulted at www.kidwelly history.co.uk. Old photographs of Llanfairfechan are available to view at www.llanfairfechan.org.uk, as well as a community discussion forum and old photos, whilst articles on many aspects of the history and archaeology of Abergwyngregyn, including historic pictures, are online at www.abergwyn gregyn.co.uk. For the history of Penmaenmawr, including information on its war memorials and village names, go to www.penmaenmawr.com.

The history of lead and gold mining in the county is explored at http:// people.exeter.ac.uk/pfclaugh/mhinf/contents.htm#wales. For information on Carmarthenshire's part in the nineteenth-century Rebecca Riots, visit the Bro Beca project at (cached version) at http://tinyurl.com/nvzrk7a.

Denbighshire

Denbighshire Record Office has several indexes at www.denbighshire. gov.uk/en-gb/DNAP-6ZQKTQ for newspapers, personal names, places and subjects in its archive holdings. The Wrexham Archives and Local Studies Service pages at www.wrexham.gov.uk/english/heritage/ archives/index .htm include a catalogue and downloadable guides of resources, with lists of parish register transcriptions and newspapers, as well as local indexes for statutory birth, marriages and deaths (1837–1950, up to 1997 for births). Similar entries for statutory records in the rest of the county are included on the North Wales BMD site (www.northwalesbmd.org.uk).

Clwyd Family History Society (www.clwydfhs.org.uk) has photos online from every church in the county, as well as a list of published monumental inscriptions for sale. Extracts from various directories and reference books are included at **www.namesfromclwyd.org.uk**, as well as a master index of names from the printed Parish Registers of Clwyd, as transcribed by volunteer members of the society.

The 1871 census for Garthgarmon is online at **http://tinyurl.com/ ydmez8f**. Details of listed buildings in Rossett are available at **www.rossett. org.uk**, and several resources for the village of Bwlchgwyn, including a gallery of old photos, can be consulted at **www.belton.me.uk**. The website for Llangollen Museum at **www.llangollenmuseum.org.uk** has an online catalogue of useful research sources for the local area, whilst the history of Chirk is briefly explored at **www.chirk.com**. Further links to various websites on neighbouring towns can also be found at the bottom of the page.

Flintshire

Local statutory records indexes for births, marriages and deaths for Flintshire are available at **www.northwalesbmd.org.uk**. The county record site at **http://tinyurl.com/ygfgkbc** has an online record gallery and family history guide, as well as various catalogues and indexes, including databases for parish-based photographic holdings, industrial records, bishops' transcripts, newspapers, and more.

As part of modern Clwyd, records for the county can also be found at **www.namesfromclwyd.org.uk**, and in the holdings of Clwyd Family History Society (see above). A brief history of the county is available at **www. flintshire.org**, whilst a study of seventeenth-century witchcraft in the county is online at the National Library of Wales website (**www.llgc.org.uk/index .php?id=witchcraftcourtofgrearsessi**).

A history of Llanasa is at **http://llanasaconservationsocie.homestead. com**, including old images, whilst a detailed history of Shotton with essays on the ships of John Summers, the railway, the Wepre Hall estate and more, can be consulted at **www.angelfire.com/fl/shotton**.

The Buckley Society (**www.buckleysociety.org.uk**) has historic photos online, as well as subject and articles indexes as featured in its journal, whilst the Bagillt Heritage Society reveals its local history at **www.bagillt.org.uk**, with various essays on topics of local interest.

Glamorgan

The Glamorgan GENUKI pages are some of the most detailed of the whole project, including various resources, and are most definitely a useful first port of call.

The Glamorgan Archives pages at **www.glamarchives.gov.uk** include parish registers listings (established and Nonconformist), and an online exhibition entitled Cardiff: the Building of a Capital. The archive also provides a guide to municipal cemeteries in the county, which can be read at **www. glamro.gov.uk/adobe/municipal.pdf**. The West Glamorgan Archive Service lists collections at **www.swansea.gov.uk/index.cfm?articleid=406**, whilst various online exhibitions can be found at **www.swansea.gov.uk/index. cfm?article id= 34045** including Guildhall Swansea 1934–2009, Swansea Hebrew Congregation and another on the fortieth anniversary of Swansea's existence as a city. There are further guides concerning records in its collection such as maritime and political papers, an index of place names, and a gazetteer of localities in West Glamorgan.

Robert Sanders' superb Wales, England and Maritime Family History Research pages at **www.glamorganfamilyhistory.co.uk** are absolutely packed with resources on Cardiff and Glamorgan, including essays on various topics of local interest, such as the history of Chartism, the Rebecca Riots, the Merthyr Uprising, the Glamorgan Militia, the history of Nonconformism and Methodism in the county, a Cardiff chronology, and much more.

The Glamorgan Family History Society website at **www.rootsweb. ancestry.com/~wlsglfhs** hosts Swansea and Neath militia lists and an article on the parish church at Llandeilo Tal-y-bont, as well as a members-only chat forum. Swansea Council (**www.swansea.gov.uk/ index.cfm?articleid=467**) has an index for the *Cambrian* newspaper from 1804–1930, as well as lists of newspapers, trade directories and electoral registers available for consultation. On the heritage front, an interactive map with links to historic images from across Swansea, as well as pages on various subjects of local historic interest, is available at **www.swanseamuseum.co.uk**. A list of Cardiff places of worship in existence in 2005 is listed in Cardiff Places of Worship Survey at **http://freepages.genealogy.rootsweb.ancestry.com/ ~cdfplacesofworship**. For resources on Caerphilly visit the Caerphilly Chronicle at **www. caerphilly.gov.uk/chronicle/english/index.htm**.

The Internet Archive has the parish registers of Llantrithyd (christenings 1597–1810, burials 1571–1810 and marriages 1571–1752) at **www.archive. org/details/registersofllant00llan**, whilst the history of Llangynwyd Parish is at **www.archive.org/details/historyllangynw00evangoog**. The Explore Gower site at **www.explore-gower.co.uk** has images of several churches and other heritage sites on the peninsula. Ogmore Valley Local History and Heritage Society's site (**www.ovlhs.co.uk**) has a timeline, a miners' deaths index (1865–1984), and a journals article index from 2000–09. A site dedicated to Whitchurch and Llandaff North is available at **www. whitchurchandllandaff.co.uk/Main%20Page.htm** containing newspaper clippings and other resources. For genealogical resources for Cymgors, Gwauncaegurwen, the parish of Llangiwg and the Amman Valley, visit **http://freepages.history.rootsweb.ancestry.com/~cwmgors/Waun.html**.

A history of the Rhondda Valley is located at **www.anglesey. info/ Rhondda_History.htm** including many photos of old coal mines from the region. The Rhondda Blue Plaque Scheme recipients are listed at **www. heritagetrailsrct.co.uk/index.php/en/blue-plaques/6-blue-plaques. html** (with biographies), whilst at **www.treorchy.net** you can access an index to papers from the former legal practice of Treharne and Treharne based in Pentre, and now held at Glamorgan Record Office. The Pillars of Faith site at **www.pillars-of-faith.com** commemorates the history of the Rhondda's Nonconformism.

For the war diaries of the 17th (Service) Battalion of the Welsh regiment (the 'First Glamorgan Bantams') visit **www.17thwelsh.org.uk**.

Merionethshire

Now mainly in Gwynedd, local statutory records indexes for post-1837 births, marriages and deaths for historic Merionethshire can be found at North Wales BMD (**www.northwalesbmd.org.uk**), whilst the online catalogue for Gwynedd Archives is at **www.gwynedd.gov.uk/gwy_doc. asp?cat=3693&doc=12971&Language=1**. A parish map for the county is available at Gwynedd Family History Society's site at **www.gwynedd fhs.org**.

Part of Merionethshire is also now included with Clwyd, and Clwyd Family History Society has photos from every church from the relevant part of the county at **www.clwydfhs.org.uk**, along with an impressive war memorials guide. Some parish register entries are also included in its index at **www.namesfromclwyd.org.uk**.

Census resources for Dolgellau, Llanelltyd, Llanfachreth, Barmouth and Dinas Mawddwy, and links to additional resources for other villages including Trawsfynydd, Maentwrog and Llandanwg can be consulted at **http://freepages. history.rootsweb.ancestry.com/~alwyn/D/census/index.htm**.

For the history of manganese mining in the county, visit **www.hend recoed.org.uk/Merioneth-Manganese**.

Monmouthshire

The 1901 Kelly's Directory for Monmouthshire has been completely transcribed and is available at **http://freepages.genealogy.rootsweb. ancestry.com/~familyalbum,** providing a useful description of the county and its residents at that point. The Bradney Collection at **https://sites. google.com/site/rhopk24324/bradney-collection** has some background to the history of the county, as well as parish register transcriptions for Llanbadog (1582–1709), Caerwent and Llanfair Discoed (1568–1812), Llanddewy Rhydderch (1670–1783), Llantilio Crisenny and Penrhos (1577– 1644), Llanfihangel Ystern Llewern (1685–1812), and Grosmont (1589– 1812).

The Forest of Dean Parish Records Project at **www.forest-of-dean.net** also includes several Monmouthshire parish records, as well as a wills index for probate at Gloucester (1858–1910).

The Monmouthshire Family History pages at **http://freepages.genealogy. rootsweb.ancestry.com/~monfamilies/monfh.htm** host a detailed parish guide and map, as well as many records for the county, including Catholic Mission and poor law records, parish registers and wills. An equally useful resource is the 1841 Census for Monmouthshire site (**www.charsbroken branches.com/Monmouthshire-files.html**), which amongst its transcriptions hosts parish records for Trelleck, Llandogo, Cymyoy and Lanthony.

For the history of Caerleon visit **www.caerleon.net**, where you will find directories, census transcriptions, an 1840 parish tithe survey and map, parish records and historic photos. Several local history resources for Crosskeys, including a timeline and Kelly's Directory entries from 1914, can be found at **www.crosskeys.me.uk.**

A site for Abertillery at **www.abertillery.net** includes an old tithe map from 1840, as well as an interesting Tillery Tales section discussing various subjects such as World War I Heroes; there is also a family history section and old photographic images. For a chronology and information about Cymtillery Colliery, visit **www.abertillery.net/picpages/cwmtillerycolliery past.html.**

Montgomeryshire

Now part of Powys, the county archive for Montgomeryshire is included at **www.powys.gov.uk/index.php?id=647&L=0&** (the Powys County Archive Office site), which has a library catalogue and a detailed guide of holdings via the link to its Local Studies Sources section. The Powys Heritage Online site at **http://history.powys.org.uk** has several resources for the county, including dedicated sections on Machynlleth and the Dovey Valley, and the district of Llandiloes, with directories listings and other materials.

Montgomeryshire Genealogical Society has placed many useful resources online at **http://home.freeuk.net/montgensoc**. These include a parish map, pictures of churches from many denominations, views of Old Montgomeryshire, a guide to the use of the Welsh language in the county, and hearth tax returns from 1664–65 for the county's seven hundreds of Cawrse, Cyfeiliog, Deuddwr, Llanfyllin, Llanidloes, Mathrafal, Montgomery, Newtown and Poole. For local statutory indexes compiled post-1837 to births, marriages and deaths, visit **www.northwalesbmd.org.uk**.

A website on the history of Machynlleth and the Dyfi Valley can be found at **www.machynlleth.info** which includes old photos, tithe maps and more.

Pembrokeshire

Pembrokeshire Record Office's site at **www.pembrokeshire.gov.uk/ content.asp?id=15732&d1=0** has various guides to its public records, official collections, ecclesiastical records and private collections. It also hosts a searchable catalogue called Calm View at **http://records.pembrokeshire. gov.uk/CalmView/default.aspx**, with a further list of holdings accessible at **http://arcw.llgc.org.uk/anw/browse_repository.php?inst_id=32?& L=0**.

As part of Dyfed, further resources can also be found on the Dyfed FHS site at **www.dyfedfhs.org.uk** (see Cardiganshire).

A history and list of mines in Pembrokeshire (also Carmarthenshire and Cardiganshire) can be explored at **http://people.exeter.ac.uk/pfclaugh/ mhinf/pembs1.htm**, whilst the story of the nineteenth-century Rebecca Riots can be read at the Bro Beca project **(http://tinyurl.com/nvzrk7a)**.

For Pembroke's history visit **www.pembrokestory.org.uk**, whilst Tenby's past can be examined at **www.tenbymuseum.org.uk**, where amongst its holdings is a page on Robert Recorde, the inventor of the equals sign! Parish birth, marriage and death indexes are online for Stackpole Elidor, St Petrox, Bosherton and St Twynnells at **www.revjones.fsnet.co.uk/stackgrpreg/ register.htm**, whilst a history of Lamphey and Hodgeston is at **www. lamphey.org.uk/sparc/sparc%20leaflet.html**.

Radnorshire

The historic county of Radnorshire now forms part of Powys, and as such its archival holdings are dealt with in the same Powys repositories as listed for Breconshire, including the Powys County Archive Office (see p.124). A guide

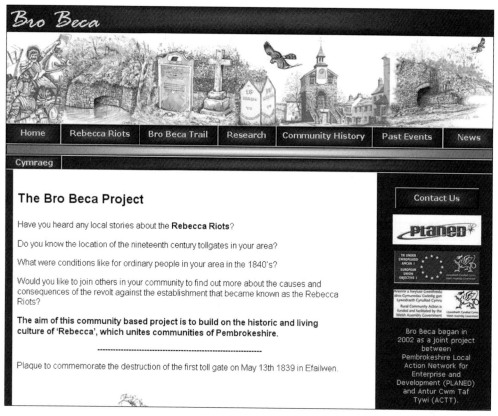

The Bro Beca Project.

to the Radnorshire Society's holdings in the county archive can be examined at **www.archiveswales.org.uk/anw/get_collection. php?inst_id=40&coll _id=12073**. The Powys Digital History Project hosts detailed studies on two communities, entitled Rhayader and the Elan Valley and Presteigne and the Marches, available at **http://history.powys.org.uk**. A name index to Powys Family History Society's journal *Cronicl Powys* (for the first thirty issues) is at **www.rootsweb.ancestry. com/~wlspfhs/Pages/intro.htm**.

The Radnorshire Churches Survey at **www.cpat.demon.co.uk/projects/ longer/churches/radnor/idxradn.htm** provides details on all churches recorded in the project in 1995–96, which was carried out by the Clwyd-Powys Archaeological Trust.

For a history of Llandrindod, including a guided walk through the town, visit **www.llandrindod.co.uk/HTML/History.htm**.

Chapter 6

SCOTLAND

Scottish resources are mainly in English, but you may find some records also written in either Scots or Gaelic (Gàidhlig). The Scots language is a variant form of the Germanic-based language that became English south of the border. Many Scots words can be deciphered from the Dictionary of the Scots Language at **www.dsl.ac.uk** or via the Online Scots Dictionary found at **www.scots-online.org**, whilst to understand older forms of Scottish handwriting visit **www.scottishhandwriting.com**.

If your research can take you that far back, two useful medieval sites are the Breaking of Britain: Cross Border Society and Scottish Independence 1216–1314 (**www.breakingofbritain.ac.uk**) and the People of Medieval Scotland (**www.poms.ac.uk**) – the latter lists all known people of Scotland between 1093 and 1314, as mentioned in over 8,600 contemporary documents. For memorials to women who have played a key part in Scottish history visit **http://womenofscotland.org.uk**.

The following additional websites may also assist with your research.

Aberdeenshire

The Aberdeen and North East Scotland Family History Society website (**http://anesfhs.org.uk**) hosts a monumental inscription index of 125,000 names from both published and unpublished sources (also covering Banffshire, Kincardineshire and Morayshire), a map of burial grounds in the Scottish north east, kirkyard photos, Aberdeenshire parish details and downloadable family history charts. Searchable databases include an Aberdeen Stent Roll 1669, St Nicholas Burials 1666–1793, St Nicholas Kirk Session Accounts 1602–1705, and St Paul's Episcopal Baptisms 1720–1793. A summary of Kirk Session accounts for St Paul's can also be downloaded. The Family History Society of Buchan's site (**www.buchanroots.co.uk**) also has contact details for local registrars and some articles from its newsletter, *Aa the Claik*.

Two maps from Aberdeen, from 1881 and 1891, have been linked to searchable data from the corresponding Post Office Directories at Addressing History (**http://addressinghistory.edina.ac.uk**). An 1895 parish map for the city is also available at **http://tinyurl.com/yjjrw9g**, whilst Tim Lambert's history of the city is at **www.localhistories.org/aberdeen.html**. *The Armorial Ensigns of the Royal Burgh of Aberdeen*, written by John Cruickshank in 1888, has been republished by the Internet Archive at **www.archive.org/details/armorialensignso00crui**. Burial records for Aberdeen and much of the surrounding county are available on Deceased Online.

Electric Scotland hosts a transcript of Ebenezer Bain's 1887 book *A History of the Aberdeen Incorporated Trades* at **www.electricscotland.com/history/guilds**, whilst the Aberdeen Built Ships Project at **www.aberdeenships.com** includes a database and history of some local shipbuilders. For the history of Grampian Police Force visit **http://tinyurl.com/n9omtq3**.

The University of Aberdeen's Manuscript and Archive Collections catalogue can be searched at **www.abdn.ac.uk/historic/Manuscripts.shtml**. The university is also responsible for the Scottish Emigration Database (**www.abdn.ac.uk/emigration**), which lists some 21,000 passengers who sailed from Glasgow and Greenock, listing voyages mainly between 1 January and 30 April 1923.

A parish map for Aberdeenshire is also available at **www.monikie.org.uk/parishmap.jpg**, whilst Colin Milne's excellent North East Scotland site (**http://myweb.tiscali.co.uk/nescotland**) includes militia records, newspaper extracts, graves photos, old school photos and more. Resources for the history of families and communities in Glenbuchat can be found at **www.glenbuchatheritage.com**. Daviot village's history is at **www.daviot.org**, with holdings including the school register from 1874–1923. The village of Birse is covered at **http://birsefolk.id.au** and includes censuses, strays, baptisms (1761–79 and 1820–21) and marriages (1782–99 and 1820–26). A Register of Baptisms from 1763–1801 at Bairnie and Tillydesk can be examined on the Internet Archive at **www.archive.org/stream/scottishrecordso19scotuoft#page/n1/mode/2up**. Census material for Kinnethmont is available at **www.kinnethmont.co.uk**, as are old school photos and war memorial transcriptions.

Records for Upper and Lower Cabrach are available at **www.threestones.co.uk** and include war memorials, local songs, local books and more, whilst the Genealogy of the Cabrach site at **http://myweb.tiscali.co.uk/stuartpetrie** has records from various sources including censuses. Vital records for Strathdon are freely available at **http://sites.google.com/site/strathdonvitals**. For the history of the Howe, visit **www.mearns.org/history.htm** to find descriptions of several villages.

Angus

Previously known as Forfarshire until 1928, the history of Angus is dominated by the city of Dundee. Historic maps of Dundee, Forfarshire and the Firth of Tay are available at **http://tinyurl.com/yjtdxsy**, whilst a maritime history of Tayside, including trade maps, essays on the flax industry, a mariners' database and more is available at **www. dmcsoft. com/tamh**. A list of some of the more prominent places and people from the area, as well as pages on the Tay Bridge Disaster of 1879, the Black Watch Museum and the Forfar Witches can be viewed at **www. tayroots.com**. Burial records for Angus can be found on Deceased Online (see p. 12).

The county archive site (**www.angus.gov.uk/history/archives**) includes several online photo collections, as well as an Angus People Index and an Angus Building Image Index relating to its holdings. Dundee has its own archive site at **www.dundeecity.gov.uk/archive** which includes council minutes dating back to 1553. The council also runs a historic images site entitled Photopolis (**http://photopolis.dundeecity.gov.uk**), which has some 5,000 old photographs of the city.

Helping the council are the Friends of Dundee City Archives, which has done some excellent work in transcribing many of the archive's holdings and placing them online at **www.fdca.org.uk**. Included are databases such as the 1801 census for Dundee, several burial collections including the Howff Cemetery, and additional resources such as the Lockit Book of Dundee, a nineteenth-century database of Dundee ships, poorhouse records for both the city and Liff and Benvie, Wesleyan Chapel records, Cowgate school records (1899–1910), and much more. The Tay Valley Family History Society, based in Dundee, has a searchable library catalogue of its resources online at **www.tayvalleyfhs.org.uk**.

The Nine Incorporated Trades of Dundee site at **http://ninetradesof dundee.co.uk** contains transcriptions from thousands of historic documents concerning the burgh's various trade incorporations, as well as detailed information on the history of each respective trade.

Unlock the Boxes (**http://tinyurl.com/yjbkvgp**) carries an interesting virtual exhibition on eighteenth-century life in Angus, whilst the Lamb Collection, available at **http://sites.scran.ac.uk/lamb**, has essays on subjects such as entertainment, cholera and crime and punishment, as derived from research into the collection compiled by Alexander Crawford Lamb (1843–97).

Various resources for Monikie and surrounding areas are available at www.monikie.org.uk, including maps and hearth tax returns. Burials for Barry (1746–1800) are recorded at **http://tinyurl.com/ygwdr8q**, whilst the Internet Archive has a reproduction of an 1895 book entitled *The Parish of Longforgan; a Sketch of its Church and People* available at **www.archive. org/details/parishoflongforg00philiala**.

Argyll
Argyll Archives, based in Lochgilphead, has provided an online guide to its resources at **www.argyll-bute.gov.uk/community-life-and-leisure/archives**, whilst a Local Studies Department guide to the council's holdings at Dunoon, including a list of newspapers held there, is at **www.argyll-bute. gov.uk/community-life-and-leisure/local-studies**.

The Lochaber And North Argyll Family History Group (**www.lochaber andnorthargyllfamilyhistorygroup.org.uk**) has parish maps for Argyll and detailed church denomination guides for the region, as well as a listing of society resources. Highland Family History Society's site (**www.highland familyhistorysociety.org**) also covers Argyll, providing a publications list, and several indexes for gravestones, articles, the 1851 census and names featured in family trees held by the society.

The censuses from 1841–71 for Kilbrandon and Kilchattan parish are available at **http://tinyurl.com/qj6pgft**, whilst a 1779 census of the Duke of Argyll's estates can be accessed at **http://web.ncf.ca/cv297/app1779 .html**. The Ralston genealogy site (**www.ralstongenealogy.com**) includes monumental inscriptions for some Kintyre-based cemeteries, as well as other local resources. A brief outline of the history of Appin is at **www. appinhistoricalsociety.co.uk**.

Records for Skipness parish, in the form of rent books, parish records, censuses, kirk session minutes, map and folklore are available at **www. rootsweb.ancestry.com/~sctcskip**. For resources covering Knapdale, visit **www.knapdalepeople.com**. Finally, if your ancestor was of the law-breaking kind, visit the Inveraray Jail site at **www.inverarayjail.co.uk** to look up the facility's prison records database.

Ayrshire
Ayrshire Roots (**www.ayrshireroots.com**) is essentially an online parish clerk site, packed with resources including parish records, gazetteer descriptions and more. Ayrshire History (**www.ayrshirehistory.org.uk**) contains many fascinating articles on the county's history, whilst historic photos from the

county are available at **http://homepages.rootsweb.ancestry.com/ ~ayrshire**. A subscription-based site at **www.ayrshireancestors.com** has several monumental inscriptions.

Ayrshire Archives has some online resources at **www.ayrshirearchives. org.uk** including a virtual exhibition on the history of Afro-Caribbean people linked to the county in the eighteenth and nineteenth century, as well as searchable databases for burgesses and guild brethren for Irvine (1715–1920) and an Irvine Harbour Trust Harbour Book Cargoes In and Out database (1821–24).

Historic maps for Ayrshire can be found at **http://tinyurl.com/yfenvfo**, and an 1819 map of Kilmarnock at **www.dangly.com/kilmarnock/maps/ Kilmarnock%202.jpg**.

For North Ayrshire, the Three Towners site at **www.threetowners.com** has material for Ardossan, Saltcoats and Stevenston, including the 1819, 1822 and 1836 censuses, headstones information, newspaper intimations and poor relief database. North Ayrshire Remembers (**http://northayrshire remembers.tripod.com**) includes information on those from Largs who fell during the two world wars, as well as a partial index of listings for Largs people noted in the *Glasgow Herald* in the nineteenth century. The site also has some links to resources for West Kilbride and Cumbrae. A history of Skelmorlie and Wemyss Bay is available at **www.scribd.com/doc/1289541 /Skelmorlie-Original-Walter-Smart-History-1968**.

The parish church page for Ochiltree at **http://ochiltreechurch.home stead.com** includes a headstone index. The Maybole community website (**www.maybole.org**) has the local 1841 census, with hearth tax rolls from 1691 for the whole county also available at **www.maybole.org/history /Archives/hearthtax1691.htm**. A baptismal register for Stair (1862– 1917) can be consulted at **http://stairchurch.homestead.com**.

There are four family history societies in the county. The site for East Ayrshire (**www.eastayrshirefhs.co.uk**) has a forum (members only) and parish list, whilst Troon@Ayrshire's site (**www.troonayrshirefhs.org.uk**) provides transcriptions from registers of applications for poor relief in Dreghorn parish (1872–1890), an Ayrshire parish list, and an article on the Hammermen of Irvine. Alloway and South Ayrshire FHS (**www.asafhs. co.uk**) also offers a parish map and a description of available resources, whilst Largs and North Ayrshire FHS (**www.largsnafhs.org.uk**) also lists resources it holds on microfiche and microfilm.

Banffshire
The Moray Burial Ground Research Group site at **www.mbgrg.org** includes

details for some headstones found within cemeteries in Banffshire (see Morayshire). Further resources are available at the Aberdeen and North East Scotland Family History Society site (see p.134)

An interesting paper on the use of aliases and patronymics in Upper Banffshire, by Stuart Mitchell, is available at **http://tinyurl.com/o947jo,** which quotes many church records as part of its source material, naming many individuals.

Berwickshire

Borders Family History Society has an interactive parish map at **www. bordersfhs.org.uk/b_shire.asp** with detailed guides to records held by both it and other repositories in Scotland. Census records from 1841–61 have been made freely available at **www.maxwellancestry. com,** with many returns linked to maps at the National Library of Scotland, as well as confirmed inter-census links to show family progressions across time. A list of heritage site locations in the county can be found at **www.scottishbordersheritage. co.uk/49842**.

An index to Berwickshire graveyard locations is online at **www.rootsweb. ancestry.com/~sctbew/Cemeteries/cemindex.htm**. Some Berwickshire death records from 1855–81, marriages from 1865, and births from 1866–67 are freely available at **http://freepages.genealogy.rootsweb.ancestry.com/ ~connochie/bdm,** whilst a one-place study for Whitsome at **http://home pages.ipact.nl/~robertson** has gravestone inscriptions, school records and the 1841 census for the parish. Monumental inscriptions from Eyemouth Cemetery and Eyemouth Old Kirk are indexed at **www.memento-mori. co.uk**. The kirk session book for Bunkle and Preston from 1665–90 is available from the Internet Archive at **www.archive.org/details/session bookbunk00clubgoog**.

Old Scottish Borders Photo Archive (**www.ettrickgraphics.com/ bordersindex.htm**) has many images from Berwickshire, whilst photos for Eyemouth, Cockburnspath and Cove can also be found online at **www. fairbairnfamily.co.uk,** along with some limited census returns.

Bute

The former county of Buteshire consisted of more than just the island of Bute, with part of the mainland to its north included as well as the two Cumbrae islands and Arran. A gazetteer description from 1868 is available at **www. genuki.org.uk/big/sct/BUT/Gaz1868.html,** and a parish map at **www. scotlandgenweb.org/buteshire**.

General resources on the heritage of the island of Bute are available at www.visitbute.com. A more comprehensive site is Bute Sons and Daughters Through the Centuries (**www.butesonsanddaughters.co.uk**), which includes a surname index of those recorded in the 1841 census, as well as some film records of Bute, a history of Rothesay pier and more. For the history of Mount Stuart House, and its family, visit **www.mountstuart.com**. The 1841 census for Cumbrae, Kilbride, Kilmory and Kingarth can be found transcribed for free at **http://freepages.genealogy.rootsweb.ancestry.com/~relys4u**.

Caithness

Whilst Caithness is included within the coverage of the Highland Family History Society (see Invernessshire), it also has its own dedicated society, the website of which (**www.caithnessfhs.org.uk**) contains a list of contents from past journals, a beginners' page and publications list. There is also a genealogical discussion forum for the county at **http://forum.caithness. org/forumdisplay.php?f=9**. For a parish map, visit **www.oddquine.co.uk/ Genealogy/index.html**.

The Highland Archives site at **www.iprom.co.uk/archives** has many resources, particularly on the local and military history of the county,

Maxwell Ancestry provides many free to access databases for the Borders counties.

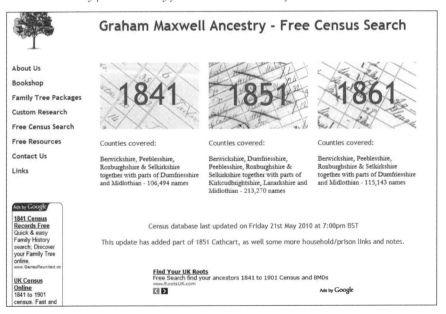

including First World War rolls of honour. The Caithness War Memorials site at **www.caithness.org/atoz/warmemorials/index.htm** also pays tribute to fallen sons of Caithness from across the county.

For people with ancestry from the Threipland estates in Caithness, it is also worth consulting the Thriepland database hosted by Perth and Kinross Archives, which lists many tenants there (see p.154).

The 1841 census for Bower, Canisbay, Dunnet and Halkirk is online at **http://freepages.genealogy.rootsweb.ancestry.com/~relys4u,** whilst the parish register of Canisbay from 1652–66 can be consulted on the Internet Archive at **www.archive.org/details/parishregisterso67cani**. Several graveyard records from the county can be sourced from Highland Memorial Inscriptions (**https://sites.google.com/site/highlandmemorial inscriptions /home**).

Clackmannanshire
Stobie's 1783 map of Clackmannanshire can be found at **www.chalmers-family.org/genuki/CLK/map.jpg**. The same map, along with maps of Westfield from 1845, 1848 and 1898 can be found at **http://freepages. genealogy. rootsweb.ancestry.com/~russellsofwestfield**. Census transcriptions for Westfield can also be browsed at the site.

For a summary of the holdings of Clackmannanshire Archives visit **www. clacksweb.org.uk/culture/archives/**. Central Scotland Family History Society lists members' interests for the county on its site at **www.csfhs.org.uk**.

Memento Mori (**www.memento-mori.co.uk**) hosts an index to monumental inscriptions for both Alva and Tillicoultry. For a fairly informative history of Tullibody village visit **www.angelfire.com/sc3/ tullibody/STORIES/stories.html**.

A history of Menstrie Castle is available at **www.menstrie.org/hist_ cas.html,** along with some photos.

Dumfriesshire
The Friends of the Archives of Dumfries and Galloway site at **www.dg community.net/historicalindexes** has many transcriptions of Dumfriesshire -based records, including census returns, kirk session minutes, jail books and bail bond registers, Dean of Guild plans, shipping registers and Poor Board minutes. The Dumfriesshire and Galloway Natural History and Antiquarian Society site (**www.dgnhas.org.uk**) hosts an index to its *Transactions* periodical (1862–2008). The Scottish Page at **http://homepages.rootsweb.ancestry. com/~scottish** has links to many resources for the county as well as details of others with research interests there.

For images of Dumfriesshire churches and graveyards visit **http://home pages.rootsweb.ancestry.com/~dfsgal**, whilst monumental inscriptions for many graveyards in the county can be found at **www.johnmacmillan. co.uk/indx_cemetery.html**.

Maxwell Ancestry has some handy resources at **www.maxwell ancestry. com** for the county, the most important of which are valuation rolls for Annan, Applegarth, Caerlaverock, Canonbie, Closeburn, Cummertrees, Dalton and Dornock from 1896–97. The site also provides free census records transcriptions from 1841–61.

For irregular marriages carried out at Gretna, an index from 1795–1895 is available at **www.achievements.co.uk/services/gretna/index.php**, though the records have also been digitised and made available at Ancestry. Also for Gretna, the Devil's Porridge (**www.devilsporridge.co.uk**) deals with the history of munitions manufacturing at HM Factory Gretna in the twentieth century.

Memorials for Sanquhar Kirkyard can be consulted at **http://freepages .history.rootsweb.ancestry.com/~cdobie/sanquhar.htm**. A history of the parish of Glencairn is at **www.archive.org/details/parishglencairn00mont goog**, and the history of the royal burgh of Annan at **www.annan.org.uk/ history/index.html**. A list of Provosts in Dumfries is at **http://homepages. rootsweb.ancestry.com/~scottish/Provosts.html**.

If your ancestors migrated overseas, a list of many born in the county who died in Canada is available at **http://homepages.rootsweb.ancestry. com/~scottish/D-GForeignBuried.html**.

Dunbartonshire

A cached version of the Vale of Leven Story (**http://tinyurl.com/op9bb6z**) contains detailed histories of towns and villages in West Dunbartonshire, as well as a discussion board and essays on various aspects of local history. Old photos of Balloch, and a transcription of the 1881 census for the village of Balloch, are available at **http://tinyurl.com/m5hhvrh**.

For Dumbarton, the More Than a Memory oral history project (**www. morethanamemory.org.uk**) has many recorded extracts in a dedicated multimedia section, as well as historic photos from the town – a highlight is cine film of the VE Day celebrations from 1945. A list of the civilian war dead from the Clydebank Blitz, during the Second World War, is available at **www.tommckendrick.com/code/casualties1.html**.

Memento Mori at **www.memento-mori.co.uk** has monumental inscriptions for Auld Isle (Kirkintilloch), Cadder, Campsie (cemetery and churchyard) and Kilsyth (cemetery and churchyard). Inscriptions for Rosneath, with a churchyard plan, can be viewed at **http://members.mad asafish.com/~fairenough**.

East Lothian (Haddingtonshire until 1921)
Until 1921, East Lothian was known as Haddingtonshire. The website for the John Gray Centre (**www.johngraycentre.org**), which houses East Lothian's Archaeology, Museum, Archive and Local History Services, has a searchable catalogue. The Lothians Family History Society covers the area, and its website (**www.lothiansfhs.org.uk**) has a map and a discussion forum. For information on friendly societies, incorporations, guilds and ancient orders in the county visit **www.historyshelf.org/shelf/friend/ index.php**.

A graveyard index and plan for St Mary's Church in Haddington is available at **www.stmaryskirk.co.uk/6_graveyard_index_plan.htm**, whilst burial ground surveys for the parish of Traprain are at **www.ejclark.force 9.co.uk**, with records for Prestonkirk, Stenton and Whittingehame.

For Bolton and Saltoun, parish records from 1998 onwards and burial records are hosted at **http://ndhm.org.uk**. The Dunbar Historical Society site at **www.dunbarhistoricalsociety.com** has a potted history and some media resources for the area, as well as an inventory of its collections.

Fife
Fife Council Archives (**http://tinyurl.com/bvhw95u**) includes a searchable catalogue and several databases – however, it is an extraordinarily difficult site to navigate around. Some apparently missing databases, recorded in the first edition of this book, do still exist on the site, but appear to have been lost in the site hierarchy, such as Escaped Prisoners and Patients in 1942 (**http:// tinyurl.com/az93ts6**) and an Index to Register of Photographs of Criminals 1912–23 (**http://tinyurl.com/y73nker**). The University of St Andrew's Special Collections Department (**www.st-andrews.ac.uk/library/ special collections**) has details on its various collections, and links to sub-sites such as the university's Photographic Collection, and its own genealogical holdings. A new portal for the library's digital collectioncollections has recently been launched online at **https://arts.st-andrews.ac.uk/digital humanities/**.

For biographical information on the great and the good, the Internet Archive hosts the *Biographical Dictionary of Eminent Men of Fife* (1866) at www.archive.org/details/biographicaldic00conogoog and *Lives of Eminent Men* (1846) at www.archive.org/details/liveseminentmen00bruc goog.

Fife Family History Society (**http://fifefamilyhistorysociety.blogspot. co.uk**) provides some free-to-access resources. A generic Fife site at **www. thefifepost.com** has many interesting sections on subjects such as the county's burghs, witches and trials, providing an interesting overview. A name index for Fife newspapers (1833–1987) held at Cupar Library is online at Ancestry.

The parish registers of Dunfermline (1561–1700) can be consulted at **www.archive.org/details/scottishrecordso32scotuoft**. Directories, voters' rolls, censuses, hearth tax records and more for Newport, Wormit and Forgan are available at **www.twentytwoflassroad.co.uk**, whilst the Scoonie 1841 census is online at **http://member.melbpc.org.au/~andes/scoonie.html**.

The history of the royal burgh of Burntisland is outlined at **www. burntisland.net** and includes the town's charter from 1541. A general history of Kincardine on Forth is recorded at **www.rocinante.demon.co.uk/ klhg/klhgindx.htm**, whilst the history of Kingsbarns is further outlined at **www.kingsbarnslinks.com/villguide/history.htm**.

The county's mining history is dealt with at **www.users.zetnet. co.uk/mmartin/fifepits** which also includes the Kingdom of Fife Mining Industry Memorial Book database.

Invernessshire

Probably the most comprehensive site for Invernessshire is Am Baile (**www. ambaile.org.uk**), meaning 'The Village' in Gaelic, which covers much of the Highlands. It hosts various materials, both indexed and digitised, including newspaper indexes, maps, plans, photos, books and Gaelic resources, all for free.

The Old Home Town Image Archive (**www.theoldhometown.com**) includes historic images of Inverness, whilst the Scottish Highlander Photo Archive at **www.scottishhighlanderphotoarchive.co.uk/html** will host some 20,000 historic black and white photos of individuals when completed, a great proportion of which come from Invernessshire.

Highland Family History Society covers the county, and its site at **www. highlandfhs.org.uk** includes an index for gravestones, a list of articles in the society's publications, members' interests, an 1851 census index and a further list of names found in compiled family trees submitted to the society. Highland Memorial Inscriptions (**https://sites.google.com/site/highland memorialinscriptions/home**) has many cemeteries indexed, including that of Tomnahurich in Inverness, and a further forty-three cemeteries from across the county (the datasets may take a while to load). You can request full inscription details from the organiser, as well as images from the individual stones themselves.

A database of some pre-1850 Invernessshire vital records can be consulted at **http://freepages.genealogy.rootsweb.ancestry.com/~ked1/Glen3.html**. The Scottish Record Society's *Commissariot Record of Inverness: Register of Testaments, 1630–1800* dataset is located on Ancestry, or for free on Electric Scotland at **www.electricscotland.com/history/records/vol04 .htm**.

The Moidart Local History Group (**www.moidart.org.uk/index.htm**) has various resources online for free, such as its Glen Moidart papers (including estate rentals), and some for members only, such as the 1841 census. A history of Ardersier and Petty can be found at **www.ardersierandpetty.cc** (via 'A Backward Glance').

If your ancestor was from Urquhart, a database of Chelsea Pension records showing soldiers discharged from the British Army who gave the parish as their birthplace is at **http://freepages.genealogy.rootsweb. ancestry.com/ ~ked1/WO97.htm**.

If your ancestor emigrated to Australia, the Invernessshire Emigrant Index (**http://freepages.genealogy.rootsweb.ancestry.com/~maddenps/INVE M1.htm**) lists many of those who sailed to New South Wales and Queensland. Databases of emigrants who sailed with the Highlands and Islands Emigration Society between 1852 and 1857 are also available through the Scottish Archive Network site at **www.scan.org.uk/researchrtools /emigration.htm** and at **www.angelfire.com/ns/bkeddy/HIES/1.html**. For the stories of many forcibly evicted in the Highland Clearances, visit **www.theclearances.org**.

Kincardineshire

Images from many of Kincardineshire's churches are available at Colin Milne's NE Scotland site at **http://myweb.tiscali.co.uk/nescotland**. The Portal to Portlethen site at **www.old-portlethen.co.uk** has many essays on the history of Portlethen, including subjects as diverse as privates and privateers, tee names, farming, and the church and clergy. For a history of Woodstone Fishing Station and St Cyrus visit **www.woodstonfishing station.com/woodston_fishing/history.shtml**.

Some census transcriptions from Garvock, Laurencekirk and Fordoun have been transcribed and made available at **http://tinyurl.com/yzetwsy**.

Am Baile, the Gateway to the Scottish Highlands.

Kinrossshire

Kinross is today jointly administered with Perth though Perth and Kinross Council. Its archive site at **www.pkc.gov.uk/archives** has a catalogue and several online databases, mainly for Perthshire, but also includes an index called Perthshire People & Kinross-shire Kin, which incorporates names from Kinross.

The 1841 census for Kinross can be consulted at **http://member.melbpc. org.au/~andes/scotland.html**. Kinross vehicle registrations, licenses and owners from 1904–52 have been transcribed from records held at Dundee Council Archives and made available at **www.fdca.org.uk/Vehicle_ Registrations.html**, which includes addresses for all those named. Kinross Museum (**www.kinrossmuseum.co.uk**) has several online exhibitions of interest, including items dedicated to burgh folk and St Serf's Island.

Kirkcudbrightshire

A modern map of Kirkcudbrightshire, along with some local family histories and researchers' interests, is available at the Scottish Page at **http:// homepages.rootsweb.ancestry.com/~scottish,** whilst free 1851 census transcriptions for part of the county are available at **www.maxwell ancestry. com**. A handful of cemetery records from twelve parishes within the county are also online at **www.johnmacmillan.co.uk/indx_cemetery. html**, whilst many more can be found at **www.kirkyards.co.uk** for various kirkyards and cemeteries in Anwoth, Borgue, Buittle, Colvend, Girthon, Parton, Rerrick, Southwick, Tongland and Twynholm. Its sister site, A Historical Index of the People and Places of the Stewartry of Kirkcudbright, is available at **www. kirkcudbright.co**.

The Old Kirkcudbright site (**www.old-kirkcudbright.net**) contains a parish and burgh history, as well as valuation rolls, parish records such as OPR deaths from 1826–53, stent rolls, census records for poorhouses in the county, and more. A history of the parish church is also available at **www. kirkcudbrightparish.org.uk,** though the site hosts no records. For the names of volunteers who joined the Urr Company Stewartry Kircudbright Volunteer Infantry on 16 July 1808, visit **http://donjaggi.net/galloway /urrvolunteers1808.html**.

Grave marker on Culloden battlefield, Invernesshire.

A town history for Dalbeattie is available at **www.dalbeattie.com/ history,** which includes information on the granite quarries, port and industrial mills in the area.

Lanarkshire (and Glasgow)

A parish list for the historic county of Lanarkshire is available at the Glasgow and West of Scotland Family History Society site at **www.gwsfhs.org.uk,** along with the society's library catalogue. The Lanarkshire Family History Society site at **www.lanarkshirefhs.org.uk** also offers an online discussion forum open to the public.

The county is dominated by Glasgow, Scotland's largest city. The Glasgow City Archives website at **www.glasgowlife.org.uk/libraries/the-mitchell-library/archives/Pages/home.aspx** provides a wealth of detail on the institution's holdings, with informative guides on collections related to schools, estates, shipbuilding, poor law material, business, police, sasines, church and more. The site also includes databases such as Boer War Burgesses (1900–04), Glasgow burgh licensed Chimney Sweeps (1852–62), and a militia registers index (1810–31).

The Virtual Mitchell photographic collection at **www.mitchelllibrary. org/virtualmitchell/** carries many free-to-view holdings from both the archive and Glasgow Museums. Historic images from the *Glasgow Herald* and the *Evening Times* can be viewed and purchased from **http://glasgow heraldandtimes.newsprints.co.uk**. The *Glasgow Herald* newspaper can itself be viewed for free from 1806–1990 at **http://news.google.co.uk/ newspapers,** along with the *Evening Times* from 1914–90 and the *Scots Bulletin and Pictorial* from 1950–60.

Glasgow University Archives Services (**www.gla.ac.uk/services/ archives**) has links to both the Scottish Business Archive and the University Archive, with searchable catalogues and guides. The university celebrates its own history at **www.universitystory.gla.ac.uk,** which includes a graduate list (1496–1896) and Rolls of Honour for the two world wars.

Radical Glasgow (**www.gcu.ac.uk/radicalglasgow**), produced by Caledonian University, has various essays on the insurrections, uprisings and protest movements to have sprung up in the past, from the weaver's strike of 1787 to the foundation of the Scottish Labour Party. The history of Glasgow's hammermen, as recorded by the Scottish Records Society in 1912, can be read at **www.archive.org/details/historyofhammerm00lums**.

The Glasgow Story (**www.theglasgowstory.com**) has various essays on the city's history, and includes digitised copies of the valuation rolls for

1913–14, as well as electoral ward maps. Maps of central Glasgow from 1881 and 1891 have been linked to searchable data from the corresponding Post Office Directories for the area at Addressing History (**http://addressing history.edina.ac.uk**). For reminiscences, mainly from Bridgeton, visit the Glesca Pals site at **www.glesga.ukpals.com,** where you will find old school photos, a forum and more. To the city's west, Anderston Then and Now (**www.glesga.ukpals.com/profiles/anderston.htm**) recalls the parish's history.

A Most Curious Murder (**www.amostcuriousmurder.com**) tells the story of the killing of Madeleine Smith in 1857, a well-compiled case study of murder and trial in nineteenth-century Scotland. With matters religious, the Diary of a Church Elder 1853–54 at **www.garrion.co.uk/diary1853** provides insights into the city's life by an elder from Hutchesontown United Presbyterian Church.

The city's urban built environment is explored at **www.bestlaidschemes. com,** whilst old streets in Glasgow which changed their names before the 1940s are listed at **www.glasgowguide.co.uk/info-streets changed1.html**.

Many monumental inscriptions for Glasgow and Lanarkshire can be found at the Memento Mori site at **www.memento-mori.co.uk,** whilst a database of interments in the city's Southern Necropolis is available at **www. southernnec.20m.com/index.html**. The *Glasgow Evening Times* Roll of Honour index for the First World War is available in PDF format at **http:// tinyurl.com/4lhuyr8**. The city's trade directories, from the 1787 Nathaniel Jones Directory of Glasgow to those up to the 1940s at the time of writing, are available on the Internet Archive via its National Library of Scotland portal at **http://archive.org/details/scottishdirectories**.

A Register of Testaments for Hamilton and Campsie (1564–1800), along with Commissariot Records for Glasgow (1547–1800) and Lanark (1595–1800) are available at **www.electricscotland.com/history/records**. The history of the county's mining, ironworks and steel industries can be explored at both **www.sorbie.net/lanarkshire_mining_industry.htm** and **http:// myweb.tiscali.co.uk/steelworks/Steelworks%20index.htm**.

For Airdrie's history visit **www.airdrie.net,** whilst names for those lost from the town in the First World War are at **www.freewebs.com/dt1078**. Nearby Monklands is covered at **www.monklands.co.uk/cigp/Irishphil. htm,** which includes a Lanarkshire parish map and resources on Irish migration to Lanarkshire.

A list of nineteenth-century Clyde Passenger Steamers, and their owners and masters, is available at **http://cook fmly.rootsweb.ancestry.com/ cps_list/**.

The Mitchell Library in Glasgow. Author's collection.

Midlothian (formerly Edinburghshire)

Until 1921 Midlothian was the County of Edinburgh, and as with Glasgow in Lanarkshire, the city dominates the county and its history. A map of the capital's parish boundaries is at **www.hoodfamily.info/misc/miscedin maplarge.html**. Contemporary maps of the city from 1784, 1865, 1881, 1891 and 1905 have been linked to the corresponding Post Office Directories for the city in the highly useful Addressing History site at **http://addressing history.edina.ac.uk**. Perform a search for a name or an occupation, and the results are plotted on the relevant map. A similar Edinburgh map project utilising historic photos instead is Visit Historic Cities (**www.visithistoric cities.com**).

The Local History and Heritage department site at **www.edinburgh. gov.uk/info/476/local_history_and_heritage** provides links to many resources at both Central Library and Edinburgh City Archives. It also connects to its Our Town Stories site at **www.ourtownstories.co.uk,** with links to projects such as the Capital Collections project (**www.capital**

collections.org.uk), depicting people and places from the seventeenth century to the present day, and other resources such as maps and historic images from the city's past.

A cached version of Scots Find at **http://tinyurl.com/k6pjd9c**) spoils you for choice with its holdings for Edinburgh and Leith, including transcriptions of apprentice registers, burgess rolls, marriages and burials, testaments, processes and decreets, and more. For the history of Leith's trade guilds, visit **www.electricscotland.com/history/leith/11.htm**. Maxwell Ancestry (**www.maxwellancestry.com**) also has some Midlothian censuses from 1841–61 and editions of *Chambers Edinburgh Journal* from 1832.

The Internet Archive has many digitised Scottish Record Society publications concerning Edinburgh. A *Register of Burials in the Chapel Royal or Abbey of Holyroodhouse 1706–1900* is at **www.archive.org/details/scottish records014scotuoft**, whilst marriages from 1564–1800 for Holyroodhouse and Canongate are online at **www.archive.org/details/scottishrecords 034scotuoft**. Edinburgh marriages from 1595–1700 are at **www.archive.org /details/registerofmarria33edin**, and from 1701–1750 at **www.archive. org/details/scottishrecordso23scotuoft**. A burial register for the churchyard of Restalrig can also be consulted by visiting **www.archive.org/details/ scottishrecordso20scotuoft**. Access to these can also be gained via Electric Scotland at **www.electricscotland.com/history/records**.

The Lothians Family History Society site (**www.lothiansfhs.org.uk**) has a discussion forum, but this does not cover Edinburgh, only the surrounding county (and East and West Lothian). The Lothian Health Services Archives site at **www.lhsa.lib.ed.ac.uk** has a searchable catalogue of holdings for medical matters, whilst the Friendly Societies in Edinburgh, the Lothians and Fife site at **www.historyshelf.org/shelf/friend/index.php** has much on the area's guilds and incorporations. For the history of coal mining in the county, visit **www.hoodfamily.info/index.html**. If your ancestors were Edinburgh-based photographers, you may find more on them at **www. edinphoto.org.uk**.

Elsewhere, a one-place study for Corstorphine at **www.angelfire.com/ ct2/corstorphine** has directories and the local 1841 census. A similar study for Duddingston at **www.ancestor.abel.co.uk/Duddingston.html** has poll tax testaments, parish records, monumental inscriptions and other resources. A history of Currie with war memorial records can be viewed at **www. ma.hw.ac.uk/ccc/history**. A blog-based site on the history of Leith is at **www.leithhistory.co.uk**, with the town also covered at **www.leithlocal historysociety.org.uk** through the Leith Local History Society, which provides a useful timeline. A host of useful resources for Granton exists at **www.grantonhistory.org,** and for a pictorial history of Niddrie visit **http://niddrie.tripod.com.**

Moray

The Local Heritage Services in Moray website at **http://libindx. moray.gov.uk/mainmenu.asp** includes searchable databases of people, places and subjects contained within the county's archives.

The Moray Burial Ground Research Group (**www.mbgrg.org**) carries a headstone index, including forename, surname, age and year of death (where known), and in the case of war memorials, regiment. Burial grounds and memorials can be searched individually, and there is a dedicated index for inscriptions found on buried headstones uncovered by the team during its survey work of old cemeteries in the region – the full transcriptions can be sourced from the society's publications. The website also hosts a gallery, a map of the area, a research progress chart and newsletters. A burial index to several Morayshire cemeteries is also available at Highland Memorial Inscriptions at **https://sites.google.com/site/highlandmemorial inscriptions /home.**

The Moray Family History Sharing site at **www.wakefieldfhs.org.uk/ morayweb/index.htm** has a message board, databases for the 1851 and 1861 censuses, photographs from the county and several further Moray-based resources.

A site for Lossiemouth is found at **www.lossiefowk.co.uk,** which contains various records and forums, including details from the war memorials and articles on local subjects such as fishing.

Nairnshire

Nairnshire, to the east of Inverness, is covered by several of the same resources focussing on the Highland capital and the Highlands. The Am Baile website at **www.ambaile.org.uk** (see Invernessshire) has many resources for Nairn-based folk, as does the Scottish Highlander Photo Archive at **www.scottishhighlanderphotoarchive.co.uk.**

Nairnshire is covered by the Highland Family History Society at **www. highlandfhs.org.uk** (see Invernessshire). A page dedicated to the war memorial in Cawdor is available at **www.spanglefish.com/CWMC,** which includes detailed information on the fallen. Memorial records for some Nairnshire cemeteries can be found indexed at Highland Memorial Inscriptions (**https://sites.google.com/site/highlandmemorial inscriptions/ home**).

Orkney

Orkney consists of several islands north of Caithness, and was not annexed to the Scottish Crown until 1472, having been under Norwegian rule for the previous six centuries.

The Orkney Library and Archive site (www.orkneylibrary.org.uk) has an online catalogue of resources held at the facility and some resources which members can access from home. It also hosts collections of photos taken by Tom Kent and William H. Houston, and has its own dedicated and often humorous blog at http://orkneyarchive.blogspot.com.

An interactive map at www.ancestralorkney.com contains lists of the most common names found on each of the islands, and information on some famous Orcadians. A parish map is located at www.genuki.org.uk/big/sct/OKI/indexpars.html. For historic images of the island, almost 8,000 photographs are hosted at www.theoldhometown.com. Further maps, and gravestones from the islands of Rousay, Egilsay, Wyre and Eynhallow, are available at www.rousayroots.com. The site also hosts censuses for these islands from 1841–1901 (with Eynhallow uninhabited since 1851), and various family histories. For a history of Ness Battery, visit www.ness battery.co.uk.

Orkney Genealogy's site (www.cursiter.com) has an impressive index of baptisms, marriages and deaths, some digitised images from *Ane Account of the Ancient & Present State of Orkney* by the minister of Kirkwall in 1684, and links to useful resources elsewhere. For South Ronaldsay and Burray visit www.southronaldsay.net for resources, including a database of the 1821 census covering the two islands, Swona and the Pentland Skerries. Various extracts from the 1841 census can be found at http://tinyurl.com/ycdbnpz. The Orkney Family History Society site (www.orkneyfhs.co.uk) has a searchable name index of the 1841 to 1901 Orkney censuses, though only provides a frequency of returns for non-members.

Peeblesshire

A History of Peeblesshire from 1864, by William Chambers, is available at http://archive.org/details/historyofpeebles00chamiala. The 1868 Imperial Gazetteer of Scotland's description of Peeblesshire can also be consulted at www.rootsweb.ancestry.com/~sctpee/genuki/peebles shire.htm.

Borders Family History Society has a page dedicated to Peeblesshire at www.bordersfhs.org.uk/p_shire.asp, containing an interactive parish map with links to pages containing information on various records held within the society's archive and elsewhere across Scotland.

The 1841–61 censuses from Peeblesshire have been transcribed and made freely available at **www.maxwellancestry.com**. As with its other borders counties holdings, the locations in most entries have links provided to connect them to an online map hosted by the National Library of Scotland, which helpfully allows you to examine the environment where your ancestors lived.

Finally for Peeblesshire, the county's most prominent heritage sites can be explored at **www.scottishbordersheritage.co.uk/49842**.

Perthshire

The Perth and Kinross Archives website (**www.pkc.gov.uk/archives**) hosts many useful databases compiled by its Friends association. These include the Perth Burial Registers 1794–1855, the Threipland's People database (listing names of people living and working in the Threipland family estates of Perthshire and Caithness), Women's Sources, three separate militia-based databases and a Perthshire People index. The Friends of the Dundee City Archives group has also uploaded details of Perthshire vehicle registrations (1909–11) within the Transport records section of the site at **www.fdca. org.uk**. Other county-wide resources for Perthshire include **www.perthshire-scotland.co.uk/towns.htm**, which hosts brief histories for main towns in the county, and the Perthshire Diary site (**www.perthshirediary.com**), which recalls 365 moments in the history of the county arranged as a daily digest.

The North Perthshire Family History Group website (**www.npfhg.org**) includes a list of the society's resources and a map of parishes covered, as well as burial and census records. The Tay Valley Family History Society (**www.tayvalleyfhs.org.uk**) carries a similar list of society holdings. The Glenlyon History Society (**www.glenlyon.org**) has several old photos and Rena Stewart's Glenlyon Memories recollections.

The Alternative Perth site (**www.alternative-perth.co.uk**) holds a virtual encyclopaedia of material related to the burgh of Perth (and Perthshire), with many biographies of important folk and gazetteer entries. My own Handloom Weavers of Perth (**www.perthweavers.bravehost.com**) names weavers found in the 1841 census for the burgh, those bearing arms in 1715, noted in rental books and charters, and paying for kirk seats in 1749. A plan of the burgh from the early 1800s is at **www.ambaile.org.uk/en/item/ item_maps.jsp?item_id=18251**.

Papers in a Trunk (**www.highlandstrathearn.com**) is another encyclopaedic project carrying essays on the history of Strathearn, with its associated clans and families. Monumental inscriptions for Little Leny in Callander are online at **www.incallander.co.uk/lit_len.htm,** whilst the names on Blairgowrie war memorial are recorded at **www.blairgowrie-sacrifice.co.uk**. Many electoral rolls for the county from 1832 can be found at **http://caledonian connectionsgenealogy.blogspot.co.uk**. For Blackford's history, visit **www.blackfordhistoricalsociety.org.uk**.

Dunning Parish Historical Society has a monumental inscriptions index at **www.dunning.uk.net,** and census entries from 1841–91. Inscriptions for Dunblane are recorded at **www.memento-mori.co.uk,** with the history of the town itself recorded at **www.dunblaneweb.co.uk**.

Renfrewshire

A gazetteer description of Renfrewshire from 1847 is available at **www.my renfrew.com/renfrew.htm**. Sources obtainable from Renfrewshire Family History Society can be found at **www.renfrewshirefhs.co.uk,** whilst the Renfrewshire Local History Forum at **http://rlhf.info** promotes all aspects of history and archaeology in both Renfrewshire and Inverclyde. For information on the county's various archive collections visit **www.renfrew shire.gov.uk/webcontent/Home/Services/Libraries/Local+and+family+ history**.

A fairly comprehensive resource is the Portal to the Past site at **www. portaltothepast.co.uk,** which displays much of East Renfrewshire's heritage. It includes a detailed family history section and hosts online exhibitions such as a history of the region in the First World War, Great Scottish Minds and Innovations, and more focussed essays such as the history of Shanks & Co. brass foundry. The site also includes a catalogue of the council's archival holdings.

The Greenock-based Watt Library has some useful online resources. A BMD index, as sourced from entries in local newspapers from the early nineteenth century to 1913, is available at **http://tinyurl.com/yd55wdm,** whilst a more generic newspaper archive index (subject based) is available at **http://tinyurl.com/ydcfn5m**. The library also has an impressive photographic site at **http://tinyurl.com/ycq3h2u**.

A register of marriages and baptisms from the parish of Kilbarchan (1649–1772) is online at **www.archive.org/details/scottishrecordso41 scotuoft,** whilst a discussion forum for Barrhead and Neilston is available at

Carr's Croft in Craigie, Perth, formerly home to a small handloom weaving community. Author's collection.

www.barrhead-scotland.com. The history of Craigends estate is discussed at **www.ourlocalhistory.co.uk**, whilst gravediggers' records for the parish of Mearns are available at **www.mearnskirkyardproject.co.uk**.

Ross and Cromarty

The Ross and Cromarty Heritage Society hosts various resources for many communities within the county at **www.rossandcromartyheritage.org**, including war memorials, parish records and more (best accessed using Internet Explorer as your browser). Ross and Cromarty Roots (**www. rosscromartyroots.co.uk**) is equally useful with contextual essays on subjects such as the Church, schools, the poor, farming and the Clearances, whilst also providing some graveyard location information. Highland Family History Society's site (**www.highlandfamilyhistorysociety.org**) includes resources for the region, whilst many of the county's folk are included in the Scottish Highlander Photo Archive (**www.scottishhighlanderphoto archive.co.uk**). An index to the monumental inscriptions to some sixty-seven cemeteries and kirkyards in Ross and Cromarty can be found at

Highland Memorial Inscriptions at **https://sites.google.com/site/highland memorialinscriptions/home**.

Am Baile (**www.ambaile.org.uk**) also covers the county, with one of its most impressive holdings being a forty-four page downloadable book on *The Cromarty Fisherfolk Dialect* at **http://tinyurl.com/y8zlxet**. For a general guide to the main towns and villages in the Black Isle visit **www.black-isle.info**.

For the royal burgh of Cromarty, an 1814 militia list for males aged between seventeen and forty-five is at **www.cali.co.uk/users/freeway/courthouse/geneal1.html**, whilst a list of householders from 1744 is at **www.cali.co.uk/users/freeway/courthouse/geneal2.html**.

Old photos of the region are available at **www.theoldhometown.com**. A history of St Michael's Kirk near Balblair village is at **www.kirkmichael.info**.

For the Coigach in the east of the county, there are considerable resources located at **http://freepages.genealogy.rootsweb.ancestry.com/~coigach/index.htm**, including militia lists, gazetteer entries, emigration records, census records and even a 1775 map showing the locations of farms in the region.

Elsewhere in the county, an 1841 census for Urray is presented at **http://tinyurl.com/y8vm5db**, along with several returns for the Isle of Lewis (see p.161). The Fearn Peninsula Graveyards Project database (**www.fearn peninsulagraveyards.com**) is another excellent resource with nearly 7,000 memorials. The index is free but access to the full records costs £2.50 for twenty-four hours.

Roxburghshire

The main archive in the former county of Roxburghshire is the Heritage Hub at Hawick, with its website at **www.heartofhawick.co.uk/heritagehub** identifying key resources and offering a catalogue. The Borders Family History Society has a web page for Roxburghshire at **www.bordersfhs. org.uk/r_shire.asp**, which includes an interactive parish map, whilst elsewhere the site also hosts a poor law records database for Jedburgh and a discussion forum. The 1841–61 censuses have been transcribed and made freely available at **www.maxwell ancestry.com**, whilst several other generic websites on the Borders include material from Roxburghshire (see Berwickshire, p.139).

Melrose Parish Registers (1642–1840), compiled by the Scottish Record Society in 1913, can be viewed at **www.archive.org/details/scottish recordso33scotuoft**. For the history of Denholm, its quarrying industry, church history, stocking industry and more, see **www.denholmvillage.co.uk**.

The History of Kelso (**www.kelso.bordernet.co.uk/history**) records the story of the town from 1113 to the First World War. For Maxton, visit **www.maxton.bordernet.co.uk** to view the history section and some black and white images. For the history of Jedburgh visit **www.jedburgh.org.uk**.

Selkirkshire
Borders Family History Society (see Berwickshire) has a page for Selkirkshire at **www.bordersfhs.org.uk/s_shire.asp**, which includes a parish map. At the time of writing the page was still under construction, but in due course will contain detailed listings of resources held by the society and elsewhere for the county.

The History of Selkirk (**www.selkirk.bordernet.co.uk/history.html**) provides introductory essays on various subjects of interest, including the Covenanters, the Reivers, Selkirk Abbey and the history of the Selkirk Common Riding.

For a list of Selkirk burgh inhabitants on 16 June 1817 visit **www.cangenealogy.com/armstrong/selkirk1817.htm**. Selkirk Antiquarian Society's pages at **www.selkirkshireantiquariansociety.co.uk** contain lists of deaths and monumental inscriptions records which can be purchased. Transcriptions of statutory death records from the county in 1874 can also be viewed at **http://tinyurl.com/yg2qt6b**, whilst census records from 1841–61 are available at **www.maxwellancestry.com**.

Shetland
Shetland Museum and Archives (**www.shetlandmuseumand archives.org.uk**) provides an online summary of local history holdings, and its fully searchable photo collection is available at **http://photos.shetland-museum.org.uk**. The islands' heritage is explored at **www.shetland-heritage.co.uk**, whilst Shetland Family History Society (**www.shetland-fhs.org.uk**) offers a map showing various parishes across the islands. The wiki-based Shetlopaedia may also help at **http://shetlopedia.com/Main_Page**.

A free database of names from across the islands, sourced from many different records, is at **www.bayanne.info/Shetland**, whilst a Shetland DNA project is hosted at **www.davidkfaux.org/shetlandislandsY-DNA**. For the 1841 and 1851 censuses for the Isle of Foula visit **http://tinyurl.com/**

yk7x6do – links on the page will also take you to the 1861, 1871 and 1891 equivalents. Census returns for other Shetland districts in 1841 are available at **http://tinyurl.com/yf4sk2y**.

Janice Halcrow's Shetland Newspaper Transactions (**www.jghalcrow. co.uk**) lists transcripts of BMD intimations from the *Shetland Times* from 1872 to 1970, as well as some historical news stories. Further intimations from the same paper from 1930–88 can also be accessed at **www.users.on.net/ ~bruce.smith**.

Stirlingshire

Transcriptions of statutory deaths in Stirlingshire in 1869 can be found at **http://tinyurl.com/ycus7qj**, whilst many monumental indexes for burial grounds across the county can be found at **www.memento-mori.co.uk**. For the history of Stirling town, and descriptions of several heritage sites, visit **www.stirling.co.uk**.

The history of Kilsyth is explored at **www.kilsyth.org.uk**, with some monumental inscriptions for the town available at **http://members.tripod. com/~Caryl_Williams/Kilsyth-7.html**, and a handful of transcribed OPR records from 1737, 1741, 1748 and 1762 further available at **http://members. iinet.net.au/~kjstew/KilsythOPRS.htm**.

The Drymen Millenium Project (**www.drymen-history.org.uk/ millennium.html**) has a useful list of publications on Drymen's history. For Killearn visit **www.killearnontheweb.co.uk**. The 1881 census for Bothkennar can be consulted freely at **http://tinyurl.com/yctb36t**.

Finally for the county, visit **www.falkirklocalhistorysociety.co.uk** for a detailed history of Falkirk.

Sutherland

The County Sutherland site (**www.countysutherland.co.uk**) contains an excellent guide to the county's communities, and includes a pay-per-view burials database. The blog at **http://cosuthtribute.blogspot.com** details those recorded on local war memorials. Sutherland is also covered by Highland Family History Society, with various resources available at its site (**www. highlandfamilyhistorysociety.org**). The Highland Memorial Inscriptions site (**https://sites.google.com/site/highlandmemorialinscriptions/home**) has an index to some twenty-six burial sites within the county.

The Internet Archive hosts a digitised facsimile at **www.archive.org/ details/scottishrecordso26scotuoft** of a Scottish Records Society publication from 1911 containing the parish register of Durness (1764–1814).

A community site for Helmsdale at **www.helmsdale.org** includes various history essays on subjects as diverse as local football, the police, the Clearances and emigration.

West Lothian
West Lothian was known as Linlithgowshire until 1921. The council's history and heritage page (**www.westlothian.gov.uk/tourism/Local History/**) has various historical resources as well as details of the council's archival holdings. Old photos from the town of Linlithgow through the decades can be found at **www.visithistoriccities.com**.

West Lothian Family History Society (**www.wlfhs.org.uk**) has several resources available, including transcriptions from war memorials across the county (and images from the Scottish Korean War Memorial), a parish list, a picture gallery and a History of West Lothian, as well as a discussion forum. Lothians Family History Society (**www.lothiansfhs.org.uk**) has a discussion forum.

For indexes to monumental inscriptions at Bo'ness, Carriden and Linlithgow visit Memento Mori (**www.memento-mori.co.uk**). The West Lothian Gravestone Photographic Resource Project has various burial sites from the county indexed at **www.gravestonephotos.com/public/area. php?area=West%20Lothian**, namely for Dalmeny, West Calder, Kirkliston, and South Queensferry, with others on the way.

A one-place study for Armadale is available at **www.armadale. org.uk/indexhistory.htm** with historic maps and more. A site on Uphall is also available at **http://uphall.org**, containing the 1841 and 1851 censuses, monumental inscriptions from St Nicholas Kirk, war memorials, and essays on life in the village's past.

Wigtownshire
The Wigtownshire Pages at **http://freepages.history.rootsweb.ancestry. com/~leighann/index.html** include separate vital records indexes from both parish registers and the Wigtownshire Free Press (starting in 1843), a parish map, death registers transcriptions, commissariat records of Wigtown Testaments (1700–1800) and much more. The Internet Archive at **www. archive.org/details/scottishrecordso38scotuoft** hosts the Parish Lists of Wigtownshire and Minnigaff from 1684, as compiled by the Scottish Records Society in 1916.

The 1851 census for the county, and shipping registers for Wigtown (1836–1908), can be consulted at **www.dgcommunity.net/historical**

indexes. The Wigtown Cultural Heritage Project (**www.wigtown-book town.co.uk/heritage/index.asp**) also hosts a list of resources which are available on a local computer database which it states 'will eventually become available on the internet'. A 1912 trade directory for the town is available at **http://homepages.rootsweb.ancestry.com/~scottish/Trade Directory1912. html**.

Dumfries and Galloway Family History Society (**www.dgfhs.org.uk**) has a map of the area from 1862. The website of the Stranraer and District Local History Trust at **www.stranraerhistory.org.uk** also contains lists of recordings in its audio archive and its books on the history of the county.

The Western Isles

The Western Isles never formed a single county historically, but as they formed a culturally distinct geographical community it is in many ways easier to deal with them in a single dedicated section.

Hebridean Connections (**www.hebrideanconnections.com**) provides various resources for the west of the Isle of Lewis, mainly for the small island of Bernera and the districts of Uig, Pairc and Kinloch, whilst the 1841 census for Lochs, Uig, Barvas and Stornoway is at http://tinyurl.com/y8vm5db. Comann Eachdraidh Uig has a blog at www.ceuig.com – amongst its gems is a map of the island, depicting place names in Old Norse, at **www.ceuig. com/archives/4021**. Comainn Eachdraidh Pairc has its own site at **www. cepairc.com** – also for the west, and for the island of St Kilda, visit the Comann Eachdraidh an Taobh Siar site at **www.ceats.org.uk/archive.htm**. Hebridean Archives (**www.cne-siar.gov.uk/archives/collections.asp**) carries school log books for both St Kilda and Mingulay. Graveyards at Dalmore, Kirvick, Sandwick, Stornoway (St Peter's Church), Ness Light House and Rodel (St Callans) on the Isle of Lewis have been recorded and indexed on the Highland Monumental Inscriptions site (**https://sites.google.com/site/ highlandmemorialinscriptions/home**).

Elsewhere on Lewis, visit www.barvasandbrue.com for a 1718 Judicial Rental roll of Nether Barvas, a Barvas School log book from 1899, and an index to articles and photographs in *Fios a'Bhaile*, the newsletter of Comann Eachdraidh Bharabhais agus Bhru. Further resources for Ness to the north of the island are to be found at **www.cenonline.org** and the Angus MacLeod Archive (**www.angusmacleod archive.org.uk**).

If your ancestors were from North Tosta, the local historical society's site (**www.tolsta.info**) has lists of emigrants, famous folk, galleries and a timeline. South of Lewis is Harris, and the Seallam Visitor Centre (**www.**

seallam.com) has details of holdings for the island's family history centre (known as Co Leis Thu). The facility has commenced the release of genealogical records as gathered over many years by locally-based genealogist Bill Lawson on a new subscription-based site called Hebrides People (**www.hebridespeople.com**), which includes an emigrants database.

For the history of Barra, Vatersay, Mingulay, Berneray, Pabbay and Sanday visit **www.barraheritage.com**. Historic images of Berneray are accessible through **www.isleofberneray.com;** for Benbecula visit **www.benbecula historysociety.co.uk.**

The holdings of the Clan Donald Centre at Armadale on Skye are explained at **www.clandonald.com,** whilst Sleat Local History Society's site (**www.sleatlocalhistorysociety.org.uk**) has a Gaelic local place-name index, old photographs and the histories of various townships. Inscriptions from some graves at Struan's municipal cemetery on the island are at **www.**

The ancient broch of Dun Carloway on the Isle of Lewis. Author's collection.

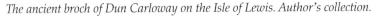

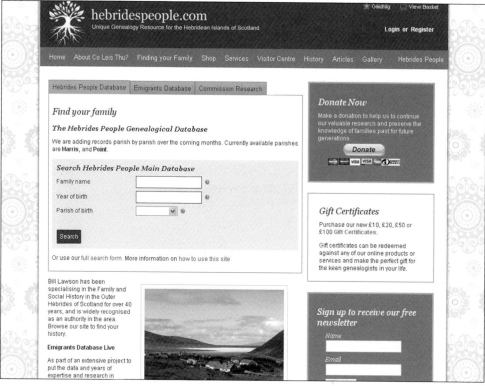

Hebrides People.

gravestonephotos.com/public/cemetery.php?cemetery=232&limit=1. Resources for Elgol and Torrin held by the local historical society are briefly noted at **www.elgolandtorrinhistoricalsociety.org.uk.**

The Isle of Eigg outlines its history at **www.isleofeigg.net,** whilst for Colonsay and Oronsay visit **www.colonsay.info** to find various census extracts, gravestones inscriptions and nineteenth-century parish records. Resources for Coll can be found at **www.collgenealogy.com,** including the censuses, a map, various vital records, lists of emigrant ships and their passengers and old newspaper articles. A similar site for Tiree at **www.tireegenealogy.com** includes overseas cemetery records and material from the Napier Commission into crofting, whilst the history of Muck is explored at **www.islemuck.com/geneal.htm,** accompanied by census transcriptions.

Mull Genealogy (**www.mullgenealogy.co.uk**) has baptism and burial indexes, and a census database for 1841, 1861, 1881 and 1901. There is also a look-up service in the Resources section of the site for books held privately, and some further databases such as rental rolls for the Torloisk estate and deaths in Kilninian. A list of Mull natives who settled in Prince Edward Island, Canada, is online at **www.islandregister.com/mullnatives.html**. The history and genealogy of the island of Lismore is explored at **www. celm.org.uk**, whilst historic images of people from the island in need of identification can be viewed at **www.isleoflismore.com**.

Parish records for Bowmore, Killarow and Kildalton on the island of Islay are online at **http://homepages.rootsweb.ancestry.com/~steve/islay/opr**. A blog-based site for genealogy on Jura is at **www.jurainfo.com/blog/ genealogy/jura-genealogy-trace-your-jura-ancestors**. For the history of Gigha and its MacNeill lairds visit www.gigha.org.uk.

Chapter 7

NORTHERN IRELAND

Despite the great loss of material caused by the Irish Civil War, a great deal of genealogical material for Northern Ireland is still accessible online.

Antrim (and Belfast)

The Glenravel Local History Project (**www.glenravel.com**) has a detailed Belfast timeline from the 1830s to 1941, available across several downloadable PDF files, as well as a history of Milltown cemetery, which can be purchased from the site as an e-book. For a history of Clifton Street Cemetery and a list of burials visit **www.cliftonstreetcemetery.com**, whilst burials in City Cemetery, Dundonald and Roselawn can be freely searched at **www. belfastcity.gov.uk/community/burialrecords/burialrecords.aspx**.

At Belfast Family and Community History (**www.belfastfamilyhistory. com**) you will find many photos of the city in the early twentieth century, rare film footage, an exhibition on Belfast and the 1911 census, and a searchable database of 60,000 people from both the 1901 and 1911 censuses, though this is predominantly for west Belfast. As well as the PRONI websites street directory listings (see p.6), several volunteers offer trade directory look-ups from the twentieth century in the Belfast Forum's *Genealogy* section at **www.belfastforum.co.uk**. Additional directories are available at **www. lennonwylie.co.uk**.

Queens University hosts a Book of Remembrance listing members of the institution and its Officers' Training Corps and Air Squadron who died on active service during the two World Wars at **http://digitalcollections. qub.ac.uk**. The site also carries a collection of personal material from Sir Robert Hart, former Inspector General of the Imperial Customs, Peking, 1863–1908, and the Edward Bunting Collection, which contains material relating to the Belfast Harpers Festival of 1792. The university's project on Poverty and Public Health in Belfast (1800-1973) is also worth visiting at **www.belfastpovhist.com**.

Away from the capital, much of the surviving 1851 census for County

Antrim has been placed online at **www.ulsterancestry.com/ua-free-pages.php**. Bill Macafee's site at **www.billmacafee.com** hosts many resources including local 1766 religious census returns, the 1796 Flaxgrowers' List and more. The Bann Valley Genealogy Church Records site includes details of many records for North Antrim at **www.torrens.org.uk/Genealogy/BannValley/church/contents.html**. Forty-one out of forty-two graveyards from the borough of Ballymena have been placed into an online database on the Braid Museum website at **www.thebraid.com/genealogy.aspx**, with the site also hosting interments for Clough from 1875–1914. For the history of churches in Larne and surrounding area, visit the Larne Historic Church Trail at **http://larnehistoricchurchtrail.co.uk**.

The Glens of Antrim Historical Society has several articles of local interest at **www.antrimhistory.net,** as well as a video tour of the Glens, transcribed returns from projects on clachans and oral history from the area (including Rathlin Island). The Internet Archive is also worth plundering for the north of Antrim (and elsewhere in the county!), with many wonderful resources such as the 1900 book *Songs from the Glens of Antrim* at **http://archive.org/details/songsglensantri00onegoog** and a 1942 book, *The Irish Language in Rathlin Island, Co. Antrim* at **http://archive.org/details/TheIrishLanguageInRathlinIslandCo.Antrim,** which shows how Rathlin's old dialect of Gaelic shared as much in common with Scottish Gaelic (Gàidhlig) as it did Irish (Gaeilge). For my home town of Carrickfergus, where many United Irishmen were jailed, the Internet Archive offers a 1909 publication, *The History and Antiquities of the County of the Town of Carrickfergus, From the Earliest Records till 1839*, at **www.archive.org/details/historyantiquiti00mcskiala**. A First World War Roll of Honour for the town is also available at **http://carrickfergusrollofhonour.blogspot.co.uk**, and historic photos at http://tinyurl.com/pmdsswk.

Many photos from across the Province, including County Antrim, are online at **www.downmemorylane.me.uk.** Ballymoney is covered at **www.ballymoneyancestry.com,** where you will find a map of the area from 1734, a timeline, discussion of famous emigrants, a townlands list and a database of 55,000 records drawn from various sources.

The story of the 1606 pre-Plantation Hamilton and Montgomery-based Scottish settlements of the Lower Clandeboye region of Antrim are explored at **www.hamiltonmontgomery1606.com**.

Armagh

Ireland's ecclesiastical heartland is superbly catered for by Dave Jassie's

The Belfast Timeline, a collection of detailed contemporary newspaper reports from the 1830s to 1941.

County Armagh Research Material Index at **http://freepages.genealogy. rootsweb.ancestry.com/~jassie/armagh/index-page9.html,** which contains databases for directories, newspapers and notices, and births and marriages. A topographical description of the county by Samuel Lewis from 1837 is available at **www.igp-web.com/armagh/index.htm.**

Hearth tax returns for the city from 1665 can be found at **www. failteromhat.com/armaghhearth.php,** whilst the history and heritage of Armagh Observatory is noted at **http://star.arm.ac.uk/history.** A list of Canadian subscribers for the building of Armagh Cathedral in 1857, as well as a list of High Sheriffs for the county from 1714–1857, can be found at **http://homepage.tinet.ie/~jbhall/index.html.**

The 1602 census of Fews barony is recorded at **www.mcconville. org/main/genealogy/census1602.html.** For Armagh tales and detailed pages on the townlands of Creggan visit **www.devlin-family.com,** whilst Creggan History Society's site at **www.creganhistory.co.uk** contains old school photos, directory entries and further townlands descriptions. Some nineteenth-century baptism and marriage records for First and Second Markethill Presbyterian Church can be found at **www.markethill presbyterian.co.uk/genealogy.htm**. Tithe Applotment records for the county, as well as other resources, can be found at **www.connorsgenealogy. net/Armagh**.

Down

The Cross Border Archives Project (**www.louthnewryarchives.ie**) is a great initiative being worked on by Newry and Mourne Museum and Louth County Archives Service. Some interesting pages deal with land holdings in Newry and Mourne and the Encumbered Estates Court. Of particular interest for County Down is Newry and Mourne Museum's online catalogue for its Reside Collection, which includes details on various landed estates' papers collections.

Family Search's Community Trees website at **http://histfam.family search.org/learnmore.php** also hosts an extensive project for the Newry

Belfast City Hall. Author's collection.

area containing extracts from newspapers, diaries, and other resources, as gathered by Francis Crossle and his son Phillip – the collection covers the period from 1600–1919.

Ros Davies' County Down site (**http://freepages.genealogy.rootsweb. ancestry.com/~rosdavies**), Raymond's County Down site (**www.ray mondscountydownwebsite.com**), and the Irish Genealogy Project (**www.igp-web.com/down/index.htm**) all offer many transcribed and free-to-access research resources. Peter Meaney's site at **http://freepages. genealogy.rootsweb.ancestry.com/~meaneypj/** has a section on Down also, containing various gems such as a name index to petty session court reports drawn from the *Belfast Newsletter*. A list of High Sheriffs for the county from 1714–1857 is at **http://homepage.tinet.ie/~jbhall/index.html**.

Down County Museum (**www.downcountymuseum.com**) offers two convicts databases of prisoners transported to Australia, maritime photos and other resources. The Carryduff Historical Society website carries a useful history of the area at **http://carryduffhistoricalsociety.org.uk**. For a 1770 map of Donaghadee and other resources visit **www.donaghadeehistorical society.org.uk**, whilst Donaghmore is catered for by the Internet Archive at **www.archive.org/details/ancientirishpari00cowarich** with the 1914 publication *An Ancient Irish Parish: Past and Present, Being the Parish of Donaghmore, County Down*. The Newry, Donaghmore, Loughbrickland and Banbridge website at **http://tinyurl.com/yfuuqe3** carries a list of landowners from 1876 and other resources, though many links are broken. For material concerning the Lecale peninsula, including a detailed lists of shipwrecks off the County Down coast, visit **www.lecalehistory.co.uk/ resources.htm**. Again, for the story of the Scottish settlements in County Down during the 1606 pre-Plantation Hamilton and Montgomery scheme, visit **www.hamiltonmontgomery1606.com**.

The history of Drumaroad and Clanvaraghan is detailed at **www.drum aroadhistory.com**, and Poyntpass at **www.poyntzpass.co.uk**. The Old Strabane Blog at **http://oldstrabane.blogspot.co.uk** has various resources including several old maps overlaid onto Google Maps, and a hefty data archive. Lisburn Historical Society's site (**www.lisburn.com/books/ historical_society/historicalsociety.html**) carries back issues of its journal from 1978–2005/6, which can be read for free.

Fermanagh

The Irish Genealogy Project's Fermanagh pages at **www.igp-web. com/fermanagh** contain many directories, maps, videos, estate records and more, whilst many additional resources and census substitutes can be accessed at **www.rootsweb.ancestry.com/~fianna/county/fermanagh /fer-1.html**. The Northern Ireland Genweb page for Fermanagh is equally packed at **www.rootsweb.ancestry.com/~nirfer** with lists of settlers from the 1610 plantations, muster rolls, freeholder lists, parish records, maps, tithes applotment records and much more. A list of electors from Fermanagh in 1788 can be found at **http://tinyurl.com/fermanagh1788**.

For over a thousand images of gravestones from across the county visit **www.tammymitchell.com/cofermanagh**, whilst Monaghan-based Clogher Historical Society's 'Record Index' has many resources for Fermanagh also at **www.clogherhistory.ie**.

On the Internet Archive at **www.archive.org** you will find several titles on Fermanagh, including *Parliamentary Memoirs of Fermanagh and Tyrone, from 1613 to 1885* (1887) and the two-volume *The History of Enniskillen with Reference to some Manors in Co. Fermanagh, and other Local Subjects* (1919).

Londonderry

PRONI hosts the digitised Londonderry Corporation Records, as sourced from both the national repository and Derry City Council Archive. The collection includes Corporation minute books from 1673–1901, as well as records of the Freemen of Derry from 1675–1945. PRONI also carries the *New Directory of the City of Londonderry and Coleraine, including Strabane with Lifford, Newtownlimavady, Portstewart and Portrush* in its Street Directories section.

Bill McAfee's site (**www.billmacafee.com**) offers a range of gems in both Microsoft Excel and PDF formats, including databases on the surviving 1831 census for County Londonderry, the 1740 Protestant Householders' Returns for the county, seventeenth-century subsidy and muster rolls, and an 1832 Townland Survey for Derry City (arranged alphabetically by street).

Discover Ever After (**www.discovereverafter.com**) has many graveyards photographed and indexed for the county. The Irish Genealogy Project pages at **www.igp-web.com/derry/index.htm** have many resources for Derry including databases such as the Flax Growers List from 1796. The Bann Valley Genealogy Church records site includes details of many records at **www.torrens.org.uk/Genealogy/BannValley/church/contents.html**.

George McIntyre's history of Drumlamph townland project (**http:// georgemcintyre.tripod.com**) includes details on the war memorial for Castledawson, and names of many people from Bellaghy Town from the 1860s to 1930s. A blog-based resource for the history of Killowen is at **www.**

The Street Directories platform on the PRONI website.

killowenhistory.com/wordpress, whilst a database of nineteenth-century Roman Catholic baptisms and marriages from Lavey is available at **www. laveyparish.com.** The Coleraine Historical Society offers a history and many historic images at **www.colerainehistoricalsociety.co.uk,** as well as details of articles published within its various journals. For burials in Glendermott Old Cemetery (mixed denominations) visit **http://members.webone.com. au/~sgrieves/cemeteries_ireland_2.htm.**

Tyrone

The County Tyrone Website at **www.cotyroneireland.com/index.html** has an excellent collection of resources, including various church records, maps, Griffith's Valuation, schools records and more. Ulster Ancestry (**www. ulsterancestry.com**) has various offerings, from an undated rent book for Strabane and land grants in 1610 to several religious census transcripts and substitutes. Although based just over the border, the Monaghan-based

Clogher Historical Society's Record Index at **www.clogherhistory.ie** also has many resources for Tyrone.

The County Tyrone Gravestone Project (**www.tammymitchell.com/ cotyrone**) carries over 1,100 gravestone photos from across the county, whilst some burials within cemeteries in Cappagh, Dumnakilly and Omagh can also be identified at **www.gravestonephotos.com/public/area.php? area=Tyrone&country=Ir**. Monumental inscriptions for Leckpatrick Old Presbyterian Cemetery in Strabane can be located at **http://members. webone.com.au/~sgrieves/cemetries_ireland.htm**.

A summary of the *Ecclesiastical Census of Clogherny* (1851–52) can be read at **www.localpopulationstudies.org.uk/PDF/LPS29/LPS29_1982_35- 49.pdf**. The history of Bready is discussed at **www.breadyancestry.com**, with the site including a townland map, and sections on Ulster Scots heritage, historical maps, and databases of 30,000 names derived from several sources.

Killeeshil and Clonaneese Historical Society has an archive with rent rolls, census returns and more at **http://killeeshilclonaneese.org/joomla**, whilst Glenelly Historical Society (**www.glenellyhistorical.org.uk**) has essays on the Great Glenelly Flood of 1680, the Plumbridge Water Scheme and other useful local articles. For the contents of past issues of Stewartstown & District Local History Society's journal *The Bell* visit **www.stewartstown history. co.uk**.

Chapter 8

CROWN DEPENDENCIES AND OVERSEAS TERRITORIES

In addition to the main counties of the United Kingdom, two important island-based communities also exist in the British Isles with their own regional identities and languages. These are the Crown Dependencies of the Channel Islands, close to the Normandy Coast, and the Isle of Man, at the heart of the Irish Sea.

Slightly further afield are the British Overseas Territories of Gibraltar and the Falkland Islands. For a concise overview of all such territories (of which there are fourteen at present), visit **http://en.wikipedia.org/wiki/British_ Overseas_Territories** and **https://familysearch.org/learn/wiki/en/ British _Overseas_Territories**.

The Channel Islands (Les Îsles de la Manche or Les Isles Anglo-Normandes)

A series of old maps depicting the Channel Islands can be found via Genmaps at **http://tinyurl.com/ybmmok3**, whilst old postcards of Jersey, Guernsey, Alderney, Sark and Herm are accessible through a series of interactive maps at **www.cipostcard.co.nz**.

A broad history of the region is available on the Island Life website (**www.islandlife.org/history.htm**), with a dedicated section for each island. For general resources, the Channel Islands are represented on GENUKI at **http://chi.genuki.weald.org.uk/**. Additional resources are freely available at **https://sites.google.com/site/channelislandsfreeancestry**.

Jersey's heritage can be explored at **www.jerseyheritage.org**, whilst the island's family history society lists details of its past journals from 2004 to the present day at **www.jerseyfamilyhistory.org/journal**. The Société Jersiaise (**www.societe-jersiaise.org**) has both library and photographic archive catalogues.

The Genealogist website carries a newspaper called the *Channel Isles Monthly Review*, which helped to keep many ex-residents of the Channel

Islands up to date with births, marriages and deaths, and other stories, during the German occupation of the Channel Islands in the Second World War. For a history of the Channel Islands and the Great War, visit **www.great warci.net**.

The Isle of Man (Ellan Vannin)

There are four vital records collections found within the UK and Ireland pages of the FamilySearch website, covering deaths and burials (1844–1911), births and baptisms (1821–1911), marriages (1849–1911) and a general database on parish registers (1598–1950). The Irish Archives Resource website at **www.iar.ie** has a catalogue entry for papers from the Isle of Man Jesuit mission from Ireland from 1825–1849 (the original records are held at the Irish Jesuit Archives).

Information about civil registration, probate and land registration for Man is available from the Manx Government at **www.gov.im/registries**. For heritage issues, visit the Manx National Heritage site at **www.manxnational heritage.im/**. Amongst its offerings is its impressive 'iMuseum' at **www. imuseum.im** which includes the Manx Newspapers 1792–1960 subscription service, and a Family History section that allows for a search of the island's censuses, vital records collections and other datasets.

Useful genealogical resources are listed at **www.ukisearch.com/isleof man.html**, whilst discussion forums are hosted by the Isle of Man Family History Society at **www.iomfhs.im**, with the site also carrying a photo gallery of images from across the island. A map of Man's seventeen parishes is online at **www.isleofman.com/places/parishes**, along with other resources such as a look-up exchange, message boards and some family GEDCOM files.

Manorial rent rolls from 1540 for several parishes can be found at **www.manxroots.info**, whilst Frances Coakley's A Manx Note Book site (**www.isle-of-man.com/manxnotebook**) hosts a packed compendium of essays and resources relating to the island. For all matters Manx Gaelic (Gaelg), the Scottish-based college Sabhal Mor Ostaig has a portal for the language, which is related to Scots Gaelic and Irish, at **www.smo.uhi .ac.uk/liosta/gaelg/**. Additional free resources for the island can be found at **https://sites.google.com/site/isleofmanfreeancestry**, whilst the Internet Archive hosts a copy of 'The Surnames & Place-names of the Isle of Man' from 1890 at **http://archive.org/details/surnamesplacenam00mooruoft**.

If your ancestors migrated to the US, check out the North American Manx Association blog at **http://namanx.blogspot.co.uk**.

Gibraltar

For the gateway to the Mediterranean, Gibraltar Genealogy (**www.gibraltar genealogy.com**) is a useful first port of call, whilst the British Library has information on its Gibraltar Collections at **www.bl.uk/reshelp/findhelp region/europe/gibraltar/gibraltarcoll/gibcol.html**.

FamilySearch (see p.4) also hosts birth records from 1704–1876 and marriages from 1879–1918.

The Falklands

For the histories of several families on the Falkland Islands visit **http:// stewartreid.tribalpages.com**.

The Falkland Islands Museum and National Trust **www.falklands-museum.com** has various essays on aspects of its history, including the two world wars and the 1982 Argentine invasion and war.

Chapter 9

EMPIRE AND MIGRATION

As an island, Britain has seen its fair share of migrants coming and going across the centuries, and this chapter examines many of the records that can help to trace their progress.

Immigration

One of the best websites for dealing with the subject of migration into Britain is Moving Here (**www.movinghere.org.uk**), with many resources on the history from the last two centuries of people arriving from the Caribbean and South Asia, as well as the Irish and Jews. Not only does the site host timelines and topical essays concerning the history of each group, it also provides handy family history research guides covering a range of subjects. It also hosts many genealogical resources, such as digitised images of crew lists for vessels sailing from Calcutta to London in the 1820s, photographs of Jewish children arriving in Britain on the Kindertransport, and maps of old Irish poor law unions.

Stories of persecution feature heavily amongst groups who have settled in Britain, and many have sought to preserve their histories online. French protestant Huguenots were one such group who started to settle in Britain in the late seventeenth century, and there are several resources that can help to establish your Huguenot ancestry. These include the website of the Huguenot Society of Great Britain and Ireland (**www.huguenotsociety. org.uk**) and the Huguenot Surnames Index (**http://huguenot.netnation. com**), which allows you to contact other families with proven lineages back to France.

A useful resource for children who fled Nazi Germany, Austria, Poland and Czechoslovakia on the Kindertransports between December 1938 and the start of the Second World War, is the Kindertransport Association site (**www.kindertransport.org**). Ancestry has also added a number of databases to its site detailing many who fled from Nazi persecution, and those who were less fortunate. For resources on how to trace Jewish families within the British Isles, see p.23.

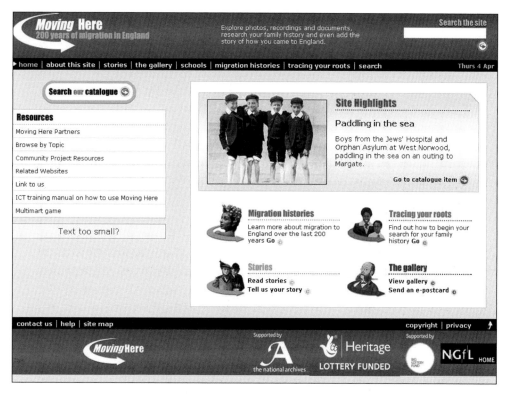

The Moving Here website.

A key problem for many is to work out exactly where our ancestors first originated. The census records from 1841–1911 can be useful in identifying a country of origin (more specifically from 1851 onwards), but it is worth noting that countries as identified today may not be the same as recorded 150 years ago – for example, a person noted as being from 'Russia' may in fact be from what is now called Poland. Naturalisation papers may also help, and TNA has a helpful guide on such records at **www.nationalarchives.gov.uk/records/research-guides/immigrants.htm**. The *England, Alien Arrivals 1810–1811, 1826–1869* collection on Ancestry is sourced from many lists compiled by the Home Office, Foreign Office and Customs records as held at TNA (FO 83/21-22, HO 2, HO 3, CUST 102/393-396), and names many settlers arriving in Britain. TNA has itself catalogued some 300,000 naturalisation records as held in its Home Office HO334 and HO409 collections. The Genealogist website has also made available a 'British naturalisation' database covering the years 1609–1960, whilst announcements on naturalisation can also be sourced via *The London Gazette* at **www.**

gazettes-online.co.uk. FindmyPast has the Manchester Naturalisation Society collection with details on 542 people who naturalised from 1896–1909, including many Jewish immigrants.

Records of an immigrant ancestor's original voyage to the UK can also provide further clues. Ancestry's UK Incoming Passenger Lists 1872–1960 database contains passenger records held by TNA as part of its Board of Trade records series (BT 26), but does not list voyages from Europe or the Mediterranean, and is incomplete prior to 1890. Where an entry can be found, however, the original manifest can be viewed, providing information such as names, ages, occupations, ports and dates of departure and arrival, vessel name and the shipping line, not to mention the details of other members of the family who may have travelled with your ancestor.

As various migrant groups arrived and settled in Britain, they established their own churches and kept their own registers. Many records for Russian Orthodox, French, Dutch, Swiss and German congregations which settled in London will be found in the Nonconformist record collections at The Genealogist website or at **www.bmdregisters.co.uk**.

The Port Cities website at **www.portcities.org.uk** provides a great deal of information on the maritime history of Bristol, Hartlepool, Liverpool, London and Southampton, and has a great deal of material on the lives of workers from ethnic communities who worked in these ports, as well as a substantial section on the history of slavery within the pages for Bristol.

For the most ethnically diverse part of the country, the Untold London website (**www.untoldlondon.org.uk**) provides a great deal of information on the various communities to have settled in the capital, with links to many exciting projects, such as that recording recent Kurdish history in London, the community having arrived en masse some twenty years ago, and today believed to number over 50,000 people. In Scotland, a useful site for the Italian migrants who settled is the Scots Italian project at **www.scots italian.com**.

If your ancestor is from an African or Caribbean background it is worth consulting TNA's online exhibition entitled *Black Presence: Asian and Black History in Britain 1500–1850* at **www.nationalarchives.gov.uk/pathways/ blackhistory**. The Caribbean Surname Index is another worthwhile site at **www.candoo.com/surnames**, which is a discussion forum-based facility that can allow you to share material with others who may be familiar with your particular ancestor. For Birmingham, a useful site on black history can be found at **www.bbohp.org.uk**, whilst a similar site for Bright and Hove's Asian and black communities is **www.black-history.org.uk**. The CASBAH website (**www.casbah.ac.uk**) provides a portal to many links for those researching Caribbean, Black and Asian peoples in the UK.

Emigration

The British Empire was first founded in the late sixteenth century and reached its zenith towards the end of the nineteenth century, before ending in the mid-twentieth century. The Royal Commonwealth Society has a massive library of resources for both the Empire and the Commonwealth, and its online catalogue at **www.lib.cam.ac.uk/deptserv/rcs** also has details of over 300,000 holdings, including books, pamphlets, periodicals, official publications, manuscripts and photographs. TNA further provides a detailed guide to the empire at **www.nationalarchives.gov.uk/education/empire-industry.htm**, and has also recently taken possession of the Foreign and Commonwealth Office's Migrated Records collections (see **www.national archives.gov.uk/about/colonial-administration-records.htm**). For the later period into the twentieth century, the outward-bound passenger manifests of journeys made from Britain and Ireland between 1890 and 1960 can be found at both **www.ancestorsonboard.com** and FindmyPast, recording some 24 million passengers from TNA's BT 27 series. The same collection is also accessible on Ancestry.

One of the empire's darker legacies was the ownership of slaves by British folk. University College London's Legacies of British Slave-Ownership site is freely accessible at **www.ucl.ac.uk/lbs**.

The following sections detail some of the resources from overseas countries which may also help with your research.

Canada

The Library and Archives Canada site (**www.collectionscanada.gc.ca**) contains many wonderful resources and indexes, such as the censuses, records for the military and migration to the country, and various online guides to help with your Canadian research. The Canadian Gazette is also available from 1998 to the present at **www.collectionscanada.gc.ca/databases/canada-gazette/index-e.html**. Ancestry also has many migration and naturalisation records, accessible through a worldwide subscription. These include Canadian Passenger Lists from 1865–1935 and Form 30A Ocean Arrivals immigration forms from 1919–24, available via a worldwide subscription package on the site. FamilySearch has a considerable range of records freely available from each of the main provinces, including several national censuses, vital records, probate material, deeds indexes and more.

For Ontario, the Upper Canada Genealogy site at **www.uppercanada genealogy.com** includes indexes to many records collections, whilst the Archives of Manitoba site at **www.gov.mb.ca/chc/archives** has several guides and catalogues including information on how to access the Hudson's Bay Company Archive. The Newfoundland's Grand Banks project at **http://ngb.chebucto.org** hosts many historic articles, passenger lists, directories, vital records, censuses, parish records and more.

Additional Canadian passenger lists can also be found at the Ships Lists site (**www.theshipslist.com**), which also covers the USA, Australia and South Africa. Finally, many Canadian history resources can be found in both English and French at **www.ourroots.ca**.

USA

A general gateway site for United States resources is the US GenWeb site at **www.rootsweb.ancestry.com/usgenweb**. The Library of Congress Online Catalog at **http://catalog.loc.gov** can help to source many American publications, photos and media of interest, whilst the National Archives site at **www.archives.gov** has a great deal of guides and resources on its site for genealogical research. For a list of state archives, visit **www.archives.gov /research/alic/reference/state-archives.html**, whilst a guide to state historical societies is found at **www. stenseth.org/us/statehs.html**. The Digital Public Library of America at **http://dp.la** provides free access to various useful resources from libraries, archives and museums across the country.

From 1892 to 1954, the federal immigration centre at Ellis Island was the main port of entry for immigrants, and digitised passenger lists for all vessels which docked there can be viewed at **www.ellisisland.org**. Prior to 1892, many who came to the States passed through Castle Garden, the nation's first official immigration centre. From 1820–92 some 11 million immigrants went through its doors, and their details can be found at **www.castle garden.org**. Further migration resources including a database of Irish immigrants who arrived from 1846–51 during the famine, naturalisation records, federal and state census records and more can be found at Ancestry, via its world subscription package. The United States Citizenship and Immigration Services also has a History and Genealogy section on its site at **www.uscis.gov**.

For earlier settlers, the Virtual Jamestown project (**www.virtualjames town.org**), commemorating America's first British colony in Virginia, has many databases such as lists of those present on indentures, court records and more. Price and Associates can also help at **www.pricegen.com** with an

Immigrant Servants database in its Resources section listing over 20,000 indentures for servants, redemptioners, and transported convicts between 1607 and 1820. For a database of Welsh Mormon immigrants, and additional resources on their emigration and settlement, visit **http://welshmormon.byu.edu**.

Many historic American newspapers have been digitised and made available online, with both Google News and My Heritage containing substantial collections. Current and historical maps from the US Geological Survey from 1884–2009 are available at **www.usgs.gov**. For access to free census transcripts visit **www.us-census.org** and the US GenWeb project at **www.usgenweb.org**.

Jamaica and the Caribbean

The Registrar General of Jamaica's site at **www.rgd.gov.jm** has information on how to apply for vital records, whilst the Jamaica Archives and Records Department has an online presence at **www.jard.gov.jm**. For the British Library's guide to Caribbean holdings, visit **www.bl.uk/reshelp/findhel pregion/americas/caribbean**.

The National Library of Jamaica has many digital collections online at **www.nlj.gov.jm**, including A Commemoration of the Abolition of the Slave Trade in the West Indies bibliography and Jamaica Unshackled, containing digitised documents and images for the 1831 Sam Sharpe rebellion, the 1865 Morant Bay Rebellion and the 1938 Labour Riots. FamilySearch hosts Jamaican births and baptisms from 1752–1920, whilst for the Caribbean in general it has births (1590–1928), marriages (1591–1905 and deaths (1790–1906).

Guy Grannum has created a useful section on the Moving Here website for tracing Caribbean ancestors at **www.moving here.org.uk/galleries/ roots/caribbean/caribbean.htm**. A guide to various holdings of archives in the Caribbean is provided at **www. heritagedocs.org**. Further gateway sites for Caribbean resources include Caribbean Roots (**www.caribbeanroots. co.uk**), the Caribbean Genweb Project (**www.rootsweb.ancestry. com/~caribgw**) and the Caribbean Genealogy Research site at **www. candoo.com/genresources**.

South America

The British Settlers in Argentina and Uruguay site at **www.argbrit.org** has many records online including baptisms, marriages, deaths and burials from the Anglican and Scots Presbyterian churches, transcripts from the National Archives in Buenos Aires and London, and returns from the Argentinean censuses.

The story of the Welsh in Patagonia, Argentina, is recalled at both **www. welshpatagonia.com** and the excellent Glaniad website at **www.glaniad. com,** whilst for Scots in Patagonia visit **http://myweb.tiscali.co.uk/scots inargpat**.

For a Dictionary of Irish Latin American Biography, and other resources, visit **www.irlandeses.org/bios1.htm**.

Australia
The National Archives of Australia (**www.naa.gov.au**) site has various resources and guides to family history including a name search feature that allows you to search for records of immigration. For a list of stowaways into Sydney from 1856–1877, visit **www.genebug.net/stowaways.html**.

The National Library of Australia site hosts a detailed web guide at **www. nla.gov.au/family-history/genealogy-selected-websites** for all Australian state libraries and archives, as well as vital records access, cemeteries databases, convicts databases, military service and other useful repositories. The library's impressive *Trove* facility (**http://trove.nla.gov.au**) is also well worth searching, containing millions of digitised records, including its superb Australian Newspapers collection, with free-to-access and fully searchable titles for the continent from 1803–1954 (and the *Australian Women's Weekly* up to 1982). The Ryerson Index (**www.ryerson index.org**) has a database of almost two and a half million death notices as extracted from contemporary newspapers.

The Australian Family History compendium site at **http://afhc. cohsoft.com.au** has guides for many useful records, institutions and genealogical vendors. The Sydney-based Society of Australian Genealogists (**www.sag.org.au**) also has various online research guides covering everything from adoptions in New South Wales to Ships and Voyages. The Australian Dictionary of National Biography can be consulted at **http:// adb.anu.edu.au**.

Convict ancestors tend to be a badge of honour Down Under these days and the Convicts to Australia site (**www.convictcentral.com**) provides a guide to researching your ancestral felons. Additional resources for convicts can also be found on The Genealogist and Ancestry. The Irish Famine Memorial site (**www.irishfaminememorial.org**) commemorates those who sailed down under from 1848–50 to escape the disaster – it includes a database listing orphan girls who were sent from Ireland's workhouses.

FindmyPast Australasia (**www.findmypast.com.au**) also has many unique offerings which can also be accessed through the British and Irish FindmyPast platforms via a worldwide subscription.

Finally, Unlock the Past is a major genealogical vendor for Australasia, with a large publishing programme, history and genealogy cruises, and expos across the continent – its offerings can be explored at **http://unlock thepast.com.au**.

New Zealand

The New Zealand Society of Genealogists site at **www.genealogy.org.nz** contains a First Families Index and many other useful resources which can help you to pursue the earliest migrants to the country. Pearl's Pad (**http://pearlspad.net.nz**) equally has many historical resources for tracing migration.

The New Zealand Government has a Births, Deaths and Marriages Online site at **www.bdmonline.dia.govt.nz,** which provides indexes for historical vital events, namely births prior to 100 years ago, marriages prior to eighty years ago and deaths prior to fifty years ago (or at least for those with a date of birth at least eighty years ago). FamilySearch has probate record images for the country from 1860–1962, as well as immigration passenger lists from 1855–1973.

Archives New Zealand has a catalogue on its site at **www.archway. archives.govt.nz** and includes access to details of New Zealand Defence Force records, some of which are digitised. The New Zealand History Online site at **www.nzhistory.net.nz** includes a war memorials register with some 450 sites listed.

Other resources to help you trace your New Zealand kin include the Papers Past website (**http://paperspast.natlib.govt.nz**) with digitised copies of seventy-seven newspaper titles from 1839–1945, whilst Victoria University's New Zealand Electronic Text Centre at **http://nzetc.victoria. ac.nz** has many transcribed entries from books and other resources. For the Dictionary of New Zealand Biography, with some 3,000 biographical entries, visit **www.teara.govt.nz/en/biographies**. The Otago Settlers Museum website at **www.otago.settlers.museum** hosts guides to both shipping lists and genealogical resources held within its archive. Further resources for Otago and the Southlands can be explored through **www.otago.ac.nz/ library** and **http://otago.ourheritage.ac.nz/**.

Africa

The South African National Archives and Records Service has many online databases at **www.national.archives.gov.za** for gravestones, heraldry, documentary archives, audio visual material and more. For early British migrants the British 1820 Settlers to South Africa site (**www.1820settlers. com**) carries many compiled genealogies, ships' lists and other resources, whilst the South African genealogy site (**www.sagenealogy. co.za**) includes a data archive with passenger lists and wrecks survivors, and operates a useful blog at **www.southafricangenealogy.blogspot. com**. At the time of writing the immensely useful data site Ancestry 24 (**http://ancestry24.com**) had just announced that it was closing, but that its data was to be relocated to a good home. If your ancestors resided in Ghana, the Gold Coast of Africa site at **http://gcdb.doortmontweb.org/index.php** is worth visiting for various resources, although the site has a strong Dutch bias.

China and Malaysia

The Chinese Maritime Customs Project at **www.bristol.ac.uk/history/ customs/ancestors/shanghai.html** has many resources concerning the cities of Hong Kong and Shanghai, as well as many northern ports. In particular, a page at **www.bris.ac.uk/history/customs/ancestors/directories. html** carries trade directories in English listing western inhabitants from 1842 to 1921. If your ancestors resided in Hong Kong, also visit the Gwulo: Old Hong Kong site at **http://gwulo.com** for a range of resources.

A useful free newspaper resource for Singapore and Malaya, including the former British Straits settlements on the Malay peninsula, is available from the National Library of Singapore at **http://newspapers.nl.sg**. Searches can be performed in English.

India

The first port of call for Indian research is the Families in British India Society site at **www.new.fibis.org**, which includes listings from cemeteries, directories, military records, photographs, publications, schools, probate indexes, vital and parish records and more. The group also has a YouTube channel at **www.youtube.com/user/fibisweb master**. The British Library's India Office Family History Search index at **http://indiafamily.bl.uk/UI** also lists some 300,000 vital records. At the time of writing FindmyPast is digitising many of the British Library's Indian records for release on its site later in 2013. Many vital records are also available in indexed form on FamilySearch, within its Asia and Middle East section.

For burials in India there are two useful projects, the British burials in India site at **www.indian-cemeteries.org,** and the British Association for Cemeteries in South Asia site at **www.bacsa.org.uk,** which carries an index to cemetery inscriptions in areas previously occupied by the East India Company. Almost 300 films depicting life in the final years of the British Raj in India have been placed online by the Centre for South Asian Studies at Cambridge University at **www.s-asian.cam.ac.uk/archome.html**.

The Digital Library of India (**www.new.dli.ernet.in**) has transcribed texts from several publications including many on British subjects in India, whilst the *Indiaman* magazine can be subscribed to online at **www.indiaman.com**. For Anglo-Indian connections visit **www.anglo-indians.com** to find a database of Famous Anglos and a detailed history.

The Moving Here website also hosts a guide at **www.movinghere. org.uk/galleries/roots/asian/asian.htm,** written by Abi Husaini, for tracing ancestors in the south of Asia. For ancestors in Sri Lanka, the International Ceylon database (**www.ceylondatabase.net/Genealogy.html**) may help.

Chapter 10

SOCIAL NETWORKING

The world of social networking is increasingly changing the way that we can collaborate and communicate with each other in our pursuit of ancestral knowledge. We can talk to one another online face-to-face or via text-based interfaces, share digitised resources, upload family trees to a community site to attract others to our research, or study online family history courses from the comfort of our own homes.

Building Family Trees

Most of the commercial record vendors offer family tree-building programmes on their sites, such as Ancestry, FindmyPast, The Genealogist and My Heritage, usually for free, with which you can integrate findings from their collections. Increasingly vendors are offering the option of being able to synchronise the tree that you are working on via your PC with an equivalent on an iPad or Android-based device. Ancestry, for example, allows you to make corrections to your online tree through a software programme called Family Tree Maker, which can be purchased and downloaded from **www.familytreemaker.com**. Its 'TreeSync' capability essentially allows the data from the PC to be uploaded to your cloud-based account every time you wish to update it. Some dedicated tree programme suppliers also make basic offerings for free. Heredis (**www.heredis.com**) offers an ability to host a tree on both a tablet and a PC or Mac at the same time – it is free to download, but at the time of writing syncing trees had to be done by importing your updated tree via email to your tablet, or by accessing it from a cloud-based storage site such as Dropbox. Legacy Family Tree (**www. legacyfamilytree.com**) is another popular free tree-building programme, which also provides a webinar service of online-based genealogy lectures (via a subscription service), with a popular following.

Several dedicated platforms allow you to upload and host a tree online, and to use such a tree as a means to generate further research. In addition to those listed above, Tribal Pages (**www.tribalpages.com**) is one such site where you can freely create a tree from scratch online. You can search in other people's trees for possible connections, and contact them if you find a match through an internal email system for members. GenesReunited (**www. genesreunited.com**) works in a similar manner, by allowing such trees to facilitate contact between descendants of the same individuals, or to post queries to establish if there is a connection in the first place.

DNA-based projects are also on the increase, with the market leader being Family Tree DNA (**www.familytreedna.com**). By testing Y-chromosome DNA (males only), profile results are generated which can be input into a database (surname or geographical) to enable genetic matches. Other tests include mitochondrial testing, or mtDNA, for tracing back on the maternal line only, and autosomal DNA, for DNA shared by both males and females, to find cousin connections within a handful of recent generations. Several projects exist, such as the Scottish DNA Project (**www. scottishdna.net**), as well as specific surname projects run by members of the Guild of One Name Studies (**www.one-name.org**), amongst others.

Located at **http://familyhistory.hhs.gov**, the US-based My Family Health Portrait site encourages people to create a form of family tree diagram known as a 'genogram', used by many within the medical profession, which specifically illustrates your family health history. GenoPro (**www. genopro. com/genogram**) is another US-based site that takes the concept of genograms much further, with a site for which you will literally need to relearn the language of family tree construction.

Other networks

Using a family tree to form the basis of a social network is one way to share information, but it is by no means the only method. Ancestral Atlas (**www. ancestralatlas.com**), for example, uses a map as its starting point. The service allows you to tag a location with a note concerning a historic event that took place there, and to view the tags placed by others in the same area. If a vital event of interest, for example, is noted on a tag on the same street where your ancestor lived, you could contact the person who placed it online for further information. The site also has additional features such as access to historic maps for the same area in question, and is subscription-based, with the most basic level being free-to-access.

Sticking on the geographic theme, Curious Fox (**www.curiousfox.com**) foregoes the maps as a connecting route, and instead forges connections by village or town names, allowing you to look up a place and to see if there are any posts for that location which tie in to your research. Lost Cousins (www.lostcousins.com) is another site which allows you to form connections, in this case with the descendants of people named in census entries that you submit to the site, so long as they too are registered and have entered the same details. The censuses it bases its network on include 1841 and 1881 for England and Wales, 1881 for Scotland and 1911 for Ireland.

Chat

The internet is increasingly becoming a useful forum to talk to other researchers face-to-face, through free platforms such as Skype (**www.nskype.com**), or FaceTime (**www.apple.com/uk/ios/facetime**) for Apple-based devices such as iPads and iPods. All you need is a webcam, a good pair of headphones and a reasonable broadband speed.

Discussion forums can also be of immense help for your research. Rootschat (**www.rootschat.com**), British Genealogy (**www.british-genealogy.com**) and Talking Scot (**www.talkingscot.com**) are just some of the many independent sites that provide thread-based discussion on a country, county or subject-defined basis. Some genealogy magazines provide forums, such as *Your Family Tree* (**www.yourfamilytreemag.co.uk/yft-forum**), *Family Tree* magazine (**www.family-tree.co.uk/Family-Tree- Magazine-Forum**) and *Who Do You Think You Are?* magazine (**www.whodo youthinkyouaremagazine.com/forum**), which provide for a degree of interactivity between the readers and with the editorial teams. Ancestry also provides the excellent Rootsweb site (**www.rootsweb.ancestry.com**) which hosts message boards and mailing lists which work in a similar way.

Genealogy Wise (**www.genealogywise.com**) hosts many dedicated research groups for names, or territories or interests, chat rooms and discussion forums, blogs, a video room and more, whilst dedicated social networking sites such as Facebook (**www.facebook.com**) and Google Plus (**http://plus.google.com**) are increasingly hosting specific community sites for genealogy enthusiasts.

Interactive community archives are also on the increase, with sites such as StoryVault (**www.storyvault.com**) hosting an archive of stories submitted by people from all over the world, in video or text format, with an online family tree capability. One type of project mentioned in the previous edition of this work – the life vault type of site where you can store memories for all eternity – is perhaps something to be somewhat more cautious of some three years later. A few, such as Arcalife, a life vault company launched in 2008 and cited in the previous edition of this book, simply came and went.

Blogs

Blogs are an incredibly useful way to share news or research, allowing you to post or read updates in a diary format on a regular basis.

Many sites offer the ability to create a blog for free, such as Blogger (**www.blogger.com**) and WordPress (**http://wordpress.org**), and there are many dedicated genealogy blogs around to keep you aware of developments in the big wide family history world. My own British GENES (Genealogy News and EventS) blog at **www.britishgenes.blogspot.co.uk**, for example, is built using Blogger, Alan Stewart's excellent Grow Your Own Family Tree news blog (**http://growyourownfamilytree.wordpress.com**) employs WordPress, whilst Dick Eastman's Online Genealogy Newsletter (**http://blog.eogn.com**) provides an American perspective on many British and Irish events. Claire Santry's Irish Genealogy News (**www.irish-genealogy-news.blogspot.ie**) is also worth adding to your daily reading fare, as is John Reid's

Keep up to date with all the latest British Isles genealogy news on the author's British GENES blog.

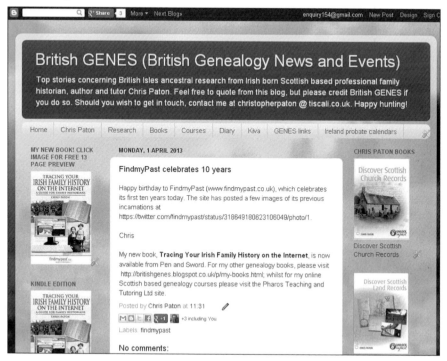

Ontario-based Anglo-Celtic-Connections (**www.anglo-celtic-connections. blogspot.ca**). Useful directory sites providing links to many genealogy blogs include Geneabloggers (**www.geneabloggers.com**) and Alltop (**http:// genealogy.alltop.com**).

Many genealogy vendors also blog regularly to communicate their latest developments, such as FindmyPast (**http://blog.findmypast.co.uk**) and Ancestry (**http://blogs.ancestry.com/uk**). Family Search also blogs updates at **https://familysearch.org/blog/en/**.

Twitter

The free-to-access Twitter site (**http://twitter.com**) allows people to leave short status messages, or 'tweets', of up to 140 characters in length only, providing for a quick update on the status of those you may wish to follow, perhaps a historian or genealogical records supplier. In many cases posters will give a quick message and provide a link to a website to follow up the story discussed, making it an effective way to stay on top of developments.

You can follow people anonymously – for example, for news of further offerings from Pen and Sword you can follow **@penswordbooks**, and for yours truly **@chrismpaton** and block those you do not wish to follow you.

FURTHER READING

BACKHURST, Marie-Louise (2011) *Tracing Your Channel Islands Ancestors.* Barnsley, Pen and Sword Books Ltd

CLARKE, Tristram (2011), *Tracing Your Scottish Ancestors – The Official Guide* (6th ed.) Edinburgh, Birlinn Ltd

FOWLER, Simon (2013) *Tracing Your Army Ancestors*, (2nd ed.) Barnsley, Pen and Sword Books Ltd

FOX-DAVIES, Arthur (1978) *A Complete Guide to Heraldry.* New York, Bonanza Books

GRANUM, Karen, & TAYLOR, Nigel (2004) *Wills and Other Probate Records.* London, The National Archives

GRENHAM, John (2012) *Tracing Your Irish Ancestors.* Dublin, Gill and MacMillan Ltd

HERBER, Mark (2005) *Ancestral Trails.* Sparkford, Sutton Publishing Ltd

HIGGS, Edward (2005) *Making Sense of the Census Revisited.* London, Institute of Historical Research/National Archives

MASTERS, Charles (2009) *Essential Maps for Family Historians.* Newbury, Countryside Books

MAXWELL, Ian (2010) *Tracing Your Northern Irish Ancestors.* Barnsley, Pen and Sword Books Ltd

PATON, Chris (2012) *Discover Scottish Church Records.* Adelaide, Unlock the Past

PATON, Chris (2010) *Researching Scottish Family History.* Bury, Family History Partnership

KENNETT, Debbie (2011) *DNA and Social Networking: A Guide to Genealogy in the Twenty-First Century.* Stroud, The History Press

RAYMOND, Stuart (2012) *The Wills of Our Ancestors.* Barnsley, Pen and Sword Books Ltd

TATE, W.E. (1983) *The Parish Chest.* Chichester, Phillimore & Co. Ltd

WENZERUL, Rosemary (2011) *A Guide to Jewish Genealogy in the United Kingdom. (2nd ed).* London, JGSGB

INDEX

Discover Your History

Ancestors • Heritage • Memories

Each issue of *Discover Your History* presents special features and regular articles on a huge variety of topics about our social history and heritage – such as our ancestors, childhood memories, military history, British culinary traditions, transport history, our rural and industrial past, health, houses, fashions, pastimes and leisure ... and much more.

Historic pictures show how we and our ancestors have lived and the changing shape of our towns, villages and landscape in Britain and beyond.

Special tips and links help you discover more about researching family and local history. Spotlights on fascinating museums, history blogs and history societies also offer plenty of scope to become more involved.

Keep up to date with news and events that celebrate our history, and reviews of the latest books and media releases.

Discover Your History presents aspects of the past partly through the eyes and voices of those who were there.

FREE BOOK
WHEN YOU SUBSCRIBE TO
Discover Your History

UK only

Discover Your History is in all good newsagents and also available on subscription for six or twelve issues. For more details on how to take out a subscription and how to choose your free book, call 01778 392013 or visit **www.discoveryourhistory.net**